NORTHSTAR 4
LISTENING & SPEAKING
FOURTH EDITION

Authors	TESS FERREE
	KIM SANABRIA
Series Editors	FRANCES BOYD
	CAROL NUMRICH

NorthStar: Listening & Speaking Level 4, Fourth Edition

Pearson Education, 10 Bank Street, White Plains, NY 10606

Staff credits: The people who made up the *NorthStar: Listening & Speaking Level 4, Fourth Edition* team, representing editorial, production, design, and manufacturing, are Kimberly Casey, Tracey Cataldo, Rosa Chapinal, Daniel Comstock, Aerin Csigay, Mindy DePalma, Dave Dickey, Graham Fisher, Nancy Flaggman, Niki Lee, Amy McCormick, Mary Perrotta Rich, Robert Ruvo, Christopher Siley, Debbie Sistino, and Ken Volcjak.

Text composition: ElectraGraphics, Inc.
Development Editing: Wayzgoose Press

Library of Congress Cataloging-in-Publication Data

Frazier, Laurie.
  Northstar 2 : Listening and speaking / Authors : Laurie Frazier, Robin Mills. — Fourth Edition. / Frazier, Laurie.
    pages cm
  ISBN-13: 978-0-13-338213-6 (Level 2) – ISBN 978-0-13-294040-5 (Level 3) –
ISBN 978-0-13-338207-5 (Level 4) – ISBN 978-0-13-338214-3 (Level 5)
  1. English language—Textbooks for foreign speakers. 2. English language—Spoken English—Problems, exercises, etc. 3. Listening—Problems, exercises, etc. I. Mills, Robin, 1962– II. Title. III. Title: Northstar two. IV. Title: Listening and speaking.
  PE1128.M586 2015
  428.2'4—dc23

                                                                    2013050585

Printed in the United States of America

ISBN-10: 0-13-338207-9
ISBN-13: 978-0-13-338207-5

4   18

ISBN-10: 0-13-404982-9 (International Edition)
ISBN-13: 978-0-13-404982-3 (International Edition)

4   17

WELCOME TO

NORTHSTAR

A BLENDED-LEARNING COURSE FOR THE 21ST CENTURY

Building on the success of previous editions, *NorthStar* continues to engage and motivate students through new and updated contemporary, authentic topics in a seamless integration of print and online content. Students will achieve their academic as well as language and personal goals in order to meet the challenges of the 21st century.

New for the FOURTH EDITION

★ **Fully Blended MyEnglishLab**

NorthStar aims to prepare students for academic success and digital literacy with its fully blended online lab. The innovative new MyEnglishLab: *NorthStar* gives learners immediate feedback— anytime, anywhere—as they complete auto-graded language activities online.

★ **NEW and UPDATED THEMES**

Current and thought-provoking topics presented in a variety of genres promote intellectual stimulation. The authentic content engages students, links them to language use outside of the classroom, and encourages personal expression and critical thinking.

★ **EXPLICIT SKILL INSTRUCTION and PRACTICE**

Language skills are highlighted in each unit, providing students with systematic and multiple exposures to language forms and structures in a variety of contexts. Concise presentations and targeted practice in print and online prepare students for academic success.

★ **LEARNING OUTCOMES and ASSESSMENT**

A variety of assessment tools, including online diagnostic, formative, and summative assessments, and a flexible gradebook, aligned with clearly identified unit learning outcomes, allow teachers to individualize instruction and track student progress.

THE NORTHSTAR APPROACH TO CRITICAL THINKING

What is critical thinking?

Most textbooks include interesting questions for students to discuss and tasks for students to engage in to develop language skills. Often these questions and tasks are labeled critical thinking. Look at this question as an example:

When you buy fruits and vegetables, do you usually look for the cheapest price? Explain.

CONTENTS

The question may inspire a lively discussion with students exploring a variety of viewpoints—but it doesn't necessarily develop critical thinking. Now look at another example:

When people in your neighborhood buy fruits and vegetables, what factors are the most important: the price, the freshness, locally grown, organic (without chemicals)? Make a prediction and explain. How can you find out if your prediction is correct? This question does develop critical thinking. It asks students to make predictions, formulate a hypothesis, and draw a conclusion—all higher-level critical thinking skills. Critical thinking, as philosophers and psychologists suggest, is a sharpening and a broadening of the mind. A critical thinker engages in true problem solving, connects information in novel ways, and challenges assumptions. A critical thinker is a skillful, responsible thinker who is open-minded and has the ability to evaluate information based on evidence. Ultimately, through this process of critical thinking, students are better able to decide what to think, what to say, or what to do.

How do we teach critical thinking?

It is not enough to teach "about" critical thinking. Teaching the theory of critical thinking will not produce critical thinkers. Additionally, it is not enough to simply expose students to good examples of critical thinking without explanation or explicit practice and hope our students will learn by imitation.

Students need to engage in specially designed exercises that aim to improve critical thinking skills. This approach practices skills both implicitly and explicitly and is embedded in thought-provoking content. Some strategies include:

- subject matter that is carefully selected and exploited so that students learn new concepts and encounter new perspectives.
- students identifying their own assumptions about the world and later challenging them.
- activities that are designed in a way that students answer questions and complete language-learning tasks that may not have black-and-white answers. (Finding THE answer is often less valuable than the process by which answers are derived.)
- activities that engage students in logical thinking, where they support their reasoning and resolve differences with their peers.

Infused throughout each unit of each book, *NorthStar* uses the principles and strategies outlined above, including:

- Make Inferences: inference comprehension questions in every unit
- Vocabulary and Comprehension: categorization activities
- Vocabulary and Synthesize: relationship analyses (analogies); comparisons (Venn diagrams)
- Synthesize: synthesis of information from two texts teaches a "multiplicity" approach rather than a "duality" approach to learning; ideas that seem to be in opposition on the surface may actually intersect and reinforce each other
- Focus on the Topic and Preview: identifying assumptions, recognizing attitudes and values, and then re-evaluating them
- Focus on Writing/Speaking: reasoning and argumentation
- Unit Project: judgment; choosing factual, unbiased information for research projects
- Focus on Writing/Speaking and Express Opinions: decision-making; proposing solutions

THE NORTHSTAR UNIT

1 FOCUS ON THE TOPIC

* **CT** Each unit begins with a photo that draws students into the topic. Focus questions motivate students and encourage them to make personal connections. Students make inferences about and predict the content of the unit.

UNIT 4

ANIMAL
Intelligence

1 FOCUS ON THE TOPIC

1. The photo shows a dolphin, considered to be one of the most intelligent animals on Earth. In what ways do you think a dolphin could demonstrate intelligence? How would you test a dolphin for intelligence?

2. Do you think that other animals think? Do *all* animals think? What kinds of things might they think about?

MyEnglishLab

CT A short self-assessment based on each unit's learning outcomes helps students check what they know and allows teachers to target instruction.

MyEnglishLab

Home | Help | Test student, reallylongname@emailaddress.com | Sign out

NORTHSTAR 4 LISTENING & SPEAKING

1   Unit 4

Check What You Know

Read the list of skills. You may already use some of them. Don't worry if you don't know about some or all of these skills. You will learn and practice them in this unit.

Check what you know. Put an *X* by the number of each skill that you already use.

If this activity was not assigned by your teacher, it will not be checked. You can still do this activity for practice.

Vocabulary

1 Infer word meaning from context
2 Identify relationships between words

Listening

3 Identify main ideas and details
4 Summarize key information
5 Infer a speaker's attitude from intonation and stress
6 Distinguish between main ideas and supporting details or examples

Speaking

7 Express opinions
8 Ask for and give examples
9 Present and defend an argument

Pronunciation

10 Identify rising or falling intonation in *yes/no* questions with *or*

Grammar

11 Recognize reported speech and use a range of reporting verbs

Vocabulary

1
2

Listening

3
4
5
6

Speaking

7
8
9

Pronunciation

10

Grammar

11

ALWAYS LEARNING

PEARSON

---

* indicates Critical Thinking

2 FOCUS ON LISTENING

Two contrasting, thought-provoking listening selections, from a variety of authentic genres, stimulate students intellectually.

CT Students predict content, verify their predictions, and follow up with a variety of tasks that ensure comprehension.

CT Students are challenged to take what they have learned and organize, integrate, and synthesize the information in a meaningful way.

My English Lab
Auto-graded vocabulary practice activities reinforce meaning and pronunciation.

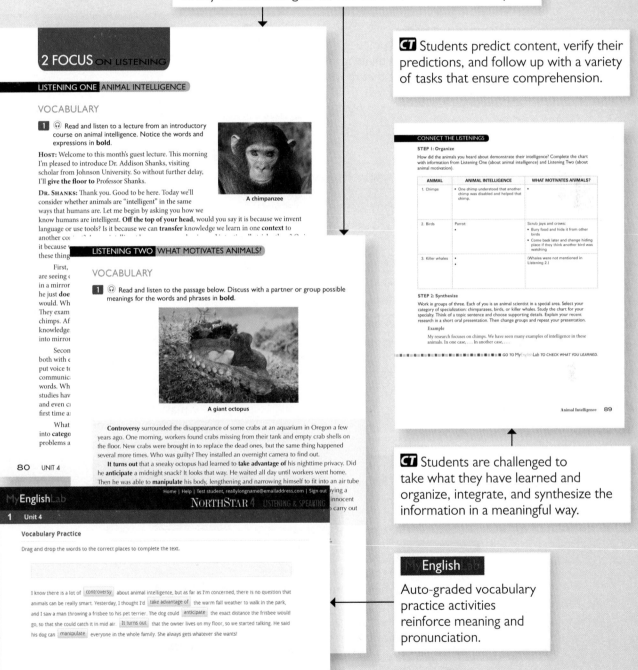

EXPLICIT SKILL INSTRUCTION AND PRACTICE

CT Step-by-step instructions and practice guide students to exercise critical thinking and to dig deeper by asking questions that move beyond the literal meaning of the text.

MAKE INFERENCES

UNDERSTANDING ATTITUDE FROM STRESSED WORDS AND HESITATION

An inference is an educated guess about something that is not directly stated in the text. We understand a speaker not only by hearing the words used, but also by noticing which words are stressed. Stressed words indicate that the speaker places more importance on something. Pauses and hesitation can also express a speaker's attitude.

🎧 Listen to the example. Notice the clues to the speaker's attitude in her stressed words and pausing.

Example

How does Dr. Boysen feel about Goodwin's question? Circle the correct answer.

  a. surprised

  b. pleased

  c. not happy

What might she say about her feelings?

  a. "I wasn't ready to speak first."

  b. "I don't know the answer to that question."

Answer: a. She feels surprised by the question. She might be thinking, "I'm not ready to speak first." Dr. Boysen begins with "Oh," showing surprise, then stresses "would" in "you *would* start with me," showing reluctance to speak, and finally hesitates on "I—I guess probably," showing that ... speak.

... rpts and circle the correct answers. Pay attention to clues in the ... stressed words, pauses, laughter, and other clues.

... oysen feel about the chimpanzee's behavior?

... ed by it.

... d by it.

... ed by it.

LISTENING SKILL

IDENTIFYING THE MAIN IDEA AND EXAMPLES IN ORAL PARAGRAPHS

Highly educated speakers often structure their speech so as to include a clear main idea (usually toward the beginning), which is sometimes supported with an example. Noticing when the oral paragraph has come to a close helps you notice when the speaker will introduce the next main idea.

🎧 Read and listen to the example.

Example

A lot of the work is done [on] chimps and other apes because they're our closest relatives. . . . So there's been a series of experiments. One of the more recent ones has to do with putting a chimp head to head with a human, and the chimp wants to reach for food, and the human has the ability to pull the food away.

Liz Pennisi says that research is being done on chimpanzees because of their similarity to humans: ". . . they're our closest relatives." She supports this main idea with an example of the experiments comparing chimps and humans. This evidence helps prove the main idea.

🎧 Listen to another oral paragraph in which Liz Pennisi explains her research. The main idea is identified for you in the outline. Complete the information about the example.

  I. Main idea: Some skills you see in chimps and humans might also exist in social birds.

    Supporting example:

    A. They started experiments on _____

      _____

    B. The experiments showed _____

      _____

Explicit skill presentation and practice lead to student mastery and success in an academic environment.

■ *GO TO MyEnglishLab FOR MORE SKILL PRACTICE.*

MyEnglishLab

Key listening skills are reinforced and practiced in new contexts. Meaningful and instant feedback provides students and teachers with essential information to monitor progress.

My**English**Lab

Home | Help | Test student, reallylongname@emailaddress.com | Sign out

NORTHSTAR 4   LISTENING & SPEAKING

1   **Unit 4**

Listening Skill: Identifying the Main Idea and Examples

Listen to the excerpts and read the questions. For each question, choose the example you hear the speaker discuss.

1 Why do we believe humans are intelligent?
    ○ opening cages at night
    ○ kitten dying, crying, not eating
    ○ stealing fish
    ○ examining teeth, getting paint off face
    ◉ using language, tools, emotions
    ○ answering questions, making new words

2 How do we know apes are conscious beings?
    ○ opening cages at night
    ○ kitten dying, crying, not eating
    ○ stealing fish
    ◉ examining teeth, getting paint off face
    ○ using language, tools, emotions
    ○ answering questions, making new words

3 What evidence do we have for gorillas being intelligent?
    ○ opening cages at night
    ○ kitten dying, crying, not eating
    ○ stealing fish
    ○ examining teeth, getting paint off face
    ○ using language, tools, emotions
    ◉ answering questions, making new words

ALWAYS LEARNING   PEARSON

Using models from the unit listening selections, the pronunciation and speaking skill sections expose students to the sounds and patterns of English, as well as to functional language that prepares them to express ideas on a higher level.

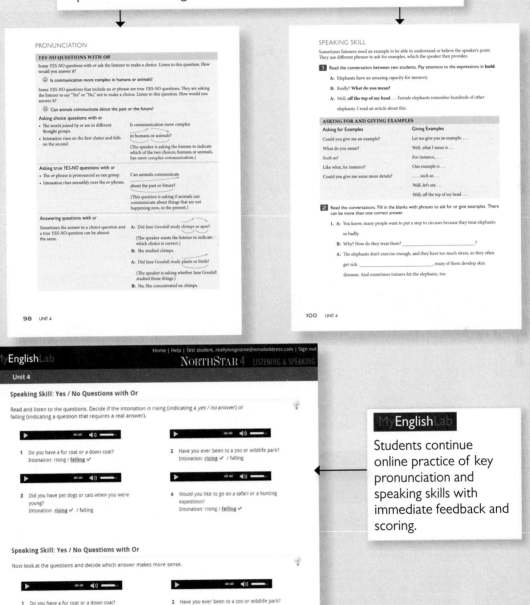

MyEnglishLab

Students continue online practice of key pronunciation and speaking skills with immediate feedback and scoring.

FOCUS ON SPEAKING

3 FOCUS ON SPEAKING

VOCABULARY

REVIEW

Work with a partner. Say the underlined word aloud. Then circle the two words that are related to the underlined word. Use a dictionary if necessary.

Example

remarkable	(incredible)	insignificant	(surprising)
1. socialized	tamed	friendly	wild
2. context	knowledge	situation	setting
3. spontaneous	thoughtful	unexpected	unplanned
4. intriguing	irrelevant	fascinating	mysterious
5. categories	types	individuals	groups
6. figure out	add	understand	solve
7. end up	get behind	finish	result in
8. doesn't get it	doesn't understand	doesn't realize	can't imagine
9. off the top of one's head	considered	not researched	quickly
10. give someone the floor	ask for an opinion	help to walk	allow to speak
11. manipulate	pull	handle	use
12. anticipate	oppose	plan	expect
13. controversy	argument	agreement	dispute

EXPAND

1. ⊙ Work with a partner. Listen to and read the transcript of a radio talk show as a host answers comments from callers.

HOST: Our guest today is Dr. James Rutledge, an expert on animal behavior. Welcome, Dr. Rutledge. I've asked our listeners to call in to tell us their stories of smart animals or animals that cause problems. We've got calls from all over. Yes, hello, Lin. You're on the air.

90 UNIT 4

Productive vocabulary targeted in the unit is reviewed, expanded upon, and used creatively in this section and in the final speaking task. Grammar structures useful for the final speaking task are presented and practiced. A concise grammar skills box serves as an excellent reference.

GRAMMAR

1. Work with a partner. Read the conversation and answer the questions.

A: I just did the assignment about animal communication. The article reported that some parrots could recognize themselves in a mirror.

B: Yeah, and it said they were able to string three or four words together, too. Actually, my professor told us that he had just written a paper on how parrots learn language. He said he was going to publish it next month.

A: What did the paper say?

B: Well, apparently it warned that researchers had to study animal intelligence more carefully before drawing conclusions.

1. Do we know the exact words of the article or the professor?

2. Why do you think Speaker B chose not to quote the article or the professor directly?

REPORTED SPEECH

Reported speech (also called indirect speech) reports what a speaker said without using his or her exact words.

Use words like *said (that), told, indicated, mentioned, reported*, etc., to show that you are reporting information that someone else said.

When you are reporting what a speaker or article said, "backshift" the verb in the indirect speech statement.

Original: "We are **are conducting** some interesting research on endangered whales."

Reported: The scientist explained that she **was conducting** some interesting research with endangered whales.

The verb in the reported speech has shifted back in time; in this case from the present continuous to the past continuous. See more examples in the chart on page 95.

NOTE: If you are reporting a person's unchanging beliefs or a general truth, rather than an event, it is not necessary to change the tense of the original verb.

Original: "Many animals **are** remarkably intelligent."

Reported: The zoologist **told her students** that many animals **are / were** remarkably intelligent.

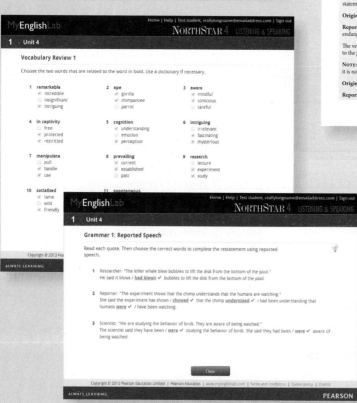

MyEnglishLab

Home | Help | Test student, reallylongname@emailaddress.com | Sign out

NORTHSTAR 4 LISTENING & SPEAKING

1 Unit 4

Vocabulary Review 1

Choose the two words that are related to the word in bold. Use a dictionary if necessary.

1 **remarkable**	2 **ape**	3 **aware**
✓ incredible	✓ gorilla	✓ mindful
insignificant	✓ chimpanzee	✓ conscious
✓ intriguing	parrot	careful

4 **in captivity**	5 **cognition**	6 **intriguing**
free	✓ understanding	irrelevant
✓ protected	emotion	✓ fascinating
✓ restricted	✓ perception	✓ mysterious

7 **manipulate**	8 **prevailing**	9 **research**
pull	✓ current	lecture
✓ handle	✓ established	✓ experiment
✓ use	past	✓ study

10 **socialized**	11 **spontaneous**
✓ tame	
wild	
✓ friendly	

Copyright © 2013 Pea

ALWAYS LEARNING

MyEnglishLab

Home | Help | Test student, reallylongname@emailaddress.com | Sign out

NORTHSTAR 4 LISTENING & SPEAKING

1 Unit 4

Grammar 1: Reported Speech

Read each quote. Then choose the correct words to complete the restatement using reported speech.

1. Researcher: "The killer whale blew bubbles to lift the disk from the bottom of the pool."
He said it blows / **had blown** ✓ bubbles to lift the disk from the bottom of the pool.

2. Reporter: "The experiment shows that the chimp understands that the humans are watching."
She said the experiment has shown / **showed** ✓ that the chimp **understood** ✓ / had been understanding that humans **were** ✓ / have been watching.

3. Scientist: "We are studying the behavior of birds. They are aware of being watched."
The scientist said they have been / **were** ✓ studying the behavior of birds. She said they had been / **were** ✓ aware of being watched

Close

Copyright © 2013 Pearson Education Limited | Pearson Education | www.myenglishlab.com | Terms and conditions | Cookie policy | Credits

ALWAYS LEARNING

PEARSON

MyEnglishLab

Auto-graded vocabulary and grammar practice activities with feedback reinforce meaning, form, and function.

CT A final speaking task gives students an opportunity to exchange ideas and express opinions in sustained speaking contexts using the vocabulary, grammar, pronunciation, listening, and speaking skills presented in the unit.

PERSON C: PROBLEM-SOLVING	PERSON D: LANGUAGE
Research finding: Crows are creative problem-solvers.	**Research finding:** Squirrels use their tails to communicate.
Researcher statement: "I filmed crows in urban Japan. They dropped nuts on the road and waited for cars to run over them and crack the shells. Then the crows went back to eat the nuts."	**Researcher statement:** "Tail flashing, or moving the tail in a wave-like motion, is one of the first indications squirrels give when they sense something disturbing. If the threat seems greater, they will add vocalizations—sounds—to the tail flashing."

GO TO MyEnglishLab TO CHECK WHAT YOU LEARNED.

FINAL SPEAKING TASK

In this activity, you will work with a group to identify arguments for and against a position related to animals and their relationship to people. You will then present the issue to the class. Use the vocabulary, grammar, pronunciation, and language for giving and asking for examples that you learned in this unit.*

STEP 1: Divide the class into groups. Each group selects a question from the list or proposes a new one. Consider the question in terms of what you have learned about animal intelligence.

1. Is it ethical to put wild animals in zoos?

2. Is it humane to raise animals as food for humans?

3. Should humans conduct experiments on animals?

4. Should we put a stop to hunting for sport?

5. Should we pass stricter laws to protect endangered species?

_____
* For Alternative Speaking Topics, see page 105.

102   UNIT 4

CT A group unit project inspires students to inquire further and prepares students to engage in real-world activities. Unit projects incorporate Internet research, helping to build students' digital literacy skills.

UNIT PROJECT

Research a famous example of an animal thought to be intelligent and present your findings to the class.

STEP 1: Select one of these famous animals, or choose your own example.

a. Akeakamai, a dolphin

b. Chaser, a dog

c. Ayumu, a chimp

d. Hank, a heron

e. Kanzi, a bonobo ape

f. Panbanisha, a bonobo ape

g. Rio, a sea lion

h. Romero, a crow

i. Tillman, a dog

Tillman

STEP 2: Research online to find the following information: what the animal was able to learn and what the scientists who worked with the animal think that means. Take notes on the information you find.

STEP 3: Present your findings to the class. Include a picture of the animal, if possible. Give your own opinion: How intelligent do you think the animal is (or was)? In what ways? For example, was it able to speak, use sign language, make or use tools, show empathy, or understand mathematical concepts?

104   UNIT 4

Welcome to *NorthStar*   xi

INNOVATIVE TEACHING TOOLS

With instant access to a wide range of online content and diagnostic tools, teachers can customize learning environments to meet the needs of every student.

USING MyEnglishLab, NORTHSTAR TEACHERS CAN:

Deliver rich online content to engage and motivate students, including:

- student audio to support listening and speaking skills.
- engaging, authentic video clips, including reports adapted from ABC, NBC, and CBS newscasts, tied to the unit themes.
- opportunities for written and recorded reactions to be submitted by students.

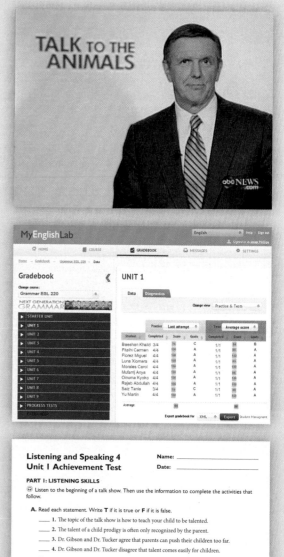

Use a powerful selection of diagnostic reports to:

- view student scores by unit, skill, and activity.
- monitor student progress on any activity or test as often as needed.
- analyze class data to determine steps for remediation and support.

Use Teacher Resource eText* to access:

- a digital copy of the student book for whole class instruction.
- downloadable achievement and placement tests.
- printable resources including lesson planners, videoscripts, and video activities.
- classroom audio.
- unit teaching notes and answer keys.

---

* Teacher Resource eText is accessible through MyEnglishLab: *NorthStar*

COMPONENTS   PRINT or eTEXT

STUDENT BOOK and MyEnglishLab

★ Student Book with MyEnglishLab

The two strands, Reading & Writing and Listening & Speaking, for each of the five levels, provide a fully blended approach with the seamless integration of print and online content. Students use MyEnglishLab to access additional practice online, view videos, listen to audio selections, and receive instant feedback on their work.

eTEXT and MyEnglishLab

★ eText with MyEnglishLab

Offering maximum flexibility for different learning styles and needs, a digital version of the student book can be used on iPad® and Android® devices.

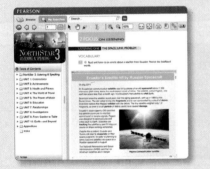

★ Instructor Access: Teacher Resource eText and MyEnglishLab (Listening & Speaking 1–5)

Teacher Resource eText

Each level and strand of *NorthStar* has an accompanying Teacher Resource eText that includes: a digital student book, unit teaching notes, answer keys, downloadable achievement tests, classroom audio, lesson planners, video activities, videoscripts, and a downloadable placement test.

MyEnglishLab

Teachers assign MyEnglishLab activities to reinforce the skills students learn in class and monitor progress through an online gradebook. The automatically-graded exercises in MyEnglishLab *NorthStar* support and build on academic skills and vocabulary presented and practiced in the Student Book/eText. The teacher-graded activities include pronunciation, speaking, and writing, and are assigned by the instructor.

★ Classroom Audio CD

The Listening & Speaking audio contains the recordings and activities, as well as audio for the achievement tests. The Reading & Writing strand contains the readings on audio.

SCOPE AND SEQUENCE

UNIT OUTCOMES	1 PRODIGIES **EXPLORING GENIUS** pages 2–25 *Listening 1: The Music in My Head* *Listening 2: Where Does Genius Come From?*	2 OVERCOMING OBSTACLES **THE ACHILLES HEEL** pages 26–51 *Listening 1: Artist Opens Others' Eyes* *Listening 2: The Achilles Track Club Climbs Mount Kilimanjaro*
LISTENING	• Make and confirm predictions • Identify main ideas and details • Summarize key information • Recognize emphasis through intonation and stress **MyEnglishLab** Vocabulary and Listening Skill Practice	• Make and confirm predictions • Identify main ideas and details • Distinguish between main ideas and supporting details and examples • Summarize key information • Analyze similarities and differences **MyEnglishLab** Vocabulary and Listening Skill Practice
SPEAKING	• Express opinions • State and report opinions and support them with relevant explanations and arguments • State others' opinions **Task:** Present scenarios and lead small-group discussions **MyEnglishLab** Speaking Skill Practice and Speaking Task	• Express opinions • Express similarities and differences • Use specific examples to support main ideas and opinions **Task:** Prepare and present a speech about an obstacle **MyEnglishLab** Speaking Skill Practice and Speaking Task
INFERENCE	• Infer important ideas through use of repeated words	• Infer meaning from figurative language
PRONUNCIATION	• Recognize and use reductions and contractions to make speech less formal **MyEnglishLab** Pronunciation Skill Practice	• Identify thought groups in sentences **MyEnglishLab** Pronunciation Skill Practice
VOCABULARY	• Infer word meaning from context • Recognize and use word forms (nouns, verbs, adjectives, adverbs) **MyEnglishLab** Vocabulary Practice	• Infer word meaning from context • Distinguish between literal and figurative meaning • Identify paraphrases **MyEnglishLab** Vocabulary Practice
GRAMMAR	• Recognize and use passive voice in the present, past, and future **MyEnglishLab** Grammar Practice	• Recognize and use gerunds and infinitives after a range of verbs and prepositions **MyEnglishLab** Grammar Practice
VIDEO	**MyEnglishLab** *Small Wonders*, ABC News, Video Activity	**MyEnglishLab** *A Child's Voice*, ABC News, Video Activity
ASSESSMENTS	**MyEnglishLab** Check What You Know, Checkpoints 1 and 2, Unit 1 Achievement Test	**MyEnglishLab** Check What You Know, Checkpoints 1 and 2, Unit 2 Achievement Test

3 MEDICINE
EARLY TO BED, EARLY TO RISE
pages 52–77

Listening 1: How Can Teenagers Get Enough Sleep?
Listening 2: Get Back in Bed!

4 ANIMAL INTELLIGENCE
ANIMAL INTELLIGENCE
pages 78–105

Listening 1: Animal Intelligence
Listening 2: What Motivates Animals?

• Make and confirm predictions • Identify main ideas and details • Recognize supporting details • Analyze problems and solutions MyEnglishLab Vocabulary and Listening Skill Practice	• Make and confirm predictions • Identify main ideas and details • Summarize key information • Distinguish between main ideas and supporting details or examples MyEnglishLab Vocabulary and Listening Skill Practice
• Express opinions • Use strategies to interrupt and to ask for clarification • Propose solutions to problems **Task:** Summarize a case study and dramatize a scenario about sleep deprivation MyEnglishLab Speaking Skill Practice and Speaking Task	• Express opinions • Ask for and give examples **Task:** Present and defend an argument MyEnglishLab Speaking Skill Practice and Speaking Task
• Infer assumptions using contextual clues	• Infer a speaker's attitude from intonation and stress
• Recognize and use contrastive stress for emphasis MyEnglishLab Pronunciation Skill Practice	• Identify rising or falling intonation in *yes/no* questions with *or* MyEnglishLab Pronunciation Skill Practice
• Infer word meaning from context MyEnglishLab Vocabulary Practice	• Infer word meaning from context • Identify relationships between words MyEnglishLab Vocabulary Practice
• Recognize and use present unreal conditionals MyEnglishLab Grammar Practice	• Recognize reported speech and use a range of reporting verbs MyEnglishLab Grammar Practice
MyEnglishLab *A Sleep Clinic,* Video Activity	MyEnglishLab *Talk to the Animals,* ABC News, Video Activity
MyEnglishLab Check What You Know, Checkpoints 1 and 2, Unit 3 Achievement Test	MyEnglishLab Check What You Know, Checkpoints 1 and 2, Unit 4 Achievement Test

SCOPE AND SEQUENCE

UNIT OUTCOMES	5 LONGEVITY **THE GOLDEN YEARS** pages 106–129 *Listening 1: The Longevity Project Report* *Listening 2: Tobey Dichter, Generations Online*	6 PHILANTHROPY **GIVING TO OTHERS** pages 130–157 *Listening 1: Why We Give* *Listening 2: The Mystery Donor*
LISTENING	• Make and confirm predictions • Identify main ideas and details • Summarize key information • Evaluate a speaker's degree of certainty MyEnglishLab Vocabulary and Listening Skill Practice	• Make and confirm predictions • Identify main ideas and details • Summarize key information • Identify the purpose of examples MyEnglishLab Vocabulary and Listening Skill Practice
SPEAKING	• Express opinions • Make suggestions **Task:** Create and dramatize a family meeting MyEnglishLab Speaking Skill Practice and Speaking Task	• Express opinions • Prioritize ideas **Task:** Create and present a Public Service Announcement (PSA) MyEnglishLab Speaking Skill Practice and Speaking Task
INFERENCE	• Infer a speaker's point of view from intonation and stress	• Infer a speaker's degree of certainty
PRONUNCIATION	• Recognize word blends with *you* MyEnglishLab Pronunciation Skill Practice	• Infer from intonation whether listed information is finished or unfinished MyEnglishLab Pronunciation Skill Practice
VOCABULARY	• Infer word meaning from context MyEnglishLab Vocabulary Practice	• Infer word meaning from context • Recognize and use word forms (nouns, verbs, adjectives, adverbs) MyEnglishLab Vocabulary Practice
GRAMMAR	• Recognize, form, and contrast simple, progressive, and perfect verbs MyEnglishLab Grammar Practice	• Recognize and use relative pronouns in adjective clauses MyEnglishLab Grammar Practice
VIDEO	MyEnglishLab *Living Longer*, ABC News. Video Activity	MyEnglishLab *Local Teen Awarded for Making Difference*, NBC News, Video Activity
ASSESSMENTS	MyEnglishLab Check What You Know, Checkpoints 1 and 2, Unit 5 Achievement Test	MyEnglishLab Check What You Know, Checkpoints 1 and 2, Unit 6 Achievement Test

7 EDUCATION	**8 COMPUTERS**
DO YOUR HOMEWORK!	**PROS AND CONS OF GAMING**
pages 158–181	pages 182–210
Listening 1: Homework Issues	Listening 1: The Darker Side of Video Games
Listening 2: Tiger Mom	Listening 2: Truths and Myths in Gaming
• Make and confirm predictions • Identify main ideas and details • Summarize key information • Recognize phrases that signal clarification MyEnglishLab Vocabulary and Listening Skill Practice	• Make and confirm predictions • Identify main ideas and details • Summarize key information • Recognize and use strategies to introduce a counterargument • Analyze pros and cons MyEnglishLab Vocabulary and Listening Skill Practice
• Express opinions • Propose suggestions • Ask for and offer clarification **Task:** Create and dramatize a public school board meeting MyEnglishLab Speaking Skill Practice and Speaking Task	• Express opinions • Discuss pros and cons • Express concessions and present counterarguments **Task:** Participate in a debate MyEnglishLab Speaking Skill Practice and Speaking Task
• Infer and recognize aspects of humor (irony, exaggeration, sarcasm)	• Infer a speaker's attitude through emphasis, stress, and intonation
• Identify and distinguish between stressed and unstressed vowel sounds MyEnglishLab Pronunciation Skill Practice	• Identify and use stress with adverbial particles MyEnglishLab Pronunciation Skill Practice
• Infer word meaning from context MyEnglishLab Vocabulary Practice	• Infer word meaning from context • Recognize and use word forms (nouns, verbs, adjectives, adverbs) MyEnglishLab Vocabulary Practice
• Recognize and use the verbs *make, have, let, help* and *get* + object + base form/infinitive MyEnglishLab Grammar Practice	• Recognize and use tag questions MyEnglishLab Grammar Practice
MyEnglishLab *Homework Holiday,* ABC News, Video Activity	MyEnglishLab *French Employers Unplug After Hours,* ABC News, Video Activity
MyEnglishLab Check What You Know, Checkpoints 1 and 2, Unit 7 Achievement Test	MyEnglishLab Check What You Know, Checkpoints 1 and 2, Unit 8 Achievement Test

ACKNOWLEDGMENTS

To friends, family, and colleagues who have supported us throughout the fourth edition of *NorthStar,* our heartfelt thanks. Each of you has left an imprint on these pages.

The project has again been enriched by the contributions of many individuals. We thank Frances Boyd and Carol Numrich, our watchful *NorthStar* series editors, as well as the wonderful editorial staff at Pearson Education, particularly Debbie Sistino for her deft management of this huge endeavor. Our gratitude goes to editors Dorothy Zemach, for her positive attitude and tactful expertise, and Mary Rich, whose help and support were critical as we finalized the manuscript. In addition, the many interviewees and commentators heard in the listenings are part of *NorthStar.* Finally, we extend our gratitude and warm wishes to students and friends at Randolph Township Schools and Eugenio María de Hostos Community College.

And, of course, we thank Jay and Miranda, Carlos, Kelly and Victor.

Tess Ferree

Kim Sanabria

REVIEWERS

Chris Antonellis, Boston University – CELOP; Gail August, Hostos; Aegina Barnes, York College; Kim Bayer, Hunter College; Mine Bellikli, Atilim University; Allison Blechman, Embassy CES; Paul Blomquist, Kaplan; Helena Botros, FLS; James Branchick, FLS; Chris Bruffee, Embassy CES; Nese Cakli, Duzce University; María Cordani Tourinho Dantas, Colégio Rainha De Paz; Jason Davis, ASC English; Lindsay Donigan, Fullerton College; Bina Dugan, BCCC; Sibel Ece Izmir, Atilim University; Érica Ferrer, Universidad del Norte; María Irma Gallegos Peláez, Universidad del Valle de México; Jeff Gano, ASA College; María Genovev a Chávez Bazán, Universidad del Valle de México; Juan Garcia, FLS; Heidi Gramlich, The New England School of English; Phillip Grayson, Kaplan; Rebecca Gross, The New England School of English; Rick Guadiana, FLS; Sebnem Guzel, Tobb University; Esra Hatipoglu, Ufuk University; Brian Henry, FLS; Josephine Horna, BCCC; Arthur Hui, Fullerton College; Zoe Isaacson, Hunter College; Kathy Johnson, Fullerton College; Marcelo Juica, Urban College of Boston; Tom Justice, North Shore Community College; Lisa Karakas, Berkeley College; Eva Kopernacki, Embassy CES; Drew Larimore, Kaplan; Heidi Lieb, BCCC; Patricia Martins, Ibeu; Cecilia Mora Espejo, Universidad del Valle de México; Kate Nyhan, The New England School of English; Julie Oni, FLS; Willard Osman, The New England School of English; Olga Pagieva, ASA College; Manish Patel, FLS; Paige Poole, Universidad del Norte; Claudia Rebello, Ibeu; Lourdes Rey, Universidad del Norte; Michelle Reynolds, FLS International Boston Commons; Mary Ritter, NYU; Minerva Santos, Hostos; Sezer Sarioz, Saint Benoit PLS; Ebru Sinar, Tobb University; Beth Soll, NYU (Columbia); Christopher Stobart, Universidad del Norte; Guliz Uludag, Ufuk University; Debra Un, NYU; Hilal Unlusu, Saint Benoit PLS; María del Carmen Viruega Trejo, Universidad del Valle de México; Reda Vural, Atilim University; Douglas Waters, Universidad del Norte; Leyla Yucklik, Duzce University; Jorge Zepeda Porras, Universidad del Valle de México

EXPLORING
Genius

1 FOCUS ON THE TOPIC

1. A *prodigy* is a young person with exceptional abilities. Do you know about anyone who could be considered a prodigy? What does this person do that is different or special?

2. If a young child shows unusual talent in one particular area, how do you think parents should react? Should they push the child to develop that talent, or allow the child to develop it naturally?

3. Why do you believe some children show advanced abilities at an early age? Are they born with a special talent, or do they learn it somehow?

GO TO MyEnglishLab *TO CHECK WHAT YOU KNOW.*

VOCABULARY

1 🎧 Read and listen to the radio report, paying particular attention to the words in **bold**.

REPORTER: Hello, everyone. Today, we have a great subject to talk about: genius, what it is, and where it comes from. I'm sure all our listeners have heard of child prodigies—people who display incredible abilities when they are very young. Let's begin by taking your calls on this interesting topic.

CALLER 1: Yes, hi, there. My husband and I have always been **fascinated** by this subject, but right now, I'm calling about our son Mike. He's only ten years old, but he can do all kinds of mathematical calculations **at the speed of light**. For example, we'll show him a rule that is completely **unfamiliar** to him—addition of large numbers, for example—and he gets it immediately. Is he a prodigy?

REPORTER: I'm not too sure, but Mike certainly sounds interested in math. Does he ever make mistakes?

CALLER 1: Well, sure, sometimes. But then he goes back to **revise** the answers he gets wrong. And he enjoys doing calculations. He has a lot of **confidence** in his own abilities.

REPORTER: That's terrific. Whether he's a prodigy or not, I think you should definitely encourage his interest.

CALLER 2: Hello? Yes, well, I'd like to know where talented young children get their abilities.

REPORTER: You know, we're not really sure. Even the most **renowned** scientists don't agree on why a few children become prodigies. Some young children become skilled in something like math, music, or chess **before our very eyes**. They don't have any training, and, most of the time, they're completely **unconscious** of their abilities. It's just the way they are. For example, Mozart started composing when he was five. It was instinctive, almost **involuntary**. And perhaps you've heard about Akrit Jaswal, the young Indian boy who performed surgery at the age of 7. Now, he really *was* a prodigy, as far as I'm concerned.

CALLER 3: Hi. . . . I wanted to point out that all children have a lot of **potential**. That's an **objective** fact.

REPORTER: Yes, you're right—and we certainly want to encourage all children to do their best. But personally, I do think that some individuals are a bit different. They seem to be born with some kind of **underlying** talent. Let's take a break now. When we return, we'll be talking about how parents should handle their children's talents.

2 Match the words on the left with their definitions on the right.

_____ **1.** at the speed of light	**a.** directly in front of us; while we watch
_____ **2.** before our very eyes	**b.** review and correct or change something
_____ **3.** confidence	**c.** the feeling that you can trust someone or something to be good or successful
_____ **4.** fascinated	**d.** a natural ability that could develop to make you very good at something
_____ **5.** involuntary	
_____ **6.** objective	**e.** unaware; not realizing what you are doing
_____ **7.** potential	**f.** very interested
_____ **8.** renowned	**g.** not influenced by your own feelings, beliefs, or ideas
_____ **9.** revise	**h.** known and admired by a lot of people
_____ **10.** unconscious	**i.** something you do without intending to
_____ **11.** underlying	**j.** extremely quickly
_____ **12.** unfamiliar	**k.** not known to you
	l. the most important part of something or reason for something, but that is not easy to discover

GO TO MyEnglishLab *FOR MORE VOCABULARY PRACTICE.*

PREVIEW

In this report, we learn about a musical prodigy named Jay. Listen to the introduction. What two points about Jay does the reporter mention?

1. A characteristic that sets Jay apart: _____

2. An unusual activity that sets Jay apart: _____

3. What might be other characteristics and activities of "the greatest [musical] talent to come along in 200 years"? Check (✓) the things you think the report might include.

_____ his role models

_____ his successes

_____ his challenges

_____ reaction of his parents

_____ his critics

MAIN IDEAS

1 Listen to the whole report. Look again at your answers and predictions in Preview. What information did you learn about Jay and how did your predictions help you understand the report?

2 Listen to the report again. Write short answers to the questions.

1. What does Jay's teacher say about his talent?

_____

2. What does Jay say about how he creates compositions?

_____

3. Why does Jay's computer frequently crash?

_____

4. Why doesn't Jay ever go back and revise his work?

_____

DETAILS

🎧 Listen again. Write **T** (true) or **F** (false) for each statement. Correct the false statements. Then discuss your answers with a partner.

_____ 1. Jay Greenberg named himself "Bluejay" because he produces a lot of sound, like a small bird.

_____ 2. Other musicians have helped Jay to compose his music.

_____ 3. Sam Zyman is a composer and teacher at the Juilliard School.

_____ 4. At 12, Jay could write a great sonata in two hours.

_____ 5. Jay doesn't need to think about his compositions.

_____ 6. Jay's parents are professional musicians.

_____ 7. At 2, Jay began drawing pictures of instruments that his parents had at home.

_____ 8. By the age of three, Jay began composing music by drawing small cellos as musical notes on a scale.

_____ 9. As a child, Jay's hero was Batman.

_____ 10. Jay creates symphonies by writing for one instrument, then thinking about how the others should come in.

■□■■□■■□■□■■■□■□■■□■□■■□■■□■□■□■■ *GO TO* MyEnglishLab *FOR MORE LISTENING PRACTICE.*

Exploring Genius 7

LISTENING FOR REPEATED WORDS

Speakers sometimes repeat words and phrases to emphasize important ideas. By repeating the same key words, the speaker helps the listener recognize and focus on the important aspects of the message.

Example

🎧 Listen to Sam Zyman commenting on Jay Greenberg's skills. Take note of repeated words.

1. Which words does the speaker repeat?_____

2. What idea does he want to emphasize? Circle the correct answer.

   a. Jay has an unusual background.

   b. Jay is incredibly talented.

Answers: 1. He repeats the words *every* (*every* note, *every* instrument) and *wrote* (*wrote* this, *wrote* every note, *wrote* it in just a few hours). 2. b.

🎧 Listen to the excerpts and answer the questions.

Excerpt One

Sam Zyman is commenting on Jay Greenberg's skills.

   1. Which words does he repeat? _____

   2. Which idea does Zyman emphasize? Circle the correct answer.

     a. Jay is one of the greatest music prodigies in history.

     b. Jay has natural musical abilities.

Excerpt Two

Jay's mother is commenting on her son.

   1. Which word does she repeat? _____

   2. What idea does Jay's mother emphasize? Circle the correct answer.

     a. Jay's mother thought she should encourage her son's interest in music.

     b. Jay became obsessed with cellos when he was a young child.

EXPRESS OPINIONS

Work in a small group. Discuss the questions.

1. What do you think of Jay? Where do you think his talent comes from?

2. Did Jay's parents do the right thing by encouraging his interest in music? Did this decision have any risks?

3. What do you predict for Jay's future in music and in life?

■ ■ ■ ■ ■ ■ ■ ■ ■ ■ ■ ■ ■ ■ ■ ■ ■ ■ ■ *GO TO* MyEnglishLab *TO GIVE YOUR OPINION ABOUT ANOTHER QUESTION.*

LISTENING TWO | WHERE DOES GENIUS COME FROM?

VOCABULARY

1 Work with a partner. Read the words aloud and discuss their meanings. Check a dictionary if necessary.

a. achievements

b. interact

c. myth

d. trait

e. versus

2 Complete the report with words from Exercise 1. Take turns reading the sentences aloud.

How do we become who we are? Where do intelligence and talent come from? Scientists

have been fascinated by this question ever since Francis Galton proposed the idea of

"nature _____ nurture" one hundred and fifty years ago. His idea
          (1)

was that people's _____ could be explained either by their genes
                    (2)

(known as "G") or their environment (known as "E.") However, scientists today say that

nature and nurture are not opposing forces: In fact, they say that the idea of nature or

(continued on next page)

nurture is a _____. After all, our characteristics are not determined
                          (3)

when we are born. For example, we can develop a particular _____
                                                                          (4)

such as confidence or optimism. We can learn to have resilience; that is, the ability

to deal with difficulties. The abilities we inherit at birth can grow and develop as we

_____ with other people in our environment.
          (5)

COMPREHENSION

🎧 Listen to writer David Shenk talk about his book *The Genius in All of Us: New Insights into Genetics, Talent, and IQ*. Then answer the questions.

1 Shenk says that genius is an "amorphous term," meaning that it is difficult to define. Instead, he mentions various things that people do to achieve success. Check (✓) three things he mentions.

_____ **a.** doing your best

_____ **b.** following your role models

_____ **c.** having good teachers

_____ **d.** doing what you love to do

_____ **e.** having intensity and resilience

2 Shenk discusses nature and nurture. Check (✓) the theory he believes is correct.

_____ **a.** Nature VERSUS nurture. Either we are born with certain traits and talents, or we get them from our environment.

_____ **b.** Nature PLUS nurture. We are born with certain abilities (nature), and other abilities are the result of our environment. This is called the additive model.

_____ **c.** Nature TIMES nurture. This means that you can't separate nature from nurture. How our genes interact with our environment determines our abilities.

3 What does Shenk say about education? Check (✓) the correct answer.

_____ **a.** It complements innate abilities.

_____ **b.** It is the most important factor in a person's life.

_____ **c.** It is less important than a person's natural talent.

■■■■■■■■■■■■■■■■■■■■■■■■■■■■■■■■ GO TO MyEnglishLab *FOR MORE VOCABULARY PRACTICE.*

LISTENING SKILL

1 🎧 Listen to an excerpt from David Shenk's talk. What do you think is his most important point?

LISTENING FOR EMPHASIS

When speakers want to emphasize an important idea, they usually slow down and speak very loudly and clearly.

🎧 Read and listen again to the example. Pay attention to the **bold** words.

Example

The idea is that we think that it's **nature versus nurture**, that there's **genes** that have all this information that kind of want to push us in a certain direction and then there's the **environment, which is nurture,** which is obviously different and kind of an opposing force.

Shenk speaks loudly and slowly when he is discussing nature and nurture, genes, and the environment. This helps the listener notice those ideas.

2 🎧 Listen to the excerpts. Each comment by Shenk is divided into two parts. Check (✓) the part of the sentence (A or B) that he emphasizes by speaking loudly and clearly.

Excerpt One

A	B
Is it 60% nature, 40% nurture _____	depending on what trait you're talking about? _____

Excerpt Two

A	B
The additive model is well, you have so much inborn intelligence and then plus what you get in the environment: _____	that would be, you know, nature plus nurture. _____

■■■■■■■■■■■■■■■■■■■■■■■■■■■■■■■■■■■ GO TO MyEnglishLab *FOR MORE SKILL PRACTICE.*

STEP 1: Organize

1 Where did you hear these statements? Check (✓) the correct column.

	LISTENING 1: The music in my head	LISTENING 2: Where does genius come from?
1. We've been living with this myth for about a hundred, hundred and fifty years . . .		
2. Genes are always interacting with the environment . . .		
3. . . . he doesn't know where the music comes from, but it comes fully written—playing like an orchestra in his head.		
4. It's like my unconscious mind is giving orders at the speed of light.		
5. You just absolutely cannot separate the effects of genes from the effects of the environment.		
6. And I was surprised, because neither of us has anything to do with string instruments. And I didn't expect him to know what a cello was.		
7. . . . all we can do, of course, is to identify the resources that we have in our environments and maximize them as best we can.		
8. . . . he started playing on it. And I was like, "How do you know how to do this?"		

2 Circle the statement that sums up the attitude of these people from Listenings One and Two.

1. Jay Greenberg's mother:

   a. Jay inherited his musical ability. Many of his relatives have musical talent.

   b. Jay was simply born with his talent.

   c. Jay's talent is due to the influence of a special early music teacher.

2. David Shenk:

   a. A person's natural talents are affected by the environment. Both of them working together create a genius.

   b. A true genius would develop no matter what environment he or she grew up in. The talent would still be expressed.

   c. Some geniuses are simply born with their talent, and others develop their talent through education and hard work.

STEP 2: Synthesize

Work with a partner. Jay Greenberg has a younger brother, Michael, who is not a prodigy or a musician. Role-play a meeting with Jay's mother and David Shenk in which you discuss these questions: 1) Where did Jay's talent come from? 2) Why is Michael not a musical prodigy?

Example

JAY'S MOTHER: I think Jay was born with his talent. He started composing when he was two! Nobody taught him anything.

DAVID SHENK: But his father is a linguist. It's possible that . . .

■■■■■■■■■■■■■■■■■■■■■■■■■■■■■■ *GO TO* MyEnglishLab *TO CHECK WHAT YOU LEARNED.*

3 FOCUS ON SPEAKING

VOCABULARY

REVIEW

1 Complete the chart with different forms of the words. Then compare your answers with a partner.

NOUN	VERB	ADJECTIVE	ADVERB
achievement			
confidence			
		fascinated	
intensity			
interaction			
	maximize		
resilience			
stimulation			
		voluntary / involuntary	

2 Work with a partner. Complete the conversation between a woman and her doctor by circling the correct word form. Then read it aloud.

Ms. Sherry: Good morning, Doctor. I have newborn identical twins, and I want to make sure I treat them differently, because I want them each to **(1)** (*achievement / achieve*) their full potential. Can you advise me?

Doctor: Raising twins is a **(2)** (*fascination / fascinating*) experience. And, of course, this experience must be very **(3)** (*intensity / intense*) for you, because even one baby is a lot of work. Two is "double the trouble," as they say! Now, every infant needs individual attention, so try to **(4)** (*maximum / maximize*) the time you can spend with each one. That way you can develop a different kind of **(5)** (*interaction / interactive*) with each twin.

Ms. Sherry: Yes, I'd like to. But I'm not feeling very **(6)** (*confidence / confident*). I'm worried that other people will treat them both the same. After all, they look identical. When people see them, they'll always assume they have the same personality and the same skills. I suppose that's a/an **(7)** (*volunteer / involuntary*) reaction when you see identical twins.

Doctor: Perhaps, but try not to be too concerned. Babies are very **(8)** (*resilience / resilient*). They overcome all kinds of obstacles. As they grow, make sure you understand how they are different and what each one is interested in. It's important to **(9)** (*stimulation / stimulate*) their individual interests and

talents. And, in the meantime, try to find someone who can **(10)** (*volunteer / voluntary*) to help you get things done. You need to take care of yourself too!

Read the opinions of three researchers about how people become geniuses. Then match the words in **bold** with a definition from the same column.

HOW DO PEOPLE BECOME GENIUSES?
Three researchers offer their opinions.

Some people are born geniuses	Everyone is full of potential	Geniuses are born *and* made
At least to some extent, genius is innate. We (1) **inherit** all kinds of personality traits from our ancestors, like a natural (2) **aptitude** for music or for math. Nature has a powerful influence on us: There is just no other explanation for the phenomenon of child prodigies. Look at the children who take up musical instruments (3) **on their own** and begin to play them. How can this be possible, if they are not genetically (4) **predisposed** to be good at music? The evidence for (5) **inborn** talent is undeniable.	In my opinion, no one is born with skills, just with potential. We (6) **acquire** skills and experiences throughout our lives. There are certainly stories of child prodigies, but, in many cases, these children have been heavily (7) **influenced** by their parents. (8) **In actual fact**, sometimes the parents even put unbelievable (9) **pressure** on these children to succeed. If children show an interest in music, the parents should encourage them to (10) **take up** an instrument. It's as simple as that.	There's no doubt that our genes (11) **interact** with our environment to make us who we are. It's a very (12) **complex** process. It's not (13) **either/or**. Current research suggests that parents should (14) **motivate** their children in any way they can. In other words, there is no way to separate (15) **heredity** from environment.
_____ a. something you have had naturally since birth _____ b. by themselves _____ c. likely to behave in a particular way _____ d. get from one of your parents _____ e. ability or skill	_____ f. begin doing a job or activity _____ g. develop or learn a skill _____ h. affected by someone else _____ i. in truth; in reality _____ j. attempt to make someone do something	_____ k. connect, work together _____ l. push, stimulate _____ m. difficult to understand or deal with _____ n. a choice between two options _____ o. genetic makeup

CREATE

1 Read the news article about a school's financial challenge.

Seabury Middle School News

Seabury Middle School has been growing very large in the last few years, and some of its students are doing very well: A few have won awards in music, math, and science. However, the school has limited funds to invest in improving the quality of education for all the students. Now, school administrators disagree about how to invest money for the next academic year. One group thinks the money should be spent on the highest achieving students, offering them additional learning experiences to improve their skills. The other group believes the money would be better spent on a larger number of weak students who are having difficulty keeping up with the existing classes.

2 Discuss your reaction in a small group, using the vocabulary in Review and Expand. Should the school invest the money in the strongest students or the weakest students? What would be the benefits of each approach?

GO TO MyEnglishLab *FOR MORE VOCABULARY PRACTICE.*

GRAMMAR

1 Look at the illustration and then read the description. Notice the verb forms that appear in **bold**.

In this cartoon, a boy is showing his teacher how to solve a complex math problem. Most likely, he **has been taught** to solve this kind of problem at home, not at school. The teacher **is surprised** when the boy gives his explanation.

PASSIVE VOICE

Forming the Passive Voice

To form the **passive**, use the correct form of *be* + **past participle**. If the agent of the action is known and important, you can use *by* + agent, although it isn't necessary.

With modals (*can, may, should,* etc.), use the base form of **past participle**.

ACTIVE	PASSIVE
Many parents **encourage** their children to explore different interests.	Some children **are encouraged by** their parents to take up sports or hobbies.
My parents **didn't allow me** to play sports until I finished my homework.	I **wasn't allowed** to play sports until I had finished my assignments.
Children **can beat** adults at some memory games.	Adults **can be beaten** by children at some memory games.

Using the Passive Voice

- Use the passive voice to shift focus from the agent of the action to the person or thing being described.

    Prodigies **are admired** by people all over the world.

    In this case, *prodigies* are more important than *people all over the world*.

- Use the passive voice when you do not know the agent of the action, or when the agent is not important.

    News about the child violinist **is being reported** in detail.

    In this case, it doesn't matter who is reporting the news in detail.

- Use the passive voice when you don't want to mention the agent, particularly to avoid blaming the agent.

    Some factual mistakes **were made** in the article about that young artist. She was five years old when she had an exhibition, not four.

    We know who made the mistakes, but we don't wish to name that person.

2 Complete the radio reports with the passive voice, using the verbs in parentheses and the verb tenses indicated. Then take turns with a partner reading the reports aloud.

Prodigies from Around the World

Audiences around the world _____ (*captivate* / present perfect) over the
(1)

past two weeks as Lang Lang, the Chinese pianist, performed his latest work. Lang Lang's recent

concert _____ (*show* / future) on public television next week.
(2)

Shakuntala Devi _____ (*know* / past) as the "human computer" because she
(3)

could calculate large numbers in her head. People thought she _____ (*give* /
(4)

past perfect) special instruction in mathematics, but in fact, she had no formal education. She

_____ (*teach* / past) to do complex calculations by her father, who was a
(5)

circus performer.

José Raúl Capablanca y Graupera, the "human chess machine," _____
(6)

(*consider* / present) one of the greatest chess players of all time. Unlike other famous players, he

_____ (*know* / past) for his simple playing style, but he played at the speed
(7)

of light. This, together with his exceptional skill, made it almost impossible for other players to

beat him.

3 Work with a partner.

Student A: Read the statements.

Student B: Respond to the statements by completing the sentence using a passive form
of the verb and the verb tense indicated.

Student A	**Student B**
1. Scientists use many different words to talk about nature and nurture.	**1.** Yes, and even letters. G and E _____ to talk about (*use* / present) genes and environment, and that means the same thing.

2. Shenk seems to have different ideas from people in the past.

3. Research into nature and nurture goes back a long way.

4. Wasn't it interesting to learn about those experiments on mice?

Now switch roles.

5. I do think Jay Greenberg is a genius, but he's had a lot of education, too.

6. Jay has become really famous.

7. I think he's going to be doing a lot of international performances.

8. I'm learning to play the piano, but I feel bad when I see young children play so much better than I do.

2. Yes. Shenk believes that nature and nurture

_____.
(can't separate / present)

3. Yes, it's incredible. Can you imagine that in the 1950s, researchers were working with rats that

_____ genetically _____?
(design / past perfect)

4. Yes, I was so surprised to learn that people who

_____ to be unintelligent
(think / past)
could become just as smart as others!

5. Right. Jay _____ to
(expose / present perfect)
all kinds of music instruction.

6. Right, now he _____
(contact / present progressive)
by musicians all over the world.

7. Yes, I heard that he _____ to
(invite / future)
Japan next fall.

8. You _____ by them. Not
(shouldn't intimidate / present)
everyone can be a prodigy!

GO TO MyEnglishLab FOR MORE GRAMMAR PRACTICE.

PRONUNCIATION

REDUCING AND CONTRACTING AUXILIARY VERBS

In speech, fluent speakers often use contractions of the verbs *be* and *have* after a pronoun. These contractions sound friendlier and less formal, and are easier to say than the full forms.

Example

I've *been reading about child prodigies, but my husband thinks there is no such thing.* *He's* *convinced that all children are equally talented.*

After nouns, the auxiliary verbs *are, have,* and *has* have reduced pronunciations.
Are sounds like an *-er* ending. It is joined with the preceding word:

Example

Scientists are *interested in prodigies.*
    (Say "Scientistser interested . . .")

Have is pronounced /əv/ (like the preposition *of*). It is joined closely with the preceding word.

Example

Some have *become world famous.*
    (Say "Someəv become . . .")

Has is pronounced /əz/ (like the "long plural") after some words.

Example

The word *genius has* *become difficult to define.*
    (Say "geniusəz.")

---

1 🎧 Listen to the sentences. Underline the auxiliary verbs that are reduced. Then read the sentences aloud to a partner, using contractions and reductions.

1. The United States has become fascinated by prodigies.

2. Americans are all aware that Einstein was a genius.

3. Critics have warned that it's unhealthy to put too much pressure on children.

4. Researchers are interested in studying children with unusual abilities.

2 🎧 Listen to the paragraph about prodigies. As you listen, fill in the auxiliary verb or contraction you hear. Then read the paragraph aloud to a partner.

Australian painting prodigy Aelita Andre has captured the world's attention with her colorful work.

However, people _____ often surprised when they hear that she's only four years
                              (1)
old. The media _____ called her the "youngest professional painter in the world."
                              (2)
Aelita's parents are artists themselves, and they _____ always encouraged their
                                                              (3)

daughter to paint. They say she can spend hours working on a canvas. The public

_____ responded enthusiastically to Aelita's work—in fact, one of her paintings
      (4)

sold for $30,000. Some critics _____ called Aelita's work "surrealist abstract
                                      (5)

expressionism."

SPEAKING SKILL

In many conversations or discussions, it is important to state your own opinion or viewpoints clearly, and to do so politely. That way, listeners will be able to understand and respect your ideas. Sometimes, however, you may wish to avoid giving an opinion—either because you don't have one or because you want to avoid an argument!

In addition, you might sometimes need to indicate which ideas are the opinions of someone else.

STATING YOUR OWN OPINION			
Offer an Opinion	Agree	Disagree	Not Give an Opinion
If you ask me, . . .	I couldn't agree more.	Maybe / Perhaps, but . . .	I'm not really sure.
In my opinion, . . .	That's just what I was going to say!	You have a good point, but . . .	I don't know what to think.
Well, as far as I know, . . .	Yes, exactly.	Yes, but on the other hand . . .	I haven't made up my mind.
As I see it, . . .		That's not exactly the way I see it. I think . . .	Beats me. (informal)

(continued on next page)

REPORTING SOMEONE ELSE'S OPINION

Read the sentences about Listenings One and Two. Notice the phrases that are used to introduce people's opinions.

David Shenk **doesn't think** there is a dividing line between high achievement and genius. He **doesn't believe** it is that important.

One hundred and fifty years ago, scientists **were sure that** nature and nurture were opposing forces. They **were convinced that** people were influenced by either their genes or their upbringing.

Composer Sam Zyman **believes** that Jay Greenberg is the most important musical prodigy in the last 200 years, and Scott Pelley **couldn't agree more**. He **thinks** Jay is amazing.

Work with a partner. Take turns presenting and responding to these ideas. Use an expression from the box when you state your opinion.

1. **A:** Most child prodigies seem to be influenced by their parents.

   Example

   B: *I think so, too. If you ask me, some parents put too much pressure on their*

   children.

2. **A:** From what I understand, a child can develop special abilities up to age four or five.

   B: _____

3. **A:** I think anyone could become a prodigy with enough work, don't you?

   B: _____

4. **A:** I bet high achievers are always happy.

   B: _____

5. **A:** I think it's unhealthy for young children to become so involved in only one area.

   B: _____

6. **A:** I don't think Shenk is right when he says that there is an interaction between our genes and our environment.

   B: _____

■■■■■■■■■■■■■■ *GO TO* MyEnglishLab *FOR MORE SKILL PRACTICE AND TO CHECK WHAT YOU LEARNED.*

FINAL SPEAKING TASK

In this activity, you will take turns presenting scenarios of child prodigies and leading a small-group discussion about their special situations. Try to use the vocabulary, grammar, pronunciation, and listening and speaking skills that you learned in this unit.*

STEP 1: Choose one of the scenarios about child prodigies. They are all based on real situations.

Scenario 1

A neighbor's five-year-old child goes jogging in the morning with her father, who is a runner. She really seems to enjoy it, even though she is so small, and she is really fast. The family says that she is going to participate in a 5K race in the next few months.

What do you think about this? Do you think that it is fair or safe for the child's parents to encourage her to participate in this race? Do you think the parents are putting pressure on the child to succeed? Or do you think they should allow their child to enter the race?

Scenario 2

At nine months old, a pair of twins swam 25 meters on their backs with no assistance. This incredible achievement made them Internet stars because, for babies, swimming this distance obviously requires strength and resilience. The parents are very relaxed about their children—they allow them to turn over in the water and do not panic if they swallow water.

What do you think? Do you think the parents might be putting their children at risk by encouraging them to exercise so much? Do you think they might make other parents want to try to teach young babies to swim? Is this safe?

Scenario 3

Your brother's seven-year-old son has shown incredible promise as a violinist. The family wants to encourage him to improve his playing. However, in order to advance, the son would have to take lessons in another city. He's too young to go alone, so the whole family, including his ten-year-old sister, would have to move.

What do you think about this? Do you think that the family should make this big change, putting financial pressure on everyone and making his sister move to a different school? Are there any other alternatives?

Scenario 4

You read about a child prodigy in the news. When he was six, he told his parents how to make the best chess moves. In the four years since then, he has become the best chess player in his town. However, the boy is also very shy and private. He never wants to spend time with other children playing outside or doing any other activities, unless it involves chess. He likes to be alone, studying the board or playing online.

(continued on next page)

---

* For Alternative Speaking Topics, see page 25.

What do you think about this? Do you think it is healthy for this child to spend so much time alone inside the house or online playing chess? Should his parents limit the time he spends playing and encourage him to do other things? Or should they let him explore his interest in chess and hope that, one day, he will become interested in other things?

STEP 2: Work in a small group. One student presents the scenario in his or her own words. The group discusses the scenario. One student takes notes on what the group says and reports back to the class. Use the vocabulary and strategies you learned in the unit.

Example

A: In this scenario, a boy was encouraged to continue playing chess—but that's all he wanted to do. Do you think that is healthy? Should children be allowed to spend so much time alone?

B: If you ask me, I think it's unhealthy. I think children need to be given more time to play outdoors.

C: I'm not so sure. Shouldn't children be permitted to develop their own interests?

STEP 3: Present your discussion to the whole class.

Listening Task

Listen to your classmates' discussions. See how many phrases you can identify that state an opinion, avoid stating an opinion, and disagree with an opinion.

UNIT PROJECT

Investigate the life and accomplishments of a prodigy in history to explore the themes in this unit.

STEP 1: Choose one of the prodigies listed on the next page, or use your own idea. Search online to find out:

- Dates he or she lived and died
- Country of origin
- Remarkable achievements
- Other interesting facts about his or her life

Take notes on the information you find.

Music	Art
Frédéric Chopin	Pablo Picasso
Yehudi Menuhin	Zhu Da
Wolfgang Amadeus Mozart	Henriett Seth F.

Mathematics	Language
Carl Friedrich Gauss	Rubén Darío
John von Neumann	Maria Gaetana Agnesi
Blaise Pascal	Giovanni Pico della Mirandola

STEP 2: Prepare a presentation to give to your class. If possible, include a picture of the prodigy. Include your opinion on the factors that helped make this person a prodigy—do you think it was more nature, more nurture, or an interaction of nature and nurture? Give support for your opinions. Prepare some follow-up questions to ask the class.

STEP 3: Give your presentation to the class. Ask your follow-up questions and lead a short discussion about the prodigy. Then listen to and discuss your classmates' presentations.

ALTERNATIVE SPEAKING TOPICS

Read the quotes and decide what they mean. Then choose one and speak about it in class. Explain the meaning and say whether you agree or disagree, and why.

Genius is one percent inspiration and ninety-nine percent perspiration.
Thomas A. Edison: American inventor, 1847–1931

There is no great genius without a mixture of madness.
Aristotle: Greek philosopher, 384–322 B.C.

Genius is eternal patience.
Michelangelo: Italian sculptor, 1475–1564

Find out what your gift is, and nurture it.
Katy Perry: American singer, 1984–

For every child prodigy that you know about, at least 50 potential ones have burned out before you even heard about them.
Itzhak Perlman: Israeli violinist, 1945–

GO TO MyEnglishLab *TO DISCUSS ONE OF THE ALTERNATIVE TOPICS, WATCH A VIDEO ABOUT CHILD PRODIGIES, AND TAKE THE UNIT I ACHIEVEMENT TEST.*

THE ACHILLES Heel

1 FOCUS ON THE TOPIC

1. The title of this unit refers to the Greek hero Achilles, whose one weakness was in his heel. The expression *Achilles heel* can refer to problems and obstacles that people face in their lives. What kinds of challenges do you predict this unit will be about?

2. The photo shows a courageous individual who has not permitted a physical challenge to get in his way. Aside from physical challenges, what other challenges do people face?

3. How would you define the word "disability"? Should conditions like obesity, memory loss, and phobias (great fear of something, like crowds or heights) be considered disabilities and protected by law?

■■■■■■■■■■■■■■■■■■■■■■■■■■■■■■■■■■■■ *GO TO* MyEnglishLab *TO CHECK WHAT YOU KNOW.*

VOCABULARY

1 Work with a partner. Take turns reading the vocabulary and definitions aloud.

average: having qualities that are typical of most people or things; ordinary

devastated: extremely sad or shocked

diagnosis: identification of what illness a person has

go far beyond: to exceed the expected or usual boundary or limit

grief: extreme sadness, especially because someone you love has died

hardships: things that make your life difficult

makes (something) look cool: makes something seem fashionable, attractive, interesting, etc. (informal)

misconceptions: ideas that are wrong or untrue, but that people still believe

persevere: to continue trying to do something difficult in a determined way

stereotypical: widely held but, sometimes, incorrect opinion

(that) was it: (that) was the end (informal)

what keeps me going: what gives me hope and encouragement

2 Read the comments to a call-in show. Fill in the blanks with a word or expression from the box.

average	go far beyond	makes . . . look cool	stereotypical
devastated	grief	misconceptions	was it
diagnosis	hardships	persevere	what keep me going

RADIO SHOW HOST: Hi. . . . Uh, well, we are asking our listeners to call in and describe a

person they admire . . . a person who has overcome an obstacle.

CALLER 1: As far as I'm concerned, my father is a hero. A few years ago,

he had a terrible car accident, and the doctors gave him a scary

_____: They told him he had severely damaged his spinal
     (1)

cord and would never walk again. My family was _____

(2)

by the news, but, you know, my father was determined to get back

on his feet. He said he wasn't going to give up—he was going to

_____. And he did! Now, he's able to get around on his

(3)

own. He's made great progress physically, but for me his achievements

_____ that. He's also become an inspiration to me because

(4)

he's shown me how to face obstacles in life.

CALLER 2: I want to talk about Helen Keller. She's a historical figure I really admire.

Helen became blind and deaf when she was a baby, and everyone had

so many _____ about her—

(5)

including her family! They thought she

lived in a world of her own, and that there

was no hope for her future. But Helen was

not a(n) _____ person. Not

(6)

only did she learn to communicate, but she

also became a world-famous speaker and

author. And she even earned a B.A. along the way. In 2003, Alabama put

her portrait on a quarter, and it's beautiful. It really _____

(7)

her _____! Sadly, some people have _____

(8)

ideas about the disabled, but Helen Keller is an incredible example that

disproves many of them.

(continued on next page)

CALLER 3: I admire Mahatma Gandhi. He overcame difficulties of his own and

helped other people overcome a lot of _____ in their
(9)

lives. He supported the poorest people in his country. His enemies made

several attempts to kill him, and, in 1948, someone was successful.

Gandhi was fatally shot as he was about to make a speech, and that

_____. After his death, there was an outpouring of
(10)

_____ across India. He was against violence, saying that
(11)

"An eye for an eye only ends up making the whole world blind." His

example and his strength are _____ when I get depressed
(12)

about world events.

■■■■■■■■■■■■■■■■■■■■■■■■■■■■■■ *GO TO* MyEnglishLab *FOR MORE VOCABULARY PRACTICE.*

PREVIEW

🎧 Think about the title of the listening and the title of this unit. What disability do you think you might hear about? Then listen to an excerpt from Carol Saylor's story. Circle the correct answer.

1. Saylor is:

    a. a painter

    b. a sculptor

    c. a musician

2. She sounds:

    a. devastated

    b. hopeful

    c. angry

MAIN IDEAS

1 🎧 Listen to the whole report. Look again at your prediction from Preview. How did your prediction help you understand the report?

2 Circle the correct answers.

1. According to Saylor, what do most sighted people think about blind people?

   a. They understand their difficulties.

   b. They have incorrect ideas about blind people.

   c. They are sympathetic to blind people.

2. Many student groups visit Saylor's studio. What does Saylor mainly want to teach them?

   a. how to make sculptures

   b. how to work with clay

   c. how to use their imagination

3. The students who visit Saylor . . .

   a. are impressed by her work.

   b. are confused about her methods.

   c. think Saylor needs to persevere with her art.

4. Saylor says her art expresses feelings such as . . .

   a. pain and unhappiness.

   b. confusion and happiness.

   c. grief and hope.

DETAILS

Listen again. Complete the summary of Saylor's story by circling the correct words or phrases.

Carol Saylor, who is **(1)** (*sixty-two / seventy-three / eighty-one*) years old, is a sculptor and art teacher. When doctors first told her she was becoming blind, she was very upset because she had many misconceptions about blindness. For example, she thought she would see **(2)** (*black images / colorful shapes / vibrating spots*). However, what she actually "sees" is **(3)** (*white / beautiful / empty*).

Kate Whitman is a teacher who brings her class to see Saylor's work. She says that Saylor's story is **(4)** (*just as important as / less important than / more important than*) her art. The students are surprised and impressed by Saylor's work. One young girl realizes that art is not just about what you see, but also what you **(5)** (*understand / believe / feel*).

Saylor emphasizes that her art is not art therapy, meaning that it is not only about helping herself feel better about her situation. She says that it is **(6)** (*a way to understand the world / part of her / a kind of medicine*).

■ **GO TO** MyEnglishLab **FOR MORE LISTENING PRACTICE.**

MAKE INFERENCES

INFERRING MEANING FROM FIGURATIVE LANGUAGE

Speakers sometimes use **figurative language** to express their feelings. Figurative language involves comparing a situation, person, or object to something else, either directly or indirectly. Often, figurative language appeals to the senses (sight, sound, smell, and touch).

Look at the example and read the explanation.

To the art students visiting her studio, Carol Saylor says:

The things that I have learned about art go far beyond, I think, what the average sighted person knows. And that is really what my art is all about.

The things that Saylor has learned do not literally "go" anywhere. She uses the figurative sense of traveling or moving ("go far beyond") to indicate the growth and expansion of her ideas.

What can you infer from Saylor's statement? Circle the correct answer.

a. People use more than just the sense of sight to create and appreciate art.

b. Sighted people do not know how to be good artists.

c. She thinks she has learned more about art than most blind people.

Answer: a.

🎧 Listen to the excerpts and circle the correct answers.

Excerpt One

A student is explaining her reaction after she visits Saylor's studio. What is the student's intended meaning?

  a. Artists don't usually tell audiences what to look for in their pictures.

  b. Carol Saylor helped the student understand art better.

  c. When Saylor became blind, she decided to turn to art.

Excerpt Two

Carol Saylor is explaining her art to the interviewer. What is Ms. Saylor's intended meaning?

  a. Creating art doesn't make Saylor feel better about being blind.

  b. Saylor doesn't believe that painting is possible for most blind people.

  c. Saylor's art allows her to express deep feelings and emotions.

Excerpt Three

Carol Saylor is explaining what art means to her. What is Ms. Saylor's intended meaning?

  a. Art has given her a reason to live.

  b. She believes she is a naturally gifted artist.

  c. She loves to teach other people to create art.

EXPRESS OPINIONS

Work in a small group. Discuss the questions.

  1. What misconceptions do sighted people have about blind people? Why? Why is it important to overcome these misconceptions?

  2. What do you think is probably the hardest challenge Carol Saylor faces as an artist? What advantages, if any, does she have over sighted artists?

■■■■■■■■■■■■■■■■■■■■ *GO TO* MyEnglishLab *TO GIVE YOUR OPINION ABOUT ANOTHER QUESTION.*

VOCABULARY

You will hear a news report about a group of athletes who climbed Mount Kilimanjaro. The athletes belong to the Achilles Track Club, an organization of athletes with physical disabilities such as blindness, deafness, or the loss of an arm.

Read the flyer about Mt. Kilimanjaro. Match the underlined items with a synonym.

General advice for hikers

Kilimanjaro is the highest mountain in Tanzania, at 19,340 feet (5,895 meters). So, climbing this mountain is **(1)** <u>no small task</u>. Take great care as you ascend. The climate is extreme, with tropical weather at the base and strong winds closer to the peak. The athletes who have made it to the top said they **(2)** <u>buckled down</u> before the climb, training for hours each day. Are you in good physical condition? Are you ready for this challenge?

The common expression: "When the going gets tough, the tough **(3)** <u>get going</u>" represents the kind of determination you will need to succeed. Past teams have made it, but sometimes by **(4)** <u>overcoming great odds</u>. Take a look at the guest book they signed after they returned from the summit. Their **(5)** <u>inspirational</u> stories will help you keep going!

_____ **a.** something that encourages others to do good

_____ **b.** started working seriously

_____ **c.** being successful even though it seemed unlikely

_____ **d.** begin or get started

_____ **e.** when a situation becomes very difficult

COMPREHENSION

(continued on next page)

Listen to the report and answer the questions. Then compare your answers with a partner.

1. How many climbers were there?

   _____

2. What disabilities did the climbers have?

   _____

3. What feelings did the climbers experience on their expedition?

   _____

4. What record did the group set?

   _____

5. Who inspired the climbers?

   _____

■■■■■■■■■■■■■■■■■■■■■■■■■■■■ *GO TO* MyEnglishLab *FOR MORE VOCABULARY PRACTICE.*

LISTENING SKILL

DISTINGUISHING MAJOR IDEAS FROM SUPPORTING EXAMPLES

Reports often include examples to explain or support a previously mentioned point. It's important for a listener to know when a piece of information is being used to explain a previously mentioned idea and when it is a major idea itself. If you hear several different examples that all support a single idea, then that idea is an important one that you should pay attention to. The individual examples are only important in helping you understand that major idea. Sometimes the major idea is even unstated and must be inferred from the examples.

(continued on next page)

🎧 Read and listen to the example.

Example

They are all disabled in some way. Five are blind. One is deaf and asthmatic. The other, a cancer survivor and amputee.

Which is the major idea? Circle the correct answer.

a. Five of the climbers were blind.

b. One of the climbers was an amputee.

c. All of the climbers were disabled in some way.

Answer: c. The other sentences are all supporting examples of the major idea that the climbers were all disabled. The speaker could have added one more or one less example without changing the meaning of that idea. Even if the major idea had not been stated first, a listener could infer it from the examples given.

🎧 Listen to the excerpts and circle the correct answers.

Excerpt One

What is the major idea?

    a. A few of the athletes were able to reach the top.

    b. The athletes persevered even when the weather was bad.

    c. The climb was more difficult than the speaker expected.

Excerpt Two

What major idea can be inferred from the examples?

    a. The outdoor experience was moving and memorable.

    b. The Track Club members normally live in a rainy climate.

    c. The wind made it difficult to climb Mt. Kilimanjaro.

■ *GO TO* MyEnglishLab *FOR MORE SKILL PRACTICE.*

STEP 1: Organize

Complete the Venn diagram with information about Carol Saylor and members of the Achilles Track Club. Inside the circles, list:

- challenges
- goals and hopes
- personal qualities

In the middle intersection of the circles, list:

- ways the stories overlap

Carol Saylor

- is a sculptor who is blind

both describe physical disabilities

Achilles Track Club

- have a variety of physical challenges, such as being blind or deaf

STEP 2: Synthesize

Work in groups of three. Role-play a reporter interviewing Carol Saylor and a member of the Achilles Track Club. The interviewer asks about each person's challenges, goals, and hopes. The interviewer comments on similarities and differences between the two people's experiences. Use information from the diagram in your questions and answers.

Example

INTERVIEWER: Carol, tell us about the challenge of painting when you can't see.

CAROL: At first I wasn't sure if I could make it as an artist or as an art teacher. Most people think that seeing is essential for creating art.

INTERVIEWER: How did you find the motivation to keep going?

CAROL: Well, I . . .

INTERVIEWER: Did you face similar challenges when you climbed Mt. Kilimanjaro?

ACHILLES TRACK CLUB MEMBER: Actually, that's an interesting question. In fact, just like Carol, I . . .

GO TO MyEnglishLab *TO CHECK WHAT YOU LEARNED.*

3 FOCUS ON SPEAKING

VOCABULARY

REVIEW

During their ascent of Mount Kilimanjaro, one of the members of the Achilles Track Club kept an online journal similar to the blog on the next page. Fill in the blanks with the words that are listed above each paragraph.

| hardships | go far beyond | what keeps me going | when the going gets tough |

Ascent of Mt. Kilimanjaro

Day One

We're at the foot of this amazing mountain. It's over 5,895 meters high. That's 19,340 feet.

We've been training at home, but this challenge will _____ what we've
(1)
done so far. I'm trying hard not to think about all the _____ that we're
(2)
going to be facing. As far as I'm concerned, we're carrying a message of hope: That's

_____. And I think that
(3)

_____, we'll support each other.
(4)

| average | misconceptions | no small task | stereotypical |

Ascent of Mt. Kilimanjaro

Day Three

We've spent the last two days getting used to the altitude. The air is kind of thin up here!

Now I see that this climb will be _____. I'm really proud of our group.
(5)
Most people have a lot of _____ about what disabled people can and
(6)
cannot do. The _____ idea of an athlete is someone with big muscles
(7)
and the full use of all his or her senses. Well, many of us just don't look like that: Five of us

are blind, one is deaf, and one is an amputee. So we are not your _____
(8)
climbers! In any case, we can't wait to begin going up this huge, beautiful mountain!

(continued on next page)

buckled down	devastated	diagnosis	overcome great odds

○○○

Ascent of Mt. Kilimanjaro

Day Five

A couple of days ago, two people in our team got sent back because they had started to

feel unwell. The _____ was altitude sickness. Of course, they were
          (9)

_____, but we told them they were a big success to have made it as far as
          (10)

they did. We couldn't risk them getting worse or injured. In any case, they had already

_____ to have made it as far as they did.
          (11)

　After that difficult experience, we _____ hard
          (12)

yesterday and made a lot of progress. Now the summit is getting close. I'm still in good

spirits. I think we are carrying a message of hope for everyone who wants to overcome a

difficult challenge in life.

---

inspirational	make (something) look cool	persevere	that was it

---

○○○

Ascent of Mt. Kilimanjaro

Day Seven

Get ready to hear this _____ news . . . We're here! When we got to the top,
          (13)

we took a photo of the group, all together. All these incredible photos will

_____ our trip _____ to our families!
          (14)

　After we rested a while, we released a bag of feathers into the air as a symbol of hope.

You can't believe how challenging this climb really was. At one point, I thought

_____: I nearly gave up. But somehow we were all able to _____
          (15)   (16)

and keep on going.

　There are birds flying below us, and the air is clear. I want to remember this day forever.

EXPAND

Certain words and phrases can have both a literal meaning and a figurative meaning. Compare the two sentences below.

Example

The view from the top of the mountain was spectacular. The climbers **turned to** each other and smiled happily.

In this sentence, the phrase "turned to" has a literal meaning. The climbers moved their bodies to face each other.

The climb was difficult for many members of the Achilles team, who **turned to** each other for inspiration.

In this sentence, the phrase "turned to" has a figurative meaning. The athletes depended on each other for inspiration.

Work with a partner. Read the sentences and focus on the **bold** phrases. Write **L** (literal) or **F** (figurative) for each sentence. Discuss your choices with each other. Then explain them to the class.

1. _____ a. The Achilles athletes **reached a high point** in their climb and stopped to admire the view.

   _____ b. I **reached a high point** in my career when I finally got a promotion.

2. _____ a. Jackie dropped his keys in the rain and had to **reach deep down** into the mud to find them.

   _____ b. When the mountain climber thought she was too weak to take another step, she **reached deep down** inside herself and found the determination to make it back to the camp.

3. _____ a. My brother was born with Down Syndrome. When he **opened his eyes**, my mother immediately knew he had a disability.

   _____ b. Down Syndrome Awareness Week tries to **open people's eyes** to the contributions that disabled people make to society.

4. _____ a. Carol Saylor wants to show her students that there is **another level** to her art. Art is not only about what you see; it's also about what you feel.

   _____ b. The climbers walked for seven hours and reached **another level** of Kilimanjaro.

5. _____ a. New devices for hearing impaired people allow them to **reach new heights** and achieve things they never thought were possible.

   _____ b. Specially designed lifts allow disabled people to **reach** items at **new heights**. Now, even the tallest cabinets are within their reach.

CREATE

Read the quotes below. Then work with a partner. Circle the paraphrase that best explains the quote's meaning, and say whether you disagree with the quote. Then give examples to support your opinion, using the vocabulary from the box. Check (✓) each word or expression as you use it.

devastated	inspirational	overcoming great odds
diagnosis	make something look cool	persevere
go far beyond	misconceptions	stereotypical
hardship	no small task	

1. "Anybody who lives long enough will eventually become disabled."
   Rachel Adams, professor and advocate for the disabled

   a. Being elderly is a type of disability.

   b. If you live a long time, certain body parts will fail; this happens to everyone.

2. "I have not been handicapped by my condition. I am physically challenged and differently able."
   Janet Barnes, the world's longest living quadriplegic[1]

   a. I don't consider my condition to be a disadvantage.

   b. I can do everything a non-quadriplegic can do.

3. "When you have a disability, knowing that you are not defined by it is the sweetest feeling."
   Anne Wafula Strike, Paralympic wheelchair racer

   a. Being in a wheelchair is not the most important thing about me.

   b. Being in a wheelchair doesn't keep me from doing things I enjoy.

4. "Aerodynamically,[2] the bumblebee shouldn't be able to fly, but the bumblebee doesn't know that so it goes on flying anyway."
   Mary Kay Ash, businesswoman and charity organizer

   a. Because of their body design, bumblebees can't fly very well.

   b. A positive attitude can help one to overcome a physical disability.

---

[1] **quadriplegic:** paralyzed in all four limbs
[2] **aerodynamically:** according to the laws of physics

■ *GO TO* MyEnglishLab *FOR MORE VOCABULARY PRACTICE.*

GRAMMAR

1 Work with a partner. Read the conversation and answer the questions.

A: My son wants to volunteer with the Achilles Track Club. He's planning **to train** with a blind athlete in the park every Sunday.

B: Isn't **running** with a blind person a bit dangerous?

A: Well, the Achilles Track Club teaches the volunteers how **to run** safely. The blind runners hold on to a short rope that the sighted people use **to guide** them.

B: **Volunteering** for this organization sounds like a very special experience.

1. In A's lines, what do the bold words have in common?

2. In B's lines, what do the bold words have in common?

GERUNDS AND INFINITIVES	
Gerunds	**Examples**
To form the gerund, add *-ing* to the base form of the verb.	It's a story of **reaching** new heights and **overcoming** great odds.
Some Uses of the Gerund	
Use the gerund as the subject of a sentence.	**Getting** to the top of the mountain was a great achievement for the athletes.
Use the gerund after a preposition, such as *for*, *in*, *of*, and *about*.	When she was diagnosed with blindness, Saylor thought **about doing** sculpture instead of painting.
Infinitives	**Examples**
To form the infinitive, use *to* and the base form of the verb.	Saylor expects visitors to her studio **to learn** about using their imagination.
Some Uses of the Infinitive	
Use the infinitive after a *be* + **adjective** combination such as *easy*, *difficult*, *hard*, *happy*, *possible*, *willing*, and *prepared*.	It **was** very **hard** for the Achilles Track Club **to climb** Mount Kilimanjaro.
Use the infinitive after certain verbs, including *allow*, *agree*, *decide*, *expect*, *hope*, *learn*, *manage*, *need*, *try*, and *want*.	One of the Achilles athletes did not **expect to reach** the summit and almost turned back several times.

2 The Universal Design Movement aims to make products and buildings **accessible to** everyone, including disabled people. Look at the flyer. It contains a list of devices that can help the disabled. Work with a partner. Discuss how these devices could improve our everyday lives. Use the expressions below the flyer with gerunds and infinitives.

Example

In the 1960s, architect Selwyn Goldsmith invented the concept of the *dropped curb*, a small ramp on street corners, **to allow** people **to cross** roads more easily. His idea made a difference for thousands of people all over the world. Nowadays, there are more innovations. For example, it is common **to find** ramps at the entrances to buildings that **make it easier** for people in wheelchairs **to access** those buildings.

Tips to Make Your Home or Community Accessible for All

ramp   **grip bar**   **mechanical lift**

- Ramps at the entrances to buildings
- Braille signs in public elevators
- Wide doorways and hallways
- Baths / showers with grip bars
- Mechanical lifts

- Contrasting colors on ledges, counter edges, and steps
- Strobe lights on smoke and burglar alarms
- Raised buttons on appliances
- New ideas? _____

. . . make it easier . . .	. . . give people freedom . . .
. . . allow people . . .	. . . good for . . .
. . . stop people from . . .	. . . make people aware of . . .
. . . make it possible . . .	. . . help people avoid . . .

3 Read the information and do the exercise that follows.

Since the Americans with Disabilities Act was passed in the United States in 1990, more people have become aware of the changes that must be made in public places to allow individuals with disabilities to deal with their challenges. Government and city officials have more responsibility to provide access to services for people with disabilities.

Work with a partner. Think about the difficulties that a person with a physical disability has doing everyday tasks. Complete the chart so that each statement indicates the view of an advocate for the disabled or the view of a government or city official. Use infinitives and gerunds. Add as much information as you can.

Discuss other innovations that might help the disabled. Then discuss whether your town or city has implemented such ideas.

ADVOCATE FOR DISABLED INDIVIDUALS	GOVERNMENT OR CITY OFFICIAL
_____ is very hard.	The city has agreed _____
_____ presents a real challenge.	We need _____
_____ must be extremely difficult.	We are willing _____
Disabled people are forced _____	We are prepared _____
They often can't manage _____	We are ready _____
I'm sure they would be happy _____	We should avoid _____

■■■■■■■■■■■■■■■■■■■■■■■■■■■ GO TO MyEnglishLab FOR MORE GRAMMAR PRACTICE.

PRONUNCIATION

THOUGHT GROUPS

When we speak, we group words together logically and join the groups into sentences. The groups are called **thought groups**. They help the listener organize the meaning of the sentence.

🎧 Listen to the thought groups in these sentences.

My Achilles heel was shyness.

I hated going to parties by myself.

And I was terrified when I had to speak in class.

Thought groups are often grammatical phrases or structures, such as prepositional phrases or short clauses.

🎧 Listen to the thought groups in this sentence.

When I first got the diagnosis, I was devastated.

(continued on next page)

The Achilles Heel 45

Words can be combined into thought groups in different ways. Speakers sometimes choose groups of similar length to create a more pleasing rhythm. In other cases, the speaker may include two phrases in one group to show that the two phrases are part of the same idea. If the speaker wants to show that the two phrases are different ideas, they will be in different thought groups.

🎧 Listen to the two ways the words in the sentence are grouped.

1. I realized that everyone is born with gifts.

2. I realized that everyone is born with gifts.

In the first sentence, the speaker emphasizes the fact that he or she realized something important. The phrase "I realized" is emphasized.

In the second sentence, what the speaker realized about everyone (the fact that everyone is "born with gifts") is most important.

Pronounce the words in a thought group together smoothly. Pause briefly after one thought group before you start the next group.

🎧 Listen to the sentences.

My Achilles heel (*pause briefly*) was shyness.

One of the misconceptions (*pause briefly*) is that you see black.

I just didn't imagine (*pause briefly*) it would be so tough.

1 🎧 Listen to the sentences. As you listen, mark the thought groups. Compare answers with a partner. Then take turns reading the sentences to each other. Remember to pause briefly at the end of a thought group before you start a new one.

1. When Saylor received her diagnosis, she thought that was it.

2. She decided to stop painting and turn to sculpture.

3. When people visit her studio, they realize that her art is amazing.

4. They realize that art can involve all of your senses.

5. Ms. Saylor's story is an inspiration for all of us.

2 Look at the two charts. Take turns creating sentences by choosing one thought group from each column. If the sentence you create is true, your partner will say, "That's right." If the sentence you create is not true, your partner will say, "I don't think that's right." Continue until you and your partner have created three true sentences for each chart.

1	2	3	4
Saylor's work	is a visual artist	she uses touch	in a different way.
A visitor to her studio	inspires other people	who is very unusual	to "see" the human body.
Carol Saylor	is impressed by the way	to think of art	because she is blind.

1	2	3	4
Organizers from the Achilles Track Club	helped each other	on the trail	in late August.
Newspaper reporters	wrote of the challenges	to the mountain summit	when the going got tough.
The inspiring athletes	accompanied the climbers	the climbers faced	as they scaled the mountain.

SPEAKING SKILL

USING SPECIFIC EXAMPLES TO SUPPORT MAIN IDEAS

In speaking, just as in writing, it is important to add specific examples to main ideas in order to help listeners understand the meaning or importance of a comment and add interest.

Listen to and read the conversation. Underline the main idea and examples that speaker A uses.

A: Carol Saylor seems to have faced many challenges in her life.

B: Really? What do you mean?

A: Well, she's a visual artist who is blind. That seems like a challenge to me. And she also said that she's experienced a lot of grief and loss.

1 Work with a partner to continue the conversations. Use examples to support the main ideas.

Conversation 1

A: Carol Saylor has accomplished so much.

B: I agree: _____

(continued on next page)

Conversation 2

    A: I think Saylor's story is very important for everyone to listen to.

    B: Really? Why do you say that?

    A: Well, _____

Conversation 3

    A: Did you hear about the Achilles Track Club who climbed Mt. Kilimanjaro? They faced so many challenges.

    B: Really? Like what?

    A: Well, _____

Conversation 4

    A: The Achilles Club story can teach us a lot.

    B: Even people who don't have disabilities?

    A: Yes, I think that they show us that _____

2 Read the sentences about Stephen Hawking and Christopher Reeve. Choose two pieces of supporting information for each sentence from the boxes on the next page. Then share your answers with a partner.

Stephen Hawking

1. Stephen Hawking, world-renowned British astrophysicist born in 1942, lived a normal life in many ways.

2. Stephen Hawking achieved incredible things in his lifetime.

3. Stephen Hawking became severely disabled.

- As a child, he was very active; for example, he enjoyed horseback riding.
- Symptoms of Lou Gehrig's disease began to appear when he was in college.
- Hawking has Lou Gehrig's disease: At age 21, he was given only three years to live and later became completely paralyzed and mute.
- He's the author of the bestseller *A Brief History of Time* (1988).
- He made a flight to space, achieving zero gravity.
- He became a happy and successful person.

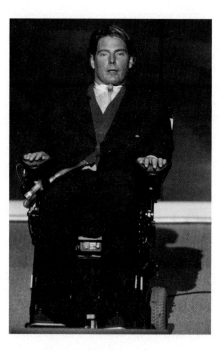

Christopher Reeve

1. Christopher Reeve, the American actor, achieved great professional success in his life.

2. Reeve suffered a serious accident when he was forty-three years old.

3. Reeve became a strong advocate for disabled people.

- Reeve played the superhero *Superman* in numerous movies.
- His book *Nothing Is Impossible* is an inspiration to many.
- A fall from a horse left Reeve unable to move.
- Reeve was not only a gifted actor, but also a film director and author.
- He taught paralyzed people to live more independently.
- Reeve needed ongoing medical care to keep him alive.

GO TO MyEnglishLab TO CHECK WHAT YOU LEARNED.

FINAL SPEAKING TASK

In this activity, you will prepare a speech about an obstacle you have overcome or a challenge you have faced. Try to use the vocabulary, grammar, pronunciation, and listening and speaking skills that you learned in this unit.*

STEP 1: Use the information in the left column of the chart below to plan a 2–3 minute speech. Take notes in the right column on examples that will illustrate your main ideas. Practice your presentation a few times aloud or in your mind.

MAIN POINTS	EXAMPLES THAT WILL ILLUSTRATE YOUR POINTS.
BACKGROUND	• Provide some information about yourself. • Describe the setting of your story.
CHALLENGE	• Give a description of the obstacle or challenge that you faced.
OUTCOME	• Explain how you met the challenge / what happened.
LIFE LESSON	• Explain what you learned from facing the challenge.

STEP 2: Present your speech to the class, or record or video it to play for the class.

Listening Task

Listen to your classmates' speeches and write at least one question to ask them about their experiences. Then ask your questions clearly and listen to the presenters' responses.

UNIT PROJECT

Work with a group or the whole class to watch and analyze a movie about overcoming disabilities.

STEP 1: Select one of the many movies that have been made about the heroism and achievements of people who have overcome obstacles, and watch it. Some examples are: *I am Sam, Benny and Joon, The Eighth Day, Shine, My Left Foot, Sound and Fury, The Mighty, Simon Birch, Girl Interrupted, The Color of Paradise, The Miracle Worker, Children of a Lesser God, The Gift, The Hero, The Keys to the House, The Little Girl Who Sold the Sun,* and *Oasis.*

STEP 2: Take notes as you watch the movie. Focus on one character who overcame obstacles.

---

* For Alternative Speaking Topics, see page 51.

STEP 3: Go online to research reactions from other viewers. What did they think of the film and how it portrayed the disabilities? Do you agree with the reactions of other viewers? Why or why not?

STEP 4: Work in a group or with the whole class. Briefly summarize the movie you watched, the reactions of other viewers, and your own opinions. Let the class know whether or not you would recommend that film to others.

ALTERNATIVE SPEAKING TOPICS

Work in a small group. Discuss the questions.

1. The Universal Design Movement aims to make the living environment easily accessible to all. It recommends having:

   - wide doors to buildings
   - lever handles for doors, not twisting knobs
   - light switches that are easy to use
   - enough restrooms for women and men
   - closed captioning on TV
   - large print labels
   - etc.

Is your campus or community accessible to everyone? Does it have any particular areas that make it difficult for anyone in particular?

2. If you could redesign your campus or community, what three changes would you make so that it is more accessible to all users?

GO TO MyEnglishLab *TO DISCUSS ONE OF THE ALTERNATIVE TOPICS, WATCH A VIDEO ABOUT A GIRL WITH AUTISM, AND TAKE THE UNIT 2 ACHIEVEMENT TEST.*

EARLY TO BED, EARLY TO Rise

1 FOCUS ON THE TOPIC

1. Work with a partner. Discuss your sleep habits:

   - Do you sleep well, or are you restless? Do you fall asleep easily?

   - Do you talk in your sleep?

   - Do you wake up well rested, or are you sleepy in the morning?

   - Are you an "early bird" (a person who gets up early) or a "night owl" (a person who stays up late)?

   - Do you have dreams? Do you have nightmares?

2. An old proverb about sleep says: "Early to bed, early to rise, makes you healthy, wealthy, and wise." What does this proverb mean? Do you agree with it?

3. What are some effects of sleep loss? Who is most affected by a lack of sleep?

 *GO TO* MyEnglishLab *TO CHECK WHAT YOU KNOW.*

VOCABULARY

1 🎧 Many parents are concerned about their children's sleep patterns. Read and listen to the online exchange between a parent and a doctor. Pay attention to the words and phrases in **bold**.

○ ○ ○

ADVICE FROM DR. JENNINGS

Hi Dr. Jennings,

I'm worried about my daughter Eden, who's a middle school student with sleep issues. She (1) **has a tendency to** stay up late, and then she's exhausted later on in the day. This sleep pattern is having a terrible effect on her schoolwork. She's falling behind in almost all her classes, and we worry that it's going to get worse (2) **over the course of** the year. (3) **That being said**, we think we're doing all we can. We have always told Eden that (4) **consistency** is really important when it comes to her bedtime routine, but she doesn't seem to be able to go to bed early. I don't know— she seems to be dealing with it (5) **pretty well**, but, obviously, we are concerned. What should we do?

Sheila Michaels

Dear Ms. Michaels,

It is normal for adolescents to have problems sleeping. Like Eden, if they go to bed too early, they suffer from wakefulness, which can also be difficult. At this age, the body's circadian rhythm—the body's "clock"—is changing. But don't worry! She'll grow out of it eventually and (6) **reset** her internal clock.

Of course, what you do need to worry about is (7) **sleep deprivation**. If she wants to sleep in on weekends, let her do so. It's not a sign of slothfulness if she doesn't get up until 1 or 2 P.M., so don't think she's being lazy. It's just the body's (8) **intrinsic** reaction to being tired. If she gets the rest she needs during the weekend, it will help her (9) **recover** from her week. If you wish, you can ask her doctor about low-dose melatonin tablets, which can sometimes help. There are even over-the-counter vitamin supplements that seem to be very effective, and most people (10) **tolerate** those quite easily. There are a lot of remedies that have been (11) **clinically proven** to work.

Good luck with Eden, and don't worry too much. Try to (12) **maintain** a positive attitude.

Dr. Jennings

2 Match the words in **bold** to their meanings.

_____ **a.** lack of sleep

_____ **b.** get better after an illness, injury, shock, etc.

_____ **c.** accept something you do not like

_____ **d.** the quality of always being the same, or always behaving in an expected way

_____ **e.** in a rather good, reasonable, or competent way

_____ **f.** return to a regular position or state

_____ **g.** in spite of what was just said

_____ **h.** during a period of time or a process

_____ **i.** part of the basic character or nature of someone or something

_____ **j.** be likely to (do something)

_____ **k.** shown scientifically through tests

_____ **l.** make something continue in the same way or at the same standard as before

■■■■■■■■■■■■■■■■■■■■■■■■■■■■■ *GO TO* MyEnglishLab *FOR MORE VOCABULARY PRACTICE.*

PREVIEW

Dr. Michael Howell, from the University of Minnesota, studies sleep patterns and sleep-related issues facing adolescents.

🎧 Read the questions and predict Dr. Howell's explanations. Then listen to the introduction to Dr. Howell's report to check your predictions.

1. Why are many teenagers always sleepy? Think of several reasons.

2. Regarding sleep issues, are human adolescents and young animals similar or different?

MAIN IDEAS

Listen to the whole report. Write **T** (true) or **F** (false). Then correct the false statements.

_____ **1.** Middle and high schools often begin classes later than elementary schools do.

_____ **2.** It is very difficult to reset your body's pattern of sleep and wakefulness, or circadian rhythm.

_____ **3.** If you lose sleep during the week, your body needs to recover about half of it on the weekend.

_____ **4.** Most teenagers who sleep in class are lazy or not interested in studying hard.

DETAILS

Listen again. Circle the correct response.

1. According to Dr. Howell, what problem is caused by adolescents' schedules?

   a. weak academic performance

   b. sleep deprivation

   c. disagreements with teachers

2. What method has been proven successful in helping people fall asleep earlier?

   a. having consistent bedtimes

   b. avoiding stressful activities

   c. limiting caffeine

3. How many minutes of sunlight can help reset a person's internal clock?

   a. 10–20

   b. 20–30

   c. 30–40

4. When should a melatonin supplement be taken?

    a. about 6 o'clock in the morning

    b. 6 hours before bedtime

    c. at 6 P.M.

5. According to Dr. Howell, about how many hours of sleep can adolescents lose each day?

    a. one

    b. two

    c. three

6. What activities for teenagers does Dr. Howell mention?

    a. theater and gym

    b. soccer and art

    c. swimming and music

■■■■■■■■■■■■■■■■■■■■■■■■■■■■■■■ *GO TO* MyEnglishLab *FOR MORE LISTENING PRACTICE.*

MAKE INFERENCES

UNDERSTANDING ASSUMPTIONS

Speakers sometimes use statements that imply that their listeners understand or share their assumptions. Listeners need to make educated guesses, or inferences, about what these assumptions are.

🎧 Read and listen to Dr. Howell from Listening One.

Example

> A couple of key things to think about when you're dealing with adolescents and sleep issues is that adolescents have a tendency to be a bit of night owls. They tend to like to go to bed later and sleep in later, and this is more than just a behavioral choice on their part. Their brains actually act differently.

Dr. Howell assumes that most people think teenagers are night owls because

    a. teens choose to go to bed late and sleep in in the morning

    b. teenagers' brains act differently, causing them to stay up late

Answer: a. Dr. Howell implies that people believe teenagers go to bed late and sleep in late because they want to, not because they need to ("this is more than just a behavioral choice"). Dr. Howell explains that teenagers' brains act differently, so they actually need this sleep pattern.

🎧 Listen to the excerpts from Listening One and circle the correct answers.

Excerpt One

Dr. Howell assumes that most people think teenagers are sleepy because . . .

    a. they are lazy.

    b. their brains are developing.

Excerpt Two

To help teenagers, Dr. Howell assumes that most people think it would be enough to . . .

    a. start activities later.

    b. start classes later.

EXPRESS OPINIONS

Work in a small group. Take turns reading the opinions. Then say whether you agree or disagree, and why.

    1. Teenagers naturally need much more sleep than older people do.

    2. Because teenagers are involved in so many additional activities these days, sleep deprivation is a more serious problem than it was in the past.

    3. High schools should change their schedules. Classes and activities should start and finish much later in the day, so that students can feel more rested.

■■■■■■■■■■■■■■■■■■■ *GO TO* MyEnglishLab *TO GIVE YOUR OPINION ABOUT ANOTHER QUESTION.*

VOCABULARY

Like teenagers, parents of small children are often sleep deprived. You will hear part of an interview from *Satellite Sisters*. Lian, one of the sisters, is talking with Dr. Joyce Walsleben, director of New York University's Sleep Disorder Center.

Use the words or phrases in the box to fill in the blanks in the conversation below. Use appropriate forms.

accumulates	get cranky	touch on
fatigue	make (something) a priority	

BRYAN: Hi, Jen, how's your new job going?

JEN: I just don't know what to do. Since my daughter was born, I'm so tired all

the time. I almost fell asleep at a meeting the other day, and I started to

_____. My boss seemed to notice I was in a bad mood. He
      (1)

told me that the meeting was really important and told everyone that we should

_____ work _____. I'm sure he was making a
      (2)

comment about me!

BRYAN: Yeah, well, you're probably just suffering from _____. What time
                                                          (3)

do you go to bed at night?

JEN: Pretty late. And my tiredness just _____ during the week. By
                                               (4)

Thursday or Friday, I'm exhausted.

BRYAN: I was watching some videos that _____ that topic. Apparently,
                                             (5)

you should sleep nine hours a night. It's absolutely critical that you get enough sleep.

Otherwise you'll be yawning all day.

JEN: Nine hours? You must be joking. I don't even get seven!

Early to Bed, Early to Rise   59

COMPREHENSION

Listen to the interview and circle the correct answers.

1. Lian complains about being constantly tired. What reason does she give?

   a. She can't fall asleep at night.

   b. She has small children.

   c. She wakes up in the middle of the night.

2. According to Dr. Walsleben, how should people combat sleep deprivation?

   a. by making sleep a priority

   b. by not combining careers and parenthood

   c. by making sure their days are active

3. Dr. Walsleben mentions the accident of the *Exxon Valdez*, an oil tanker that crashed and spilled 750,000 barrels of oil in Alaska. What do some people suspect about the causes of the accident?

   a. The captain of the ship was sleep deprived.

   b. The mate driving the ship had been working for too many hours.

   c. The crew was sleeping when the accident occurred.

4. How does sleep deprivation affect Lian, the interviewer?

   a. She's too tired to see her parents.

   b. She's too tired to decide what to eat.

   c. She's too tired to make good parenting decisions.

5. How do most people feel about the effects of sleep deprivation?

   a. They don't feel any effects.

   b. They worry about its effects on their health.

   c. They accept that they are sleep deprived.

6. What happens to many workers by the end of the workweek?

   a. They accumulate a large sleep debt.

   b. They often need to take Fridays off.

   c. They can no longer get things done at work.

7. About how many hours of sleep are many people missing by Friday?

   a. four

   b. five

   c. seven

■■■■■■■■■■■■■■■■■■■■■■■■■■■ *GO TO* MyEnglishLab *FOR MORE VOCABULARY PRACTICE.*

LISTENING SKILL

RECOGNIZING SUPPORTING DETAILS

Like writers, speakers state main ideas and offer supporting details. They sometimes speak in "oral paragraphs," especially when they want to inform or persuade. In this interview, the intention of the speakers is to do both: to inform us about the problem and to persuade us that the problem is serious. Listen for supporting details that prove the validity of the speaker's point.

🎧 Read and listen to the example.

Example

> **INTERVIEWER:** Dr. Walsleben, why are we all so tired?
>
> **DR. WALSLEBEN:** We're probably tired because we don't make sleep a priority. And I think, as a young mother and a career woman, your days are pretty well filled, and I would suspect that you probably think you can do without sleep.

Dr. Walsleben's main idea is "we don't make sleep a priority." She supports this main idea with four reasons why Lian probably doesn't make sleep a priority:

   1. She is a young mother.
   2. She is a career woman.
   3. Her days are filled.
   4. She thinks she can do without sleep.

In this example, the main idea and details are linked in the oral paragraph by two connecting phrases:

And I think. . . .

And I would suspect . . .

🎧 Listen to the excerpts. Read the main ideas, and then identify the supporting ideas.

Excerpt One

Main idea: Sleep deprivation can be very serious because lack of sleep can affect our performance.

Dr. Walsleben supports the main idea with examples of two different types of accidents. What are these?

1. _____

2. _____

Excerpt Two

Main idea: Sleep deprivation affects us a lot.

Lian supports her main idea with details from her own life. Complete the list:

1. She is tired and cranky.

2. _____

3. _____

4. _____

■■■■■■■■■■■■■■■■■■■■■■■■■■■■■■■■■■■■ *GO TO* MyEnglishLab *FOR MORE SKILL PRACTICE.*

STEP 1: Organize

Work in a small group. Use information from Listening One (about teenagers) and Listening Two (about the parents of young children) to fill in the chart.

	TEENAGERS	PARENTS OF YOUNG CHILDREN
CAUSES OF SLEEP DEPRIVATION	• teenagers have a natural tendency to go to sleep late • •	• their children may sleep a little and wake up a lot • •
SYMPTOMS OF SLEEP DEPRIVATION	• •	• • •
RECOMMENDATIONS FROM PROFESSIONALS	• • • •	• • •

STEP 2: Synthesize

Role-play a radio call-in show with a public health doctor. Work in groups of three: the doctor, a teenager, and the parent of a young child. The doctor asks the callers to describe the symptoms of their sleep deprivation. Then the doctor explains the dangers of sleep deprivation and recommends solutions. Use the information from the chart above.

Example

DOCTOR: Hi, thank you for calling. I understand you're a teenager who has sleep deprivation. Can you describe your symptoms to me?

TEEN: Thanks, doctor. Yeah, I can't fall asleep at night. Then I have to get up early for school. I'm yawning all day!

DOCTOR: Well, one cause of that is a hormone called melatonin, which . . . Not getting enough sleep is dangerous for you because . . . What I recommend is . . .

GO TO MyEnglishLab TO CHECK WHAT YOU LEARNED.

3 FOCUS ON SPEAKING

VOCABULARY

REVIEW

Read the website about sleep disorders. Circle the correct word.

Sleep Disorders: Are You a Victim?

Are you constantly exhausted? You might want to educate yourself about these common sleep disorders. Being (1) *critical / sleep-deprived* is much more common than you think!

Insomnia
People with insomnia have difficulty falling asleep at night or (2) *have a tendency to / make it a priority* to wake up in the middle of the night. Believe it or not, at least 50% of people have this problem!

Apnea
This is when your normal breathing gets blocked as you sleep. You may snore or sleep restlessly, and you can (3) *get cranky / reset* during the day. If you think you are suffering from apnea, it is (4) *consistent / critical* for you to see a doctor.

Restless Legs Syndrome (RLS)
This is a painful feeling in your legs that makes you kick while you are asleep. RLS can lead to severe (5) *fatigue / recovery*, which is obviously dangerous.

Sleepwalking
Although it is not as common as other syndromes, sleepwalking can have a terrible effect on sleepwalkers and their families. If someone in your family gets out of bed and walks around while still asleep, (6) *have a tendency / make it a priority* to send him or her to a doctor for a physical checkup!

Daydreaming
(7) *That being said / Over the course* of their lives, most people daydream from time to time, and daydreaming can be caused by boredom, not just tiredness. In general, you should be sure to get plenty of sleep, and don't worry if you daydream occasionally!

Nightmares
If your tiredness (8) *accumulates / maintains*, you may find that you have more nightmares. It's not fun to have scary dreams in the middle of the night, but most people (9) *tolerate / recover* quickly from these experiences if they get enough sleep.

EXPAND

Work with a partner. Look at the expressions and their definitions. Read the conversations below between (1) an employee and his boss, and (2) two friends. Complete the conversations with words from the box. Then practice the conversations aloud.

burn the midnight oil: work very late at night

irritable: easily annoyed or made angry

naps: short sleeps during the day

nod off: fall asleep by accident

power nap: an extra-short sleep in the middle of the working day

run by: have someone consider

shut-eye: sleep (informal)

be drowsy: be tired and almost asleep

demonstrate: show a fact clearly

a major concern: something important that worries or involves you greatly

Conversation 1: Sleep Pods

drowsy	irritable	naps	power nap	run by

WILL MARTIN: Uh, Mr. Rogers? Could I have a word?

JACK ROGERS: Sure. Come on in. What's up?

WILL MARTIN: Well, a few of us had an idea that we wanted to _____ you.
(1)
We've thought of a way you could increase productivity and make your employees really happy at work. Sleep pods!

JACK ROGERS: Sleep pods? I'm not following you. What are you talking about?

WILL MARTIN: Well, you know how sometimes people are _____ in the
(2)
afternoons? Sleep pods are private, reclining chairs that allow employees to take short _____. Here, take a look at this brochure . . .
(3)

JACK ROGERS: Hmm. Sleep pods, huh? They look expensive.

(continued on next page)

WILL MARTIN: But they would practically pay for themselves. Think about it, sir. Everyone would work more productively. Everyone would be nicer, too. You know how some of us get _____ by Friday and start shouting at each other? Well, that's because we're all so tired.
(4)

JACK ROGERS: Well, I'll think it over, but really, are you saying I should pay people to sleep on the job?

WILL MARTIN: That's not it, sir. It's more like taking a _____, something executives do to restore themselves so they can work harder and longer. Just 10 minutes and a person can feel refreshed and ready to work again.
(5)

JACK ROGERS: Heh, heh. Very clever. Well, as I said, I'll think about it.

Conversation 2: Research on Sleep and Memory

| burning the midnight oil | demonstrate | a major concern | nod off | shut-eye |

HELEN: Psst, wake up! You've been snoring. Did you _____?
(6)

NEIL: What? Oh . . . sorry. I guess I did. I went to bed so late last night.

HELEN: You're always _____. That can't be good for you.
(7)

NEIL: Yes, I know. I got home really late from work last night. Lately I'm having trouble keeping track of everything I need to do.

HELEN: Well, you'd better take more care. You know, sleep deprivation is _____.
(8)
Some researchers just discovered that when you get plenty of sleep, your memory improves.

NEIL: Really? How did they _____ that?
(9)

HELEN: They took brain images of people while they were in bed. Apparently your brain moves your memories from one place to another while you're asleep.

NEIL: That's amazing. I think I'd better go home and get some _____ right
(10)
away!

CREATE

Work with a partner. Cover your partner's column. Ask and answer each other's questions in a few sentences. Use as many of the vocabulary items in your column as you can.

STUDENT A	STUDENT B
1. Does reading in bed keep you alert or help you relax? Explain.	*rub your eyes*
	priority
2. Does exercising before bed keep you awake, or does it help you sleep? Why do you think this happens?	*yawn*
	snore
3. Have you ever felt drowsy or fallen asleep on a bus or train? Explain.	*fatigue*
	power nap
accumulate	4. Does drinking tea, coffee, or cola stop you from sleeping? Why or why not?
alert	
awake	5. Do you feel better or worse after a nap? Explain.
burn the midnight oil	
do without	6. Do you ever try to sleep late on weekends? Why or why not?
drowsy	
nod off	

GO TO MyEnglishLab *FOR MORE VOCABULARY PRACTICE.*

GRAMMAR

1 Work with a partner. Read the conversation aloud. Then answer the questions.

PATIENT: I'm exhausted. I just can't keep my eyes open during the day.

DOCTOR: It seems that you are quite sleep deprived and don't get to bed early enough. If you went to sleep earlier, you would feel a lot better.

PATIENT: That's the problem, doctor: I can't go to bed early. I work the late shift, and I don't get home until 10:00 or 11:00 P.M.

DOCTOR: Well, perhaps you could take naps instead. If you took regular naps, you'd feel less sleepy.

1. What two suggestions does the doctor make?

2. What verb tense does the doctor use to make the suggestions?

PRESENT UNREAL CONDITIONALS

A **present unreal conditional** sentence has two clauses: the *if-clause*, which states the condition, and the **result clause**, which states the result. Use the present unreal conditional to talk about something that is untrue, impossible, or imagined.

To form the present unreal conditional, use the *past form* of the verb in the *if-*clause. Note that the sentence is not in the past tense, however.	If I **didn't work** at night, I **could go** to bed early. (I work at night, so I can't go to bed early.)
Use *would* + **base form** of the verb in the main clause to describe a definite result.	If Lian **didn't have** such a hectic lifestyle, she **would spend** more time asleep. If more people **paid attention** to their sleep habits, the problem **would not be** so serious.
Use *might* or *could* to describe a possible result.	If people **knew** more about the dangers of sleep deprivation, they **might treat** their sleep habits more seriously.
To make a question, use question order in the main clause.	If you **were sleep deprived, would you be** able to tell?
The *if-*clause is not needed if the condition is understood by the listener.	How **would you be** able to tell?
For the verb *be*, use *were* for all subjects.	If I **were** a doctor, I would tell my patients about sleep debt.
You can begin the sentence with either the *if-*clause or the main clause. When writing, put a comma between the clauses in sentences that start with the *if-*clause.	**If I went to bed earlier,** I would feel better. (comma) I would feel better **if I went to bed earlier**. (no comma)

2 Read the interviews. Complete the sentences using present unreal conditionals. Then work with a partner. Read the conversations aloud, with expression.

Interview between a Sleep Researcher and a Medical Worker

SLEEP RESEARCHER: Thank you for taking the time to share your experience with me.

Can you tell me about the sleep problems that medical workers have?

MEDICAL WORKER: Well, one of the problems is that medical residents and

interns can work up to 100 hours a week. They can get really overtired. If they

_____worked_____ less, they _____ so tired.
     (1) (work)   (2) (not / get)

SLEEP RESEARCHER: And does this fatigue cause serious problems in the health profession?

MEDICAL WORKER: Sure. Just think about your own work. How well _____ (3) (do) your job if you _____ only five or six hours a night?
(4) (sleep)

SLEEP RESEARCHER: Aren't there any rules about how much you can work?

MEDICAL WORKER: Yes, but they are not strict enough. For example, if interns

_____ for work for six days and _____ for 16
(5) (show up)   (6) (work)
hours, they _____ following the regulations, as long as they
(7) (be)
_____ less the following week.
(8) (work)

SLEEP RESEARCHER: That's terrible! What can be done to make getting sleep a priority?

MEDICAL WORKER: We need to raise public awareness. For example, surgeons

and medical technicians can be on call for many nights every week. If they

_____ to do that, there _____ fewer problems.
(9) (not / be allowed)   (10) (be)

Interview between a Sleep Researcher and a Pilots' Association Official

SLEEP RESEARCHER: Hello there. I'd like to ask you about sleep regulations in the airline industry.

PILOTS' ASSOCIATION OFFICIAL: Well, luckily there have been several studies about

the importance of adequate sleep. Sleep is important for everyone, but pilots, in

particular, cannot be tired or distracted. Can you imagine what _____
(11) (happen)
if a pilot _____ asleep on the job?
(12) (fall)

SLEEP RESEARCHER: Asleep? I can't imagine that!

(continued on next page)

PILOTS' ASSOCIATION OFFICIAL: Well, many people take what we call "microsleeps,"

which last from five to ten seconds. But if a pilot _____ one of these
                                                        (13) (take)
little naps during takeoff or landing, the results _____ disastrous.
                                                        (14) (be)

SLEEP RESEARCHER: I see. So you need to make sure pilots are awake and alert.

PILOTS' ASSOCIATION OFFICIAL: Yes, alert is the right word. For example, if you yourself

_____ adequate sleep, your reaction time _____
         (15) (not / get)   (16) (be)
affected. The same thing _____ to a pilot who _____
                              (17) (happen)   (18) (not / sleep)
enough.

SLEEP RESEARCHER: Are all pilots made aware of the dangers of sleep deprivation?

PILOTS' ASSOCIATION OFFICIAL: Certainly. The number of accidents

_____ significantly if we _____ some serious regulations
         (19) (increase)   (20) (not / enforce)
about sufficient sleep.

3 Work with a partner. One person works for the *Satellite Sisters* radio talk show, and the other is calling to get advice about a sleep problem. Take turns describing the problems and making suggestions using the present unreal conditional.

Example

CALLER:	My schedule changes from day to day. Sometimes I go to bed early, sometimes late, depending on how much homework I have to do. When I finally do go to bed, I can't sleep.
SATELLITE SISTER:	Why don't you take a bath before going to bed? If you took a warm bath, you would find it easier to go to sleep.

1. I have trouble sleeping in warm weather. I often wake up feeling really hot and cranky.

2. My husband / wife / roommate gets home from work at nine o'clock every evening, so I have dinner very late.

3. I get really tired in the evenings. I usually drink a coffee after dinner, but then I can't fall asleep at night.

4. I fall asleep in the living room with the TV on. I usually wake up at two or three o'clock in the morning, go to bed, and can't fall asleep again.

5. I get home from sports activities at 9:00 P.M. Then I go online and chat with my friends. I usually don't get to bed until after midnight.

6. I get a surge of energy late at night, a second wind. I keep remembering things I need to do for the next day, so I stay up until two or three o'clock in the morning taking care of them.

■■■■■■■■■■■■■■■■■■■■■■■■■■■ *GO TO* MyEnglishLab *FOR MORE GRAMMAR PRACTICE.*

PRONUNCIATION

CONTRASTIVE STRESS

Native speakers contrast information in a sentence by emphasizing the words they want to contrast or the accented syllables in those words. The emphasized words or syllables are said louder, more slowly, and with a higher pitch.

🎧 Listen. In the following example, the speaker is contrasting *body* with *brain*, and *classroom* with *pillow*:

Example

My BOdy's in the CLASSroom, but my BRAIN's still on the PILlow.

1 🎧 Listen to the sentences. As you listen, underline the contrasted words. Then repeat the sentences with a partner.

1. I need to go to bed, but I'm feeling energetic.

2. Adolescents wake up late, but children wake up early.

3. Lian is fast asleep, but her children are awake.

4. My husband has insomnia, but I need to sleep.

5. I'm sleepy in the morning, but I'm wide awake at night.

2 Work in pairs. Look at the contrasting information in columns A and B. Create and say sentences that emphasize the information.

Example

What are some obvious effects of sleep deprivation? (absenteeism)

What are some subtle effects of sleep deprivation? (emotional problems)

ABSENTEEISM is an OBVIOUS effect of sleep deprivation, but EMOTIONAL problems are a more SUBTLE effect.

Column A

1. When is melatonin secreted in adults? (early evening)

2. When does melatonin "turn on"? (evening)

3. Why do adults think that teenagers stay up late? (because they are having fun)

4. How do many parents feel on Monday morning? (tired)

Column B

1. When is melatonin secreted in adolescents? (late at night)

2. When does melatonin "turn off"? (morning)

3. Why do teenagers say they stay up late? (because they are night owls)

4. How do many parents feel by Friday night? (completely exhausted)

3 Complete the survey and compare your answers with a partner. Then report any differences back to the class using sentences that contrast your partner's response and your own. Use contrastive stress to indicate your comparisons.

Example

I OFten wake up at night, but JOE NEVer does.

OR

I take naps in the MORning, but CElia takes naps in the afterNOON.

	YOU	YOUR PARTNER
1. Do you often wake up at night?		
2. Do you snore?		
3. Do you daydream?		
4. Do you take naps?		
5. Do you use an alarm clock?		
6. What time do you wake up in the morning?		
7. How much coffee do you drink?		

SPEAKING SKILL

INTERRUPTING TO ASK FOR CLARIFICATION

Sometimes you might not hear a speaker's information clearly: It is spoken too fast, there is background noise, or you have difficulty understanding the speaker.

To clarify information, especially facts, you can (1) interrupt the speaker and ask about what you thought you heard, or (2) ask the speaker to repeat what he or she said.

Example

A: Joelle, I heard some horrifying statistics—over thirty percent of traffic accidents are caused by sleepiness! People should be more careful!

B: What did you say? Thirteen percent?

A: No, I said over thirty percent. That's a lot, don't you think?

B: Thirty percent! I see what you mean! Wow! That's a very high figure.

Here are some expressions you can use to interrupt a speaker when you do not understand something. Use rising intonation for the questions.

REQUESTS TO CLARIFY INFORMATION	
Excuse me? What did you say?	Could you repeat that?
What? (*informal*)	Sorry, I didn't hear you. What was that?
Sorry?	Could you say that another way?
I'm sorry. I didn't catch that. Could you say it again?	Did you say . . . ?

Work with a partner.

Student A: Read each statement aloud. Speak too softly or too quickly, or mispronounce an important word, so that Student B won't understand and will have to ask you a question.

Student B: Listen to your partner. Interrupt to ask a question or to ask your partner to repeat information you didn't understand. Use one of the expressions in the box above when you interrupt.

Example

A: I read that 17 percent of Americans are insomniacs!

B: *Sorry, could you repeat that?* _____

(continued on next page)

Student A

1. There are about 1,500 sleep-disorder clinics in the United States.

2. Almost 20 percent of Americans are shift workers, meaning that they often have changes in their work schedules.

3. During the winter, there are 14½ hours of darkness in some parts of the United States. There's no excuse for not sleeping!

Now switch roles.

Student B

4. Even if a person is seriously sleep deprived, he or she can get back on a regular pattern of sleep after only three weeks.

5. If rats are completely deprived of sleep for 2½ weeks, they die.

6. Sleeping pills first became popular in the United States in the 1970s.

■■■■■■■■■■■■■■■■■■■■■■■■■■■■■■■■■■ *GO TO* MyEnglishLab *FOR MORE SKILL PRACTICE.*

FINAL SPEAKING TASK

In this activity, you will role-play a meeting about sleep deprivation between hospital administrators, medical interns, and members of a patients' rights group. You will study a situation at the fictional Hilldale General Hospital and then try to resolve some problems through discussion. The situation is based on real cases at many hospitals. Try to use the vocabulary, grammar, pronunciation, and listening and speaking skills that you learned in this unit.*

STEP 1: Read the situation. Then divide the class into three groups. Each group will study one of the roles to prepare for a meeting to establish hospital policies on how long medical personnel can work until rest is required.

Situation

Two weeks ago, a ten-year-old boy was admitted to a private hospital for some routine surgery.

In preparation for the operation, he was accidentally given an overdose of his medication. He

became very ill for several days, but fortunately he recovered and was not seriously affected.

---

* For Alternative Speaking Topics, see page 77.

Investigations revealed that both the intern who ordered the medication that night and the nurse who administered it were seriously sleep deprived. They had both been on duty for 15 hours when the boy received his medicine. The intern had worked ten hours per day for the previous eight days, while the nurse had worked the same shifts for six days in a row. Just before checking on the boy and ordering his medicine, the intern and the nurse had spent five hours in the operating room working on victims of a car accident emergency. The story appeared in the local newspaper, and the hospital received a general review.

In addition to this latest case, Hilldale General Hospital is having serious financial problems. The only other hospital in the community of Hilldale closed down two years ago due to lack of funding, leaving Hilldale General to cope with too many patients and too little money.

ROLES		
A. *Hospital Administrators:* You are worried. There is so little money to operate the hospital, and you are seriously understaffed. Your staff works long hours to cover all the shifts and keep the emergency room open 24 hours a day. Doctors' shifts cannot last longer than 16 hours a day, with one continuous 24-hour period off every week. You do what you can for your staff, but you know it's not enough. Hilldale General is in serious financial trouble.	**B.** *Interns:* You are worried. You are dedicated professionals. You work long, hard hours for very little pay, but you are committed to helping the community of Hilldale. You know that sometimes you don't perform well because you are sleep deprived, but you don't feel you have a choice. There is no one else to take your place.	**C.** *Patients' Rights Group:* You are concerned about the patients. You fear that someone will be hurt because the hospital staff is overworked and sleep deprived. You want the administration to take action. Other hospitals in the country are using innovative ways to prevent mistakes from happening, such as using videotapes to assess staff performance and using computers to regulate doses of medicine.

STEP 2: Work with your group to clarify your viewpoint on the issue. Make a list of points you want to discuss.

STEP 3: Divide into groups of three, with one student representing each of the roles (A, B, and C). Role-play a meeting. Try to reach some solutions that will satisfy everyone.

Example

HOSPITAL ADMINISTRATOR: We are seriously understaffed. If we had more staff members, we would not be so concerned about sleep deprivation among the interns.

INTERN: Yes, that's true. For example, there are only two of us on the ward at night. If my partner and I didn't show up for work one evening, there would be no one available to help incoming patients.

PATIENTS' RIGHTS GROUP MEMBER: Excuse me? Did you say there were only two people on the ward?

Listening Task

Share your answers to the following questions with the whole class:

- What are the causes of the crisis at Hilldale General Hospital?

- What are some possible solutions? (Use conditionals.)

- Who should be responsible for addressing the problems?

Listen to everyone's ideas. Then write down what you think is the best possible solution to the problem. Vote as a class.

UNIT PROJECT

Investigate the causes and remedies for jet lag.

STEP 1: Talk with a partner or group about **jet lag**. What is it? Have you experienced it before? If so, what did it feel like?

STEP 2: Research jet lag online. Complete the chart with your findings.

EFFECTS OF JET LAG	FACTORS THAT MAKE JET LAG WORSE	METHODS TO PREVENT OR REDUCE JET LAG

STEP 3: Make a presentation to the class about the dangers of jet lag and how to cope with it or avoid it when you travel.

ALTERNATIVE SPEAKING TOPICS

Work in a small group. Discuss the questions.

1. The National Sleep Foundation recommends that adults get between 7 and 9 hours of sleep a night. Look at the chart below. It shows how much sleep people actually get. Answer the questions with a partner.

   - What does the graph show about how much most people sleep?
   - Which category of people best represents you?
   - What could be the consequences of these habits at school, home, and work?
   - What changes should people make?

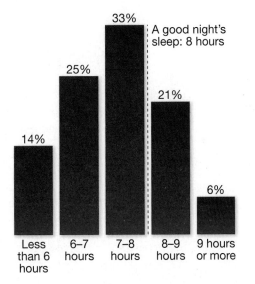

2. When teenagers get enough sleep, they are in better moods and tend to do better in school. Should schools redesign their schedules to help teenagers sleep more? How? What would be some advantages and disadvantages to a school schedule that lets teens sleep later?

3. Interns and residents (doctors-in-training), as well as drivers, pilots, and factory workers, are often sleep deprived, which leads to accidents. Should there be laws to require that these professionals get a certain amount of sleep? How could these laws be administered and enforced?

■■■■■■■■■■■■■■■■■GO TO MyEnglishLab TO DISCUSS ONE OF THE ALTERNATIVE TOPICS, WATCH A VIDEO ABOUT A SLEEP CLINIC, AND TAKE THE UNIT 3 ACHIEVEMENT TEST. ■■■■■■■■■■■■■■■■■■

ANIMAL
Intelligence

1 FOCUS ON THE TOPIC

1. The photo shows a dolphin, considered to be one of the most intelligent animals on Earth. In what ways do you think a dolphin could demonstrate intelligence? How would you test a dolphin for intelligence?

2. Do you think that other animals think? Do *all* animals think? What kinds of things might they think about?

GO TO MyEnglishLab *TO CHECK WHAT YOU KNOW.*

LISTENING ONE | ANIMAL INTELLIGENCE

VOCABULARY

1 🎧 Read and listen to a lecture from an introductory course on animal intelligence. Notice the words and expressions in **bold**.

A chimpanzee

HOST: Welcome to this month's guest lecture. This morning I'm pleased to introduce Dr. Addison Shanks, visiting scholar from Johnson University. So without further delay, I'll **give the floor to** Professor Shanks.

DR. SHANKS: Thank you. Good to be here. Today we'll consider whether animals are "intelligent" in the same ways that humans are. Let me begin by asking you how we know humans are intelligent. **Off the top of your head**, would you say it is because we invent language or use tools? Is it because we can **transfer** knowledge we learn in one **context** to another context? Are we intelligent because we can deceive and intentionally trick others? Or is it because we empathize with others, understanding how they feel? Are other animals capable of these things as well? Let's consider some recent research.

First, humans are conscious beings. When we look into a mirror, for example, we know we are seeing our own image. What about other animals? If you show a chimp his own reflection in a mirror, one might assume that he thinks he's looking at another chimp. But is it true that he just **doesn't get it**, or would the chimp understand he's looking at himself? Apparently, he would. When some apes look into a mirror for the first time, their reaction is **spontaneous**: They examine their teeth. In some studies, researchers put paint on the faces of sleeping chimps. After waking, the chimps used a mirror to get the paint off. This shows awareness, or knowledge, of self. Dolphins and elephants have also demonstrated self-awareness: They look into mirrors to examine themselves after researchers place marks or objects on their heads.

Second, we've learned some **intriguing** things about the ability of animals to communicate, both with each other and with humans. Of course, most animals aren't able to vocalize; that is, put voice to words. However, a growing number of animals raised in captivity have learned to communicate with humans through computers or gestures, sometimes learning thousands of words. While we could claim that this is just **rote** memorization and not true communication, studies have shown that certain apes can ask and answer questions they have never heard before and even create new "words." For example, a gorilla named Koko saw a picture of a mask for the first time and called it an "eye hat."

What other abilities are unique to humans? We humans show intelligence by putting items into **categories** according to color, size, shape, and so on. Humans also find answers to complex problems and apply the answers in a different context, or new situation. However, many examples show that animals can **figure out** complicated problems and transfer knowledge as well. Crows, for instance, figure out how to steal when fishermen aren't looking, by pulling the fishing line out of the water inch by inch until they get the fish.

Finally, consider emotions. Are humans alone in feeling love, sadness, empathy, compassion? Consider the research gorilla who showed distress and stopped eating when her pet kitten died, or recall that elephants display grief when family members die. Like humans, can animals be **socialized** to help one another? And do animals lie and use deception to trick others? Do animals guess what others are thinking and then take advantage of that knowledge? At this point, you can safely predict yes. Case in point: An elephant secretly learned how to open his cage at a zoo. After the humans had left for the night, the elephant opened all the other elephant cages, releasing his friends for midnight walks.

So we **end up** asking if animal intelligence is really so different from that of humans, and, if so, to what degree? Furthermore, if animals can categorize, perform simple mathematics, intentionally deceive others, make and carry out plans, and communicate with humans, what kind of relationship should we have with them? A growing body of research is pushing the edge of the envelope on what we consider "human" when we think about these questions.

2 Match the words and expressions on the left with their definitions on the right.

_____ 1. give the floor to someone

_____ 2. off the top of one's head

_____ 3. transfer

_____ 4. context

_____ 5. doesn't get it

_____ 6. spontaneous

_____ 7. intriguing

_____ 8. rote

_____ 9. categories

_____ 10. figure out

_____ 11. socialized

_____ 12. end up

a. interesting because it's unusual or unexpected

b. understand

c. not planned

d. doesn't understand

e. the situation, events, or information related to something

f. trained to behave in a way that is acceptable to others in your group

g. finish by

h. groups based on similar qualities

i. habitual, mechanical

j. spoken without thought or planning beforehand

k. move from one place to another

l. give someone else the opportunity to speak

GO TO MyEnglishLab *FOR MORE VOCABULARY PRACTICE.*

PREVIEW

Recent research has changed our view of animal emotions and animal intelligence. Three researchers discuss their experiments in a radio interview:

Dr. Sally Boysen, professor of psychology, Ohio State University

Dr. Stan Kuczaj, professor of psychology, University of Southern Mississippi

Dr. Irene Pepperberg, University of Arizona

🎧 Listen to the introduction. Write the type of animal to be discussed. Talk with a partner and predict what information you might hear about each.

1. _____

_____

2. _____

_____

3. _____

_____

An African grey parrot

MAIN IDEAS

1 🎧 Listen to the whole interview. Look again at your predictions from the Preview section. How did your predictions help you understand the interview?

2 What did the animals do? Check (✓) the correct picture. Then compare your answers with your predictions in Preview.

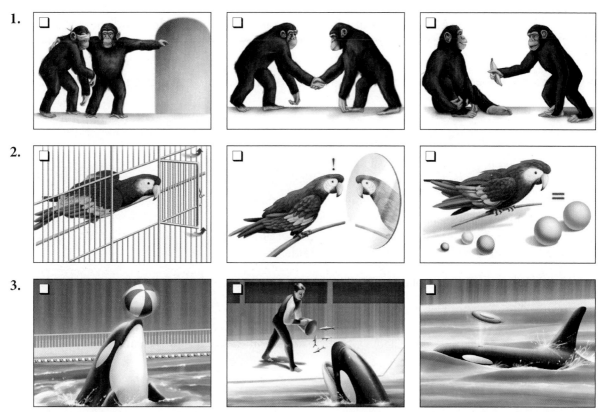

1. 2. 3.

DETAILS

Listen to the interview again. Write **T** (true) or **F** (false) for each statement. Correct the false statements. Then discuss your answers with a partner.

_____ **1.** The older chimp, Sara, helped the new, disabled chimp by giving her some food.

_____ **2.** Sara's behavior is remarkable to Dr. Boysen because Sara has not been socialized with other chimps.

_____ **3.** Alex, the parrot, uses a computer to communicate.

_____ **4.** Alex can answer questions about where he wants to go.

_____ **5.** Dr. Kuczaj's killer whale used fish to attract seagulls.

_____ **6.** Dr. Pepperberg says that talking to Alex is like talking to a very young human.

(continued on next page)

_____ **7.** Dr. Pepperberg doesn't call Alex's talk "language;" she calls it "two-way communication."

_____ **8.** When Alex answers questions, he doesn't seem to understand the questions; instead, he is answering in a rote manner.

■■■■■■■■■■■■■■■■■■■■■■■■■■■■■■■ *GO TO* MyEnglishLab *FOR MORE LISTENING PRACTICE.*

MAKE INFERENCES

UNDERSTANDING ATTITUDE FROM STRESSED WORDS AND HESITATION

An inference is an educated guess about something that is not directly stated in the text. We understand a speaker not only by hearing the words used, but also by noticing which words are stressed. Stressed words indicate that the speaker places more importance on something. Pauses and hesitation can also express a speaker's attitude.

🎧 Listen to the example. Notice the clues to the speaker's attitude in her stressed words and pausing.

Example

How does Dr. Boysen feel about Goodwin's question? Circle the correct answer.

a. surprised

b. pleased

c. not happy

What might she say about her feelings?

a. "I wasn't ready to speak first."

b. "I don't know the answer to that question."

Answer: a. She feels surprised by the question. She might be thinking, "I'm not ready to speak first." Dr. Boysen begins with "Oh," showing surprise, then stresses "would" in "you *would* start with me," showing reluctance to speak, and finally hesitates on "I—I guess probably," showing that she isn't quite ready to speak.

🎧 Listen to the excerpts and circle the correct answers. Pay attention to clues in the speakers' tone of voice, stressed words, pauses, laughter, and other clues.

Excerpt One

1. How does Dr. Boysen feel about the chimpanzee's behavior?

a. She's impressed by it.

b. She's confused by it.

c. She's saddened by it.

2. What might Dr. Boysen say about what Sara, the chimp, did?

   a. "This shows that animals have emotions and feelings."

   b. "This shows that animals can teach each other."

Excerpt Two

1. What is Goodwin's attitude about the parrot's behavior?

   a. He is impressed by what the bird did.

   b. He can't believe the behavior really happened.

   c. He doesn't think the behavior shows intelligence.

2. What might Goodwin say about what Alex, the parrot, did?

   a. "He is easily confused by new situations."

   b. "He understood that we were trying to trick him."

EXPRESS OPINIONS

Work in a small group. Discuss the questions.

1. Do you think the research shows that these animals are intelligent? Why or why not?
   Give reasons for your answers.
   - Sara, the chimp
   - Alex, the parrot
   - the killer whales

2. Have you ever observed intelligence or emotional expression in an animal, either a wild animal or a pet? If so, describe it and what you think it showed.

■■■■■■■■■■■■■■■■■■ *GO TO* MyEnglishLab *TO GIVE YOUR OPINION ABOUT ANOTHER QUESTION.*

VOCABULARY

1 🎧 Read and listen to the passage below. Discuss with a partner or group possible meanings for the words and phrases in **bold**.

A giant octopus

Controversy surrounded the disappearance of some crabs at an aquarium in Oregon a few years ago. One morning, workers found crabs missing from their tank and empty crab shells on the floor. New crabs were brought in to replace the dead ones, but the same thing happened several more times. Who was guilty? They installed an overnight camera to find out.

It turns out that a sneaky octopus had learned to **take advantage of** his nighttime privacy. Did he **anticipate** a midnight snack? It looks that way. He waited all day until workers went home. Then he was able to **manipulate** his body, lengthening and narrowing himself to fit into an air tube that led out of his covered tank. He moved across the floor into the crab tank. After enjoying a midnight crab meal, he went back to his own tank the way he had come, looking quite innocent in the morning. Workers were amazed that a seemingly unintelligent animal was able to carry out such a trick.

2 Match the words and expressions on the left with the definitions on the right.

_____ **1.** controversy   **a.** has a particular result

_____ **2.** it turns out   **b.** skillfully handle or control

_____ **3.** take advantage of   **c.** expect something to happen

_____ **4.** anticipate   **d.** profit from

_____ **5.** manipulate   **e.** serious disagreement

COMPREHENSION

Other scientists have added to our knowledge of large ape and bird intelligence. In this podcast interview, Liz Pennisi, a writer for *Science Magazine*, discusses some new research on animal cognition.

A scrub jay hiding food

1 🎧 Listen to the interview. Check (✓) the answers.

The speakers say that apes and / or birds can . . .	YES	NO
1. understand when a human is watching.	❑	❑
2. manipulate humans to get what they want.	❑	❑
3. operate robots.	❑	❑
4. teach what they've learned to their offspring.	❑	❑
5. remember.	❑	❑
6. create works of art.	❑	❑
7. plan.	❑	❑
8. anticipate the future.	❑	❑
9. judge what someone else might be doing.	❑	❑
10. deceive others who might steal their food.	❑	❑

2 Discuss the question with a partner. Then share your answer with another pair or the whole class.

In both reports, you heard research that investigates the meaning of intelligence. In your opinion, what is a useful definition of "intelligence"?

■■■■■■■■■■■■■■■■■■■■■■■■■■■■ GO TO MyEnglishLab FOR MORE VOCABULARY PRACTICE.

IDENTIFYING THE MAIN IDEA AND EXAMPLES IN ORAL PARAGRAPHS

Highly educated speakers often structure their speech so as to include a clear main idea (usually toward the beginning), which is sometimes supported with an example. Noticing when the oral paragraph has come to a close helps you notice when the speaker will introduce the next main idea.

🎧 Read and listen to the example.

Example

A lot of the work is done [on] chimps and other apes because they're our closest relatives. . . . So there's been a series of experiments. One of the more recent ones has to do with putting a chimp head to head with a human, and the chimp wants to reach for food, and the human has the ability to pull the food away.

Liz Pennisi says that research is being done on chimpanzees because of their similarity to humans: ". . . they're our closest relatives." She supports this main idea with an example of the experiments comparing chimps and humans. This evidence helps prove the main idea.

🎧 Listen to another oral paragraph in which Liz Pennisi explains her research. The main idea is identified for you in the outline. Complete the information about the example.

I. Main idea: Some skills you see in chimps and humans might also exist in social birds.

Supporting example:

A. They started experiments on _____

_____

B. The experiments showed _____

_____

■■■■■■■■■■■■■■■■■■■■■■■■■■■■■■■■■ GO TO MyEnglishLab FOR MORE SKILL PRACTICE.

STEP 1: Organize

How did the animals you heard about demonstrate their intelligence? Complete the chart with information from Listening One (about animal intelligence) and Listening Two (about animal motivation).

ANIMAL	ANIMAL INTELLIGENCE	WHAT MOTIVATES ANIMALS?
1. Chimps	• One chimp understood that another chimp was disabled and helped that chimp.	•
2. Birds	Parrot: •	Scrub jays and crows: • Bury food and hide it from other birds • Come back later and change hiding place if they think another bird was watching
3. Killer whales	• •	(Whales were not mentioned in Listening 2.)

STEP 2: Synthesize

Work in groups of three. Each of you is an animal scientist in a special area. Select your category of specialization: chimpanzees, birds, or killer whales. Study the chart for your specialty. Think of a topic sentence and choose supporting details. Explain your recent research in a short oral presentation. Then change groups and repeat your presentation.

Example

My research focuses on chimps. We have seen many examples of intelligence in these animals. In one case, . . . In another case, . . .

■■■■■■■■■■■■■■■■■■■■■■■■■■■■■■■ GO TO MyEnglishLab TO CHECK WHAT YOU LEARNED.

3 FOCUS ON SPEAKING

VOCABULARY

REVIEW

Work with a partner. Say the underlined word aloud. Then circle the two words that are related to the underlined word. Use a dictionary if necessary.

Example

remarkable	(incredible)	insignificant	(surprising)
1. socialized	tamed	friendly	wild
2. context	knowledge	situation	setting
3. spontaneous	thoughtful	unexpected	unplanned
4. intriguing	irrelevant	fascinating	mysterious
5. categories	types	individuals	groups
6. figure out	add	understand	solve
7. end up	get behind	finish	result in
8. doesn't get it	doesn't understand	doesn't realize	can't imagine
9. off the top of one's head	considered	not researched	quickly
10. give someone the floor	ask for an opinion	help to walk	allow to speak
11. manipulate	pull	handle	use
12. anticipate	oppose	plan	expect
13. controversy	argument	agreement	dispute

EXPAND

1 🎧 Work with a partner. Listen to and read the transcript of a radio talk show as a host answers comments from callers.

> **HOST:** Our guest today is Dr. James Rutledge, an expert on animal behavior. Welcome, Dr. Rutledge. I've asked our listeners to call in to tell us their stories of smart animals or animals that cause problems. We've got calls from all over. Yes, hello, Lin. You're on the air.

LIN: Hi, I'm calling about a smart animal that's causing me problems. I have a bird feeder hanging in my yard. No matter what I do, squirrels eat all the food. They're such a nuisance! I've tried to **put a stop to** it every way I can think of, but the squirrels always figure out a solution. How can I outsmart them? And, also, raccoons are getting into my attic . . .

A squirrel

HOST: Sorry to **butt in** here, Lin, but I want to stick to one question at a time. Dr. Rutledge, what about Lin's squirrel problem?

DR. RUTLEDGE: Well, squirrels are clever at getting food and enjoy a challenge. However, you *can* outwit them. Most likely, they're getting at your feeder from above. Raise it higher and move it to an open space so they can't jump down from the house or trees.

HOST: Thanks for calling, Lin. OK, Janek . . . Janek? Are you there? You have the floor.

JANEK: Yes, hello. I'm calling about problems with deer, which are not very intelligent animals. I **make a living** selling garden plants, but deer jump my fence at night and eat everything. It's costing me a fortune. What's more, they're dangerous.

HOST: Dangerous? What do you mean?

JANEK: Deer often run into the street and cause car accidents. I like animals as much as the next person, but at some point we have to admit that humans are more, well, superior to animals. Deer are not **endangered** animals. We just have to **get rid of** them if they become problems.

HOST: You mean kill them? Some people might think killing them is **pushing the envelope** a bit, no? Callers, what do you think? The phone lines are already ringing. Alicia, you're on.

ALICIA: Hi. I just heard your last caller, and I **take issue with** his cruel solution to the deer problem. Animals are helpless next to humans, so it's our responsibility to protect them, not kill them because they're in our way. The **humane** thing to do is stop thinking that wild animals are a nuisance, and just learn to live with them.

HOST: Dr. Rutledge, would you like to **weigh in** here?

DR. RUTLEDGE: Both callers have good points. We have to allow for human activity, but we also want to be **ethical** in our treatment of animals. And we want to preserve what we can of the natural world for our children, of course.

(continued on next page)

HOST: OK, time for one last caller. Kenna, you're on the air.

KENNA: I saw a very smart cat on my local news and on YouTube. He's called the "Cat Burglar" because he sneaks out at night and steals from families in the neighborhood. He takes bathing suits, shoes, toys, all kinds of things, and delivers them all to his embarrassed owners. He's taken hundreds of items in a couple of years.

DR. RUTLEDGE: (*laughing*) Intriguing case! It would be fun to study this cat's behavior and figure out his motivation. For example, maybe he's categorizing these objects by smell or taste.

HOST: Or maybe he's just having fun! At any rate, we're out of time for today. So thanks, callers, and thank you for joining us today, Dr. Rutledge!

2 Match the words and phrases on the left with the definitions on the right.

_____ 1. put a stop to   **a.** not cruel

_____ 2. butt in   **b.** remove; throw away

_____ 3. make a living   **c.** give an opinion about something

_____ 4. endangered   **d.** threatened with extinction

_____ 5. get rid of   **e.** interrupt

_____ 6. pushing the envelope   **f.** disagree with

_____ 7. take issue with   **g.** earn enough money to support oneself

_____ 8. humane   **h.** moving beyond the limit of what has usually been done

_____ 9. ethical   **i.** morally good and correct

_____ 10. weigh in   **j.** end an activity

CREATE

Work with a partner. Take turns asking and answering these questions using vocabulary from this section. The words are listed in the box below. Check them off as you use them. Before beginning, look at the questions and write a few notes to help you speak.

anticipate	figure out	pushing the edge of the envelope
butt in	get rid of	put a stop to
categories	give the floor to someone	rote
context	humane	socialized
controversy	intriguing	spontaneous
doesn't get it	it turns out	take advantage of
endangered	make a living	take issue with
end up	manipulate	transfer
ethical	off the top of one's head	

1. What is your reaction to the comments of these callers?
   - Lin (squirrels)
   - Janek (deer)
   - Alicia (deer and other wild animals)
   - Kenna (cat)

2. Do you think the animals mentioned in the interview—squirrels, deer, and cats—are intelligent? Why or why not?

3. What other animals do people consider a nuisance? Are they just annoying, or do they pose a danger to humans?

4. What abilities do animals have that people don't have? What abilities do people have that animals don't have?

5. Do you think people are sometimes unethical in the way they treat animals? Can you think of examples in which animals are not treated in a humane way?

6. There is controversy over whether animals should be used in scientific experiments, just as some people debate whether we should stop eating meat. Are people pushing the envelope if they consider putting an end to either of these two activities?

GO TO MyEnglishLab *FOR MORE VOCABULARY PRACTICE.*

1 Work with a partner. Read the conversation and answer the questions.

A: I just did the assignment about animal communication. The article reported that some parrots could recognize themselves in a mirror.

B: Yeah, and it said they were able to string three or four words together, too. Actually, my professor told us that he had just written a paper on how parrots learn language. He said he was going to publish it next month.

A: What did the paper say?

B: Well, apparently it warned that researchers had to study animal intelligence more carefully before drawing conclusions.

1. Do we know the exact words of the article or the professor?

2. Why do you think Speaker B chose not to quote the article or the professor directly?

REPORTED SPEECH

Reported speech (also called indirect speech) reports what a speaker said without using his or her exact words.

Use words like *said (that), told, indicated, mentioned, reported,* etc., to show that you are reporting information that someone else said.

When you are reporting what a speaker or article said, "backshift" the verb in the indirect speech statement.

Original: "We are **are conducting** some interesting research on endangered whales."

Reported: The scientist explained that she **was conducting** some interesting research with endangered whales.

The verb in the reported speech has shifted back in time; in this case from the present continuous to the past continuous. See more examples in the chart on page 95.

NOTE: If you are reporting a person's unchanging beliefs or a general truth, rather than an event, it is not necessary to change the tense of the original verb.

Original: "Many animals **are** remarkably intelligent."

Reported: The zoologist **told her students** that many animals **are / were** remarkably intelligent.

COMMON VERB CHANGES

Change:	Direct Speech	Indirect Speech
present tense → past tense	"I**'m** a researcher, studying animals' use of tools."	The zoologist said (that) she **was** a researcher, studying animals' use of tools.
present progressive tense → past progressive tense	"I**'m conducting** an experiment on crows."	She said (that) she **was conducting** an experiment on crows.
past tense and **present perfect tense → past perfect tense**	"The crows **made** a hook to get food from a tree."	The researcher reported (that) the crows **had made** a hook to get food from a tree.
	"We **have** never **studied** this behavior before."	She said (that) they **had** never **studied** this behavior before.
will → would	"I **won't** be at the meeting."	She explained (that) she **wouldn't** be at the meeting.
can → could	"I **can** ask my colleague to take notes."	She said (that) she **could** ask her colleague to take notes.
may → might	"I **may** be able to send my secretary."	She mentioned (that) she **might** be able to send her secretary.
must → had to	"I **must** find a way to repeat my experiment."	She said (that) she **had to** find a way to repeat her experiment.
The modals *should, could, might*, and *ought to* do not change.	"I **should** publish my results."	She said (that) she **should** publish her results.
Change the pronouns, possessives, and time words to reflect the original meaning.	"I can't access **my** computer because it broke down **yesterday**."	The student claimed (that) **she** couldn't access **her** computer because it had broken down **the day before**.

Work with a partner.

Student A: Read the first statement aloud.

Student B: Cover Student A's statements. After Student A reads each statement, report it using indirect speech. Use a variety of reporting verbs. Follow the example.

Student A: Check Student B's response. The correct response is in parentheses.

Example

A: I'm reading an article about Jane Goodall.

B: You mentioned you were reading an article about Jane Goodall, right?

A: That's right.

Student A

1. Jane Goodall is the world authority on chimpanzees.

   (B: You said she was the world authority on chimpanzees.)

2. She has studied chimpanzees for over 45 years.

   (B: You said she had studied chimpanzees for over 45 years.)

3. She discovered tool-making among chimps.

   (B: You explained she had discovered tool-making among chimps.)

4. Her work will affect generations of people.

   (B: You told me her work would affect generations of people.)

Now switch roles.

Student B

5. I'm reading about a dolphin research center.

   (A: You said you were reading about a dolphin research center.)

6. I'm going to visit the center in August.

   (A: You indicated you were going to visit the center in August.)

7. I've always wanted to swim with dolphins.

   (A: You claimed you'd always wanted to swim with dolphins.)

8. The dolphins at the center are used to interacting with humans.

   (A: You reported that the dolphins at the center were used to interacting with humans.)

3 Work with a partner. Role-play a conversation between A, who believes that animals are quite intelligent, and B, who does not. A and B each use information and reasons they've heard (see pages 80–81) to support their positions.

Example

A: My professor told me that a recent study had shown that an ape had learned to use sign language to communicate.

B: Well, my uncle, who's a zookeeper, claimed that when the chimp he worked with made signs, he . . .

SUPPORT FOR A'S POSITION	SUPPORT FOR B'S POSITION
College professor: "A few studies have shown that apes can learn to use sign language to communicate."	**Uncle who is a zookeeper:** "When the chimp I work with makes signs, he is just copying humans. He doesn't know what he is doing."
Radio report: "Crows have been filmed carrying clams high into the air. They drop the clams, and the clam shells break. Then the crows pick up the food."	**Teacher:** "Some dogs and other animals can be trained to do tricks. That doesn't prove that they are intelligent."
Neighbor: "I have a cat who senses when I'm sick and stays by my side. When I'm well, she usually keeps to herself."	**Parents who have had cats for years:** "Some people think their pets are smart. But the pets that we've seen can't understand even basic ideas."
Friend: "Animals have feelings, too. Whenever I'm away on a short business trip, my family says my dog stops eating."	**Roommate:** "Animals don't feel love for people. They're only motivated by food or fear. No pet will ever be able to experience human emotions."

■■■■■■■■■■■■■■■■■■■■■■■■■■■■■■■ *GO TO* MyEnglishLab *FOR MORE GRAMMAR PRACTICE.*

PRONUNCIATION

YES-NO QUESTIONS WITH OR

Some *YES-NO* questions with *or* ask the listener to make a choice. Listen to this question. How would you answer it?

🎧 Is communication more complex in humans or animals?

Some *YES-NO* questions that include an *or* phrase are true *YES-NO* questions. They are asking the listener to say "Yes" or "No," not to make a choice. Listen to this question. How would you answer it?

🎧 Can animals communicate about the past or the future?

Asking choice questions with *or*

- The words joined by *or* are in different thought groups.
- Intonation rises on the first choice and falls on the second.

Is communication more complex

in humans or animals?

(The speaker is asking the listener to indicate which of the two choices, humans or animals, has more complex communication.)

Asking true *YES-NO* questions with *or*

- The *or*-phrase is pronounced as one group.
- Intonation rises smoothly over the *or*-phrase.

Can animals communicate

about the past or future?

(This question is asking if animals can communicate about things that are not happening now, in the present.)

Answering questions with *or*

Sometimes the answer to a choice question and a true *YES-NO* question can be almost the same.

A: Did Jane Goodall study chimps or apes?

(The speaker wants the listener to indicate which choice is correct.)

B: She studied chimps.

A: Did Jane Goodall study plants or birds?

(The speaker is asking whether Jane Goodall studied those things.)

B: No. She concentrated on chimps.

1 🎧 Listen to the questions and repeat them. The questions are all true *YES-NO* questions. Say the words in the *or*-phrase as one thought group. Your voice should rise smoothly over the *or*-phrase.

1. Do you have a cat or a dog?

2. Do you like to visit zoos or parks?

3. Do chimps communicate with sounds or gestures?

4. Can your dog shake hands or roll over?

5. Can that parrot ask or answer questions?

6. Did the speaker talk about the intelligence of cows or chickens?

7. Have you read about seagulls or crows?

8. Do you have a fur coat or a leather jacket?

2 🎧 Listen to the same questions, said differently, and repeat them. This time the speaker is asking choice questions. Say the words in the *or*-phrase in two thought groups. Your voice rises on the first choice and falls on the second.

3 Work with a partner. Read the questions below. Some of the questions make more sense as choice questions, some make more sense as true *YES-NO* questions, and some could be either choice questions or true *YES-NO* questions. Have short conversations using each question. Take turns asking and answering the questions. Group words carefully and use intonation clearly.

1. Can animals manipulate or deceive?

2. Are you a meat-eater or a vegetarian?

3. Do pets prefer human food or pet food?

4. Are you more afraid of snakes or spiders?

5. Would you like to see a tiger or a lion?

6. Should people wear real fur or fake fur?

SPEAKING SKILL

Sometimes listeners need an example to be able to understand or believe the speaker's point. They use different phrases to ask for examples, which the speaker then provides.

1 Read the conversation between two students. Pay attention to the expressions in **bold**.

A: Elephants have an amazing capacity for memory.

B: Really? **What do you mean?**

A: Well, **off the top of my head** . . . Female elephants remember hundreds of other

elephants. I read an article about this.

ASKING FOR AND GIVING EXAMPLES	
Asking for Examples	Giving Examples
Could you give me an example?	Let me give you an example: . . .
What do you mean?	Well, what I mean is . . .
Such as?	For instance, . . .
Like what, for instance?	One example is . . .
Could you give me some more details?	. . . , such as . . .
	Well, let's see . . .
	Well, off the top of my head . . .

2 Read the conversations. Fill in the blanks with phrases to ask for or give examples. There can be more than one correct answer.

1. A: You know, many people want to put a stop to circuses because they treat elephants

so badly.

B: Why? How do they treat them? _____?

A: The elephants don't exercise enough, and they have too much stress, so they often

get sick. _____, many of them develop skin

diseases. And sometimes trainers hit the elephants, too.

2. A: People should be more aware of the problems elephants face.

    B: _____?

    A: Well, _____ African elephants are hunted for ivory,

    and many hundreds of them are killed every year. And Asian elephants are losing

    their natural habitat because of humans.

3. A: I read that female elephants find several "babysitters" to help them raise their babies.

    The babysitters help with all kinds of things.

    B: _____?

    A: Well, _____ they protect the young elephants when

    the group moves from place to place.

3 Work in small groups and share information about types of animal intelligence. Each person selects one square in the box and reads the corresponding information. Then take turns explaining the finding to the other members of the group, giving and asking for examples. Use reported speech to restate the words of the researcher.

PERSON A: **Expression of Emotions**	PERSON B: **Self-Recognition**
Research finding: Chimps recognize and express emotions such as happiness and fear.	**Research finding:** Dolphins are able to recognize themselves in mirrors.
Researcher statement: "We showed them TV scenes of other chimps playing and fighting. We used thermometers to measure their brain temperature. We found that the chimps had physical reactions to the other chimps' feelings."	**Researcher statement:** "Our research team used markers to draw lines on the bodies of two captive dolphins. Once the dolphins felt the marker, they swam over to mirrors to inspect various parts of themselves. Then they tried to get rid of the marks by rubbing themselves on the tank."

(continued on next page)

PERSON C: PROBLEM-SOLVING	PERSON D: LANGUAGE
Research finding: Crows are creative problem-solvers. **Researcher statement:** "I filmed crows in urban Japan. They dropped nuts on the road and waited for cars to run over them and crack the shells. Then the crows went back to eat the nuts."	**Research finding:** Squirrels use their tails to communicate. **Researcher statement:** "Tail flashing, or moving the tail in a wave-like motion, is one of the first indications squirrels give when they sense something disturbing. If the threat seems greater, they will add vocalizations—sounds—to the tail flashing."

■ *GO TO* MyEnglishLab *TO CHECK WHAT YOU LEARNED.*

FINAL SPEAKING TASK

In this activity, you will work with a group to identify arguments for and against a position related to animals and their relationship to people. You will then present the issue to the class. Use the vocabulary, grammar, pronunciation, and language for giving and asking for examples that you learned in this unit.*

STEP 1: Divide the class into groups. Each group selects a question from the list or proposes a new one. Consider the question in terms of what you have learned about animal intelligence.

1. Is it ethical to put wild animals in zoos?

2. Is it humane to raise animals as food for humans?

3. Should humans conduct experiments on animals?

4. Should we put a stop to hunting for sport?

5. Should we pass stricter laws to protect endangered species?

---

* For Alternative Speaking Topics, see page 105.

STEP 2: Study the example outline. Then organize your ideas in the outline below. Be sure to think of reasons and examples for both sides of the argument.

Example

Topic: Should people wear fur or leather?
I. People should not wear fur or leather.
  A: Killing animals for fur is not humane.
    1. Animals raised for fur are kept in inhumane conditions.
    2. They are killed before they reach old age.
  B: Fur is not necessary for people.
    1. They can wear other materials.
    2. Example:
	II. People should be allowed to wear fur or leather.
	  A: Animals are raised specifically for fur.
	    1. Many animals such as rabbits, minks, and chinchillas wouldn't be alive unless people bred them for their fur. They weren't wild animals that were shot.
	    2. Example:
	  B: Reason:
	    1. Example:
	    2. Example:

Topic:
I. One side of the argument:
 	
  A: Reason:
  1. Example:
  2. Example:
 	
  B: Reason:
  1.
  2.
	II. Other side of the argument:
	
	  A: Reason:
	  1. Example:
	  2. Example:
	
	  B: Reason:
	  1.
	  2.

STEP 3: Choose one person in your group to present the group's arguments and examples to the class.

Listening Task

Listen to your classmates' arguments. Then conduct a class vote to see which side of the issue most people support.

UNIT PROJECT

Research a famous example of an animal thought to be intelligent and present your findings to the class.

STEP 1: Select one of these famous animals, or choose your own example.

a. Akeakamai, a dolphin

b. Chaser, a dog

c. Ayumu, a chimp

d. Hank, a heron

e. Kanzi, a bonobo ape

f. Panbanisha, a bonobo ape

g. Rio, a sea lion

h. Romero, a crow

i. Tillman, a dog

Tillman

STEP 2: Research online to find the following information: what the animal was able to learn and what the scientists who worked with the animal think that means. Take notes on the information you find.

STEP 3: Present your findings to the class. Include a picture of the animal, if possible. Give your own opinion: How intelligent do you think the animal is (or was)? In what ways? For example, was it able to speak, use sign language, make or use tools, show empathy, or understand mathematical concepts?

ALTERNATIVE SPEAKING TOPICS

Work with a small group and read the quotations. Paraphrase each quotation and then choose one that you agree with and explain its meaning to the class. Organize your arguments by stating a main idea and supporting it with details and examples.

1. *If an animal does something, we call it instinct; if we do the same thing for the same reason, we call it intelligence.* (Will Cuppy, 1884–1949, author)

2. *The greatness of a nation and its moral progress can be judged by the way its animals are treated.* (Mohandas Gandhi, 1869–1948, statesman and philosopher)

3. *The soul of man is divided into three parts: intelligence, reason, and passion. Intelligence and passion are possessed by other animals, but reason by man alone.* (Pythagoras, about 569 B.C.–about 475 B.C., mathematician and philosopher)

■■■■■■■■■■■■■■■■■*GO TO* MyEnglishLab *TO DISCUSS ONE OF THE ALTERNATIVE TOPICS, WATCH A VIDEO ABOUT TALKING TO ANIMALS, AND TAKE THE UNIT 4 ACHIEVEMENT TEST.* ■■■■■■■■■■■■■■■■■■

THE GOLDEN Years

1 FOCUS ON THE TOPIC

1. *Longevity* means the length of a person's life. At what age do you consider someone "elderly"?

2. The photo shows an older man surfing. Do you think this is a good hobby for older people? What kinds of activities do you think senior citizens enjoy?

3. What do you think are some factors that might help a person live for a long time? That might help a whole community have a longer life expectancy?

GO TO MyEnglishLab *TO CHECK WHAT YOU KNOW.*

VOCABULARY

1 🎧 More and more seniors, or older people, are active members of society. Listen and read a blog discussing some issues modern seniors face. Pay special attention to the words and expressions in **bold**.

○ ○ ○

Golden Life Blog, Volume 9

by Eileen Julian

Is Peace of Mind for Seniors Just a Myth?

There's a **myth** out there that too many people believe: that when we reach a certain age, we can no longer be happy, independent, and productive members of society. How wrong that is!

I recently had a serious hip injury that landed me in the hospital. I was frightened at first, but I was only **facing a short-term crisis**. Now, after good medical treatment, I'm **back on my feet**, back to work, and feeling great. Sure, I have my aches and pains, and I move a little slower than I did when I was 18, but who doesn't? And then last night, I was touched when my niece said, "Aunt Eileen, I want to be like you when I'm older. You're 76 years old, yet you're happy, healthy, and still working. You're actually **thriving**!"

She was right; I am thriving. However, I haven't always felt so secure. Years ago, my grandmother **encountered** serious financial problems. Fortunately, our family was able to take her in, and she eventually lived to the ripe old age of 94. However, her situation made me think about my own financial future. I was in my early 30's. Would I have **sufficient** resources to live comfortably for another 50 or 60 years? The answer was probably no, so I decided to take action to **improve the odds**. I used to worry about becoming old, poor, and alone, but not anymore. I'm not wealthy, but I am well-off compared to many others my age. So how did I accomplish this?

Well, first I **recruited** a financial advisor. She said I had been too **happy-go-lucky** with my spending. As a result, I might run out of money and should **ameliorate the risks** by saving more right away.

When I finally retired, I had to face some **straightforward** choices about what to do next. Did I want to move to an inexpensive apartment in a warmer climate, pursuing hobbies all day? No, I did not! So, I took some courses to improve my skills. Then I found a part-time job I really like. Although I started this second career mostly for additional income, I now believe that working keeps me alive and mentally alert.

When my niece asked if I had a list of **dos and don'ts** for being happy and healthy at 76, I told her this: Keep working at something you love, think positive, do whatever you like in moderation, and surround yourself with loving people. Oh, and eat chocolate!

Today, I feel secure knowing that I won't be a financial burden to my nieces later on. And that thought gives me great peace of mind.

2 Match the words and expressions on the left with their definitions on the right.

_____ **1.** myth

_____ **2.** facing a short-term crisis

_____ **3.** back on your feet

_____ **4.** thriving

_____ **5.** encountered

_____ **6.** sufficient

_____ **7.** improve the odds

_____ **8.** recruited

_____ **9.** happy-go-lucky

_____ **10.** ameliorate the risk

_____ **11.** straightforward

_____ **12.** dos and don'ts

a. recovered from a problem or setback

b. enjoying life and not worrying about things

c. as much as you need for a particular purpose

d. simple or easy to understand

e. a story that many people believe, that is not true

g. asked to join a new club, company, or organization

h. things that you should or should not do in a particular situation

i. experienced something bad that you had to deal with

j. reduce or lessen the chance that something bad will happen

k. dealing with an immediate problem

l. increase the chances that you will be successful

m. very successful; strong and healthy

■■■■■■■■■■■■■■■■■■■■■■■■■■■ *GO TO* MyEnglishLab *FOR MORE VOCABULARY PRACTICE.*

The Golden Years 109

PREVIEW

An infomercial is a commercial that provides information about a product in the style of a radio or TV report. In this presentation, you will hear an infomercial for a book that summarizes research on longevity. The book synthesizes information from a study started long ago with new research.

🎧 Listen to the two researchers. Then make predictions.

Some of the subjects, the children in these studies, lived longer than others. Predict what factors might have made the difference.

_____

_____

MAIN IDEAS

1 🎧 Listen to the whole report. Look again at your predictions from Preview. How did your predictions help you understand the interview?

2 Check (✓) the items that are myths, according to the listening.

_____ **a.** By following a lot of steps, you can probably live a long life.

_____ **b.** Stress at work should be avoided whenever possible.

_____ **c.** A healthy diet is key to living a long life.

_____ **d.** Genes and heredity have nothing to do with who lives longest in these studies.

_____ **e.** People who are the happiest live the longest.

DETAILS

🎧 Listen again. Write **T** (true) or **F** (false) for each statement. Correct the false statements. Then discuss your answers with a partner.

_____ **1.** The subjects of this study were 1,500 boys, and no girls.

_____ **2.** Subjects were followed for more than 80 years.

_____ **3.** This presentation is the product of a group of studies following the same subjects.

_____ **4.** Stress at work will probably not shorten a person's life.

_____ **5.** At least forty minutes of a strenuous exercise every day will improve longevity.

_____ **6.** People who live the longest don't necessarily have healthy diets.

_____ **7.** People who take risks and have the most exciting lives live the longest.

_____ **8.** Divorced men who marry again increase their chances of living longer, but women do not.

_____ **9.** People who do physical exercise at the same time every day live the longest.

_____ **10.** People who live the longest start school before age five.

■■■■■■■■■■■■■■■■■■■■■■■■■ *GO TO* MyEnglishLab *FOR MORE LISTENING PRACTICE.*

MAKE INFERENCES

UNDERSTANDING THE MEANING OF STRESSED WORDS

Speakers stress, or emphasize, particular words, to convey extra meaning.

🎧 Read the sentence. Notice which words you naturally stressed. Then listen to the sentence from Listening One and answer the questions.

Example

HOWARD S. FRIEDMAN: One of those that amazed me the most was that hard work, and even stressful hard work, was not harmful.

1. Which words does the speaker emphasize most?

2. Based on the speaker's choice of word stress, which of the following statements would he be likely to say?

   a. "Before this study, most people probably believed that any hard work was harmful."

   b. "Before this study, most people probably believed that stressful hard work was more harmful than non-stressful hard work."

Answers: 1. The speaker stresses *stressful*, and *not*. 2. a. He thinks most people assume that any kind of stress is bad for living a long life. He emphasizes these words so the listener will take special notice *not* to rely on earlier assumptions.

🎧 Listen to the excerpts from Listening One and answer the questions.

Excerpt One

1. Which words are stressed? _____

2. From the speaker's word stress, which statement would he be likely to say?

   a. "People used to think that only men could improve their longevity by getting remarried after divorce."

   b. "People used to think that both men and women could improve their longevity by getting remarried after divorce."

Excerpt Two

1. Which words are stressed? _____

2. From the speaker's word stress, which statement would he be likely to say?

   a. "Exercise is one factor in keeping us healthy."

   b. "Exercise is the most important factor in keeping us healthy."

Excerpt Three

1. Which words are stressed? _____

2. From the speaker's word stress, which statement would he be likely to say?

   a. "These patterns are not inherited but are learned."

   b. "All people could develop these patterns."

EXPRESS OPINIONS

Work with a partner. Discuss whether you agree with the statements. Give reasons for your opinion. After two short discussions, work with a different partner.

1. I take steps now to live a longer life.

2. I'd like to live as long as possible, no matter what.

3. I don't care if I live a very long life, I just want to be happy and healthy until the end.

4. Thinking about how long I might live makes me appreciate everything more.

■■■■■■■■■■■■■■■■■■■■ *GO TO* MyEnglishLab *TO GIVE YOUR OPINION ABOUT ANOTHER QUESTION.*

VOCABULARY

You will hear a report by a woman who is doing something she feels is worthwhile in her senior years. She helps other, less knowledgeable, seniors.

1 Work with a partner. Take turns reading the sentences aloud. Pay attention to the phrases in **bold**.

1. I didn't get to visit my grandparents last weekend. That thought has been **tugging at me** all week.

2. After my grandmother broke her hip, her life changed **radically**. She could no longer drive, so she learned how to do most of her shopping online.

3. Her injury now **sets the parameters** of what she can and cannot do. She simply has to do less, but she's still witty and fun to be around. She spends lots of time online,

4. Grandpa says he's too old to learn how to use a computer, but if he were motivated, he would **catch on** easily.

5. On the other hand, Grandpa can be quite cheerful. After he retired from a job he loved, he started volunteering at a hospital. He says he's glad he stopped working and has **never looked back**.

2 Match the expressions on the left with the definitions on the right.

_____ **a.** tugging at me   **1.** determines the boundaries or limits

_____ **b.** radically   **2.** bothering me; weighing on my mind

_____ **c.** sets the parameters   **3.** understand

_____ **d.** catch on   **4.** had no regrets

_____ **e.** never looked back   **5.** extremely; in a significant way

COMPREHENSION

Listen to the report and circle the correct answers.

1. Tobey Dichter started the program in
   a. places where seniors live and get together.
   b. places where families meet.
   c. hospitals and health-care centers.

2. Tobey Dichter knew older people could be witty, wise, and cool. She learned this from
   a. her grandmother.
   b. her mother.
   c. her neighbor.

3. Dorothy Gray
   a. had a difficult time learning to use computers.
   b. had little trouble learning to use computers.
   c. had her own computer.

4. Before Tobey Dichter left her life-long career,
   a. she wasn't actually happy with her job.
   b. she had sometimes thought about helping older people.
   c. she had never thought of starting this kind of project.

5. One motivation for learning about computers that is mentioned by seniors is
   a. to shop and bank online.
   b. to become more independent.
   c. to email their families.

6. Tobey Dichter's project
   a. has changed her a lot.
   b. requires a lot of work.
   c. is successful for each individual she teaches.

GO TO MyEnglishLab FOR MORE VOCABULARY PRACTICE.

LISTENING SKILL

EVALUATING A SPEAKER'S DEGREE OF CERTAINTY

The first-person examples in this piece illustrate seniors with different levels of certainty about their success learning to use computers with Tobey Dichter's course. A person's confidence level and general attitude are reflected in intonation, strength of voice, and choice of words.

🎧 Listen to the example and determine how confident this person sounds. Generally, rising intonation at the end of a statement indicates a question or a doubt. Falling intonation usually indicates more confidence.

Example

1. How certain does the speaker sound? Circle the correct level.

   uncertain   somewhat certain   very certain

2. What clues do you hear in her tone of voice?

Answers:

1. Dorothy's choice of words shows she feels somewhat or very certain. She compares her successful attempt to learn one skill, cooking, to learning the new skill—using a computer. She points out that the key to both is following directions.

2. Her voice is quite strong and the words are clear. Her intonation drops rather than rises at the end of sentences.

🎧 Listen to the excerpts. How certain does the speaker sound? Circle the best answer. Then answer the questions.

Excerpt One

1. How certain does the speaker sound?

   uncertain   somewhat certain   very certain

2. What clues do you hear? _____

Excerpt Two

1. How certain does the speaker sound?

   uncertain   somewhat certain   very certain

2. What clues do you hear? _____

■■■■■■■■■■■■■■■■■■■■■■■■■■■■■■ *GO TO* MyEnglishLab *FOR MORE SKILL PRACTICE.*

STEP 1: Organize

Summarize the types of behavior and attitudes that help people live a long and happy life. Complete the chart with answers to the questions from Listenings One and Two.

QUESTIONS ABOUT LONGEVITY	GENERAL ADVICE: THE LONGEVITY PROJECT	SPECIFIC ADVICE: TOBEY DICHTER
What kinds of interactions are important?	• marriage makes a difference • helps men live longer, happier lives	Important: • •
How do people's attitudes and behavior affect their longevity and happiness?	• •	• stay independent • help others • do something emotionally fulfilling
What kinds of activity are helpful?	• work stress not necessarily bad Important factors: • hard work • reasonable amounts of physical exercise	Important to do: • •

STEP 2: Synthesize

Work in groups of three. Role-play a reporter interviewing two people: a researcher from the Longevity Project and Tobey Dichter.

REPORTER: Use the chart to ask questions about longevity research. Ask for specific examples.

RESEARCHER: Give general trends from the research. Comment on surprising results.

TOBEY DICHTER: Give examples from your own experience and from your students' experience.

Example

REPORTER: What interactions are important that help people live long, happy lives?

RESEARCHER: Well, getting married after a divorce helps certain people.

■■■■■■■■■■■■■■■■■■■■■■■■■■■■■■■■■■■■■ *GO TO* MyEnglishLab *TO CHECK WHAT YOU LEARNED.*

VOCABULARY

REVIEW

Read the podcast interview. Complete the sentences with words from the box. Then read the passage aloud with a partner.

back on our feet	happy-go-lucky	radically
caught on	improve the odds	recruited
encountered	myth	sufficient
facing a short-term crisis	never looked back	thriving

INTERVIEWER: Welcome to "Business Talks." According to recent government statistics, nearly one-fifth of Americans over 65 have paying jobs, and that number is rising. By 2020, one-quarter of all workers will be 55 and over, a big change from 15 years ago. My guests today are a business owner, a retired/rehired engineer, and a young engineer.

So, guests, is it true that a carefree, _____ retirement
(1)
life isn't really possible? Sandy Heinz, you were a retired engineer. Why are folks like you who are able to retire not doing so?

SANDY HEINZ: Yes, for many of us, being "able" to retire is just a

_____. When I was near retirement age, my
(2)
company went out of business. The pension I was counting on disappeared, and I had very little savings.

INTERVIEWER: A shock for you, I guess.

(continued on next page)

HEINZ: Absolutely. The company's decline was a big secret. By the time I _____ (3) that something bad was happening, I started saving as much money as I could to _____ (4) that I'd have enough money later. Too late, though. So, at 67, here I am working again—part-time. But a good surprise is how much I enjoy it.

INTERVIEWER: Michael Grange, you're the owner of a growing manufacturing company. You've hired a number of seniors besides Sandy.

MICHAEL GRANGE: Yes, my engineering department ran into some design problems that the younger workers had never _____ (5). The kids were good; they just didn't have _____ (6) experience. Sales were seriously dropping.

INTERVIEWER: So you _____ (7) experienced engineers.

GRANGE: Yes, people like Sandy who had actually built the kind of parts that we make in my plant. I had to get this design problem solved and get us _____ (8).

INTERVIEWER: What besides experience do older employees offer?

GRANGE: A terrific work ethic. They're really focused on the task, and they're very reliable. They call in sick less often than the younger ones do. They will also work part-time. We were _____ (9) and couldn't afford to hire full-time employees.

INTERVIEWER: Kyle Stanwicz, you're 24. You had trouble finding your first job, despite excellent college records. Why?

KYLE STANWICZ: Every employer wanted someone with experience. But how can you get experience if you can't get hired to begin with? Fortunately, Mr. Grange took a chance on me.

GRANGE: That's right, Kyle, and I _____ (10).

INTERVIEWER: Kyle, what's it like working with the senior guys?

STANWICZ: It was strange at first. Sandy and the other senior guys have

_____ different work styles. They don't socialize as
(11)

much. But now we get along fine. They've helped us a lot.

INTERVIEWER: Michael Grange, what's the final word on hiring retirees?

GRANGE: It works for my business. I hire the best people for the job, young or old.

Sales are up now, and the company's _____ again.
(12)

INTERVIEWER: Congratulations and good luck, all of you!

EXPAND

1 Read the online magazine article.

Smart Senior Today:
The Online Magazine for Modern Adults

Gray Divorce: A National Trend for the Over-50s

Although divorce rates nationwide have been declining since the 1980s, divorce rates for the over-50 crowd have more than doubled. Experts predict that those over 50 who are in a second or third marriage have a 150% greater chance of divorcing.

Why the Increase?

People in their 50s are more independent and educated than any previous generation, and they're better off financially. If they stayed in unhappy marriages to raise their children, they're able to consider their own dreams and interests after the children leave home. In addition, thanks to technology, it's easier for folks of all ages to connect with people they knew long ago and to make new friends. That means meeting a new spouse isn't the difficult ordeal it might have been years ago.

Divorce is not as frightening as it used to be, so don't despair if it strikes your marriage. Take heart in knowing that many over-50s who divorce will marry again, and will do so happily!

2 Complete the conversations with words and expressions from the box. Then practice the conversations with a partner.

> **broke my heart:** caused emotional pain
>
> **knows what she's getting into:** understands the result of her action
>
> **ordeal:** suffering; trouble

A COUPLE IN THEIR 60S:

TRENT: Did you read that piece about divorce and the over-50 crowd?

KATE: Yes, and I immediately thought of Sue. It _____ when she and (1) Frank split up after all those years together.

TRENT: It's hard to start over. I hope Sue _____ . (2)

KATE: Sue's pretty sharp. And so is Frank, for that matter. I think they'll be fine.

TRENT: I hope this doesn't turn out to be a painful _____ for them. And I (3) sure hope you don't have similar plans.

KATE: After all we've been through together? No thanks! I'm quite happy and have no desire to start over!

TEENAGE SIBLINGS:

> **light a fire under (someone):** make (someone) take action
>
> **losing it:** no longer making sense; losing mental clarity
>
> **put up with:** tolerate
>
> **set in his ways:** resistant to change

ALLISON: Did you hear that Grandma told Granddad she might want a divorce?

KYLE: Oh, no! That can't be right! She must really be _____ ! (4)

ALLISON: No, she's still sharp as a tack. I think she doesn't want to _____ (5) Granddad's stubbornness. He's more _____ than ever. He barely (6) leaves the house anymore. She thinks he's getting too lazy.

KYLE: But they've been married for 48 years. Do you think they'll really divorce?

ALLISON: No. I think Grandma just wanted to _____ Granddad. And it
(7)
worked. They're now planning a vacation to Hawaii!

KYLE: Those two never stop surprising me!

CREATE

Work with a partner. Student A asks a question and Student B answers. Take turns with the roles. In your answers, use words from the vocabulary exercises in Review and Expand, whenever possible. Use several sentences to answer. Some suggestions are given.

Before you begin, look at the questions you will be asked and write a few notes to use in your answers.

Student A asks:

1. What advice would you give someone worried about a grandmother who wants to live alone? What questions would you ask about the grandmother first?

2. What might you do to increase your own longevity?

Student B asks:

3. How would you advise an elderly man who isn't sure whether to marry again? He thinks he's too set in his ways.

4. Would you hire a senior over a young person?

Student B possible vocabulary:

1. *set the parameters, improve the odds, know what she's getting into, losing it, radically, set in her ways*

2. *happy-go-lucky, ameliorate the risks, dos and don'ts, improve the odds*

3. *ameliorate the risks, catch on, light a fire under, thriving, put up with, know what he's getting into*

4. *straightforward, recruited, sufficient, facing a short-term crisis*

■■■■■■■■■■■■■■■■■■■■■■■■■■■■■ GO TO MyEnglishLab FOR MORE VOCABULARY PRACTICE.

GRAMMAR

1 Read the following information. Notice the verb forms that appear in **bold**.

Sociologists knew that average age **was rising** in the 20th century; many people believe it **will continue** in the future. In addition, the elderly population **has been growing** steadily in the United States over the past century. In 2004, most people **were** under the age of 50, but in the next few decades, the population **will be aging** dramatically. These changes **have affected** every aspect of society.

(continued on next page)

The Golden Years 121

CONTRASTING SIMPLE, PROGRESSIVE, AND PERFECT VERBS

Simple Past and Past Progressive

The **past progressive** is used to describe an action that was in progress at a specific time in the past.

The **simple past** is used to describe an action that was completed in the past.

The **simple past** is also used to describe two actions that happened in a sequence, one after the other.

The **past progressive** is used with the **simple past** to describe one action that was interrupted by another action.

Examples

At last month's Global Population conference, experts **were discussing** reasons for the aging of the world's population.

They noted that medical care **was** less advanced in the past than it is today.

In their slide show, they showed that every time the standard of living **improved**, the world population **grew**.

When the chairman of the conference **was speaking**, various experts **raised** their hands to make a comment.

Present Perfect and Present Perfect Progressive

The **present perfect** and **present perfect progressive** are used to talk about things that started in the past, continue to the present, and may continue in the future.

The **present perfect** is used to talk about things that happened

- at an unspecified time in the past;
- more than one time in the past.

The **present perfect progressive** puts greater emphasis on a continuing action.

Examples

Experts **have been discussing** several possible explanations of these trends. For example, there **have been** many improvements in agriculture and health care.

Most developed countries **have made** access to clean water a priority. Many improvements **have been made** to city infrastructures.

The average age **has been rising** sharply in many industrialized countries in recent years.

Future Simple, Future Progressive, and Future Perfect

The **future simple** is used to make predictions about the future.

The **future progressive** is used to describe actions that will be in progress at a specific time in the future.

The **future perfect** is used to talk about a future action that will be completed before a further future point or action.

Examples

If current trends continue, world population **will reach** 9 billion by the middle of the century.

In the future, governments **will be considering** ways to deal with larger and older populations.

By 2050, global aging **will have become** a worldwide challenge.

2 Complete the conversation. Circle the correct form of the verb. Then read the interview aloud with a partner.

SCARLET: Dr. Rubio, thank you for helping me with my research paper. My professor (**1**) *has assigned / was assigning* a report on the elderly population in Chicago.

DR. RUBIO: You're welcome, Scarlet. Well, as you know, I (**2**) *moved / have moved* to the city in the 1970s, and since then, I (**3**) *have been working / will be working* in the city with an organization called Elderly Matters.

SCARLET: What does the organization do? I mean, I (**4**) *am reading / was reading* some of your materials right before I came here, but I'd like to hear more about your work.

DR. RUBIO: Well, our philosophy is that the elderly need both physical and emotional care, and let me give you an example. One of the women we serve—her name's Edna O'Sullivan—is in her 90s. When she was younger, she was a nurse, so obviously she (**5**) *took care / takes care* of others: that was her job. But now, it's hard for her to accept the fact that she herself needs help. We make sure she gets food and medical care, of course, but it's not just that. (**6**) She *was crying / has cried* the other day because she felt so lonely.

SCARLET: That's sad. How do you deal with a situation like that?

DR. RUBIO: Yes, it is sad. Recently, we (**7**) *have been talking it over / will be talking it over* in our team. We finally made the decision to invite her to our intergenerational program, where she (**8**) *was able / will be able* to meet up with young people and tell them about life when she was a young girl.

SCARLET: That's a great idea! What (**9**) *did she tell / will she tell* them about?

DR. RUBIO: We're not sure yet. She (**10**) *has met / will be meeting* the kids this time next week.

SCARLET: Well, thank you Dr. Rubio. I (**11**) *have written / will be writing* my report next week at that time. Hopefully, I (**12**) *have finished / will have finished* it two weeks from now, and I'll be sure to send you a copy. Maybe I could even come and meet Mrs. O'Sullivan!

DR. RUBIO: I'm so glad to meet you. You know, I (**13**) *have done / will have done* a lot of thinking about issues like these over the years. So, if you have any other questions, please don't hesitate to contact me. Maybe we (**14**) *will start / will have started* our intergenerational program by the time you call, and I can give you an update.

3 Work with a partner. Discuss the lives of seniors in the future. Use the ideas below and your own ideas to make predictions about what people will and won't be doing, and what will and won't have happened.

Examples

In 30 years, a greater percentage of seniors **will** probably **be living** active lives.

By 2040, a greater percentage of seniors **will** probably **not be alone**.

- live past the age of 100
- take medicine
- participate in extreme sports
- divorce and remarry
- go back to school
- travel more easily
- retire early / work into their 70s
- see family members less
- have surgery to repair or replace aging parts
- have cosmetic surgery

■■■■■■■■■■■■■■■■■■■■■■■■■■■■■ *GO TO* MyEnglishLab *FOR MORE GRAMMAR PRACTICE.*

PRONUNCIATION

 Native speakers often blend words together when they speak. Listen to the words in **bold** in the conversation.

A: **Who did you** go to the movies with?

B: My 80-year-old grandmother. **You know**, she's **a lot of** fun.

RECOGNIZING WORD BLENDS WITH *YOU*	
The pronoun *you* often has a short, reduced sound in informal speaking situations.	See **yə** later. (See you later.) I'll call **yə**. (I'll call you.)
When *you* follows common words that end in a /t/ or /d/ sound—for example, words like *what* or *did*—those words often blend with *you*.	**Didjə** see the parade? (Did you see the parade?) You'll come with me, **wontchə**? (You'll come with me, won't you?)

You don't have to blend words together when you speak. However, using blends when you speak will make it easier for you to recognize them when you hear them, and native speakers use them often.

1 🎧 Listen to the conversation and notice how the words in **bold** sound. Then practice the conversation with a partner. Blend the words in **bold**.

A: **What did you** do last night?

B: Nothing special. My roommate and I rented a movie. **How about you**?

A: We went to the parade. I called to see **if you** wanted to come, **but your** cell phone was off.

B: Yeah, I turned it off during the movie. How was the parade? **Did you** see anything interesting?

A: Yeah. There were a **bunch of** older women wearing some pretty colorful clothes.

B: Oh—the Red Hat Society. You've heard of them, **haven't you**?

A: No. **But you** know, I heard people at the parade talking about the red hats.

B: It's an organization of women who led pretty conservative lives when they were young. The parade **gives them** a chance to be bold and dress in bright colors.

2 🎧 Listen to the sentences in Column 1 and repeat them. Then listen again. Complete the questions in Column 1 with phrases from Column 2.

Column 1

1. _____ Why did you _____ go there?

2. _____ see at the parade?

3. You can come, _____ ?

4. They won't _____ in without an ID card.

5. _____ get there?

6. _____ live?

7. You can't come, _____ ?

8. _____ go after class?

9. _____ think about that?

Column 2

a. How do you

b. can you

c. ~~Why did you~~

d. Where did you

e. can't you

f. Where do you

g. let you

h. What do you

i. What did you

SPEAKING SKILL

1 Work with a partner. Read the conversations. Underline the suggestions.

A: I've always wanted to fly an airplane. Too late now, I guess.

B: What if you took piloting lessons this summer?

A: I've always wanted to be an actor, but that will never happen.

B. How about trying out for the local theater production in town? My friend was in a show there last year.

A. When I was a kid, I wanted to visit every state in the country. Now I can't afford that much time from work.

B. If I were you, I'd visit four or five new states every year.

MAKING SUGGESTIONS

Why don't you . . . Why doesn't he . . . don't we . . . (+ base form)

You / he / we could . . . (+ base form)

Have you thought about . . . (+ -ing), Have you considered . . . (+ -ing)

What if you . . . (+ unreal conditional)

If I were you, I . . . (+ unreal conditional)

In your position, I (+ unreal conditional)

---

2 A "bucket list" is a list of goals and accomplishments people create to complete before they die, or "kick the bucket." Some of our bucket list goals seem a little crazy or impossible to accomplish, but they are fun to consider.

Create your own bucket list.

Fill in the boxes with something you'd like to accomplish in each category, no matter how "impossible" they seem. Some examples are provided. Then read one item to your partner. Ask your partner to help you narrow your goal to a beginning first step that is possible to achieve. Then switch roles. Use terms for making suggestions when you help your partner.

MY BUCKET LIST

Travel / Entertainment:	Relationships:
• Become a concert violinist	• Find my great-grandfather's grave
• Win a salsa-dancing contest	• "Re-marry" my spouse on a beach
•	•
•	•
Career / Financial:	**Education:**
• Become an archaeologist	•
•	•
•	•
Health / Spiritual:	**Other:**
• Learn to meditate	•
•	•

■▪■▪■▪■▪■▪■▪■ *GO TO* MyEnglishLab *FOR MORE SKILL PRACTICE AND TO CHECK WHAT YOU LEARNED.*

FINAL SPEAKING TASK

In this activity, you will role-play a family meeting about how to best take care of a family member. You will take the roles of different family members with different points of view. Try to use the vocabulary, grammar, pronunciation, and listening and speaking skills that you learned in this unit.*

STEP 1: Work in groups of four. Consider this situation:

You are concerned about George, your 80-year-old relative whose wife died six years ago. George is independent and stubborn and wants to continue living alone. However, his physical and mental health are declining, and you are worried about his future. He is alone most days and seems to be depressed. When his wife was alive, George had hobbies. He also had several good friends, many of whom have passed away. George is close to his eldest grandson, Andy.

(continued on next page)

---

* For Alternative Speaking Topics, see page 129.

Choose one of the roles and study the information. Think about what you would like to recommend for George and how you will try to convince other family members.

LISA (George's daughter)	RAY (Lisa's husband; George's son-in-law)	ANDY (Ray and Lisa's 14-year-old son; George's eldest grandson)	JOSH (George's son; Andy's uncle)
lives with Ray and their children, ages 8 and 14 doesn't work would like George to live with her family wants to see her father frequently and make sure he is well cared for wants her children to know their grandfather	lives with Lisa and their two children, ages 8 and 14 works full-time believes their house is too small to accommodate another person is worried that his wife will not be able to take care of an elderly parent along with their two children is worried about having enough money to help Lisa's father	plays on his school baseball team four days a week after school is close to his grandfather (learned how to play baseball from Gramps) doesn't want to share a bedroom with his little brother likes to visit Gramps by himself; spends time at grandfather's house almost every week.	lives alone in a large apartment with two extra bedrooms lives one hour from sister Lisa's family works full-time travels a lot is worried about his father's health and believes he needs professional care thinks his sister is good at taking care of people

STEP 2: After studying your part, role-play a family meeting with Lisa, Ray, Andy, and Josh. Discuss each option for George, and evaluate its advantages and disadvantages. Then choose one option or think of your own idea.

- George could continue to live alone.
- He could live in his own house, but have a nurse living with him or visiting frequently.
- He could live with Josh.
- He could live with Lisa and Ray and their children.
- He could move to an assisted-living facility.
- He could be taken to an adult day-care facility each weekday.

Listening Task

Listen to others' decisions. Take notes to help you remember all the decisions. Then, as a class, vote on which decision you like best.

UNIT PROJECT

Work individually or in a small group to investigate the images of seniors in advertisements.

STEP 1: Go online to find advertisements that show elderly men and women. You may include video ads. Make notes about what products they are advertising. If possible, copy and save some examples of the ads.

STEP 2: Organize your information. Do you see any trends? What products are most often associated with the elderly? Do you think the image of the elderly portrayed in advertisements is positive or negative? Why?

STEP 3: Report your findings to the group or class. Share some of the ads you found.

STEP 4: Discuss the findings. As a class, discuss any common results brought up by all or most groups. What conclusions can you draw?

ALTERNATIVE SPEAKING TOPICS

Work in a small group. Discuss answers to the questions.

1. Look at the graph below. As the percentage of children in the world population declines, the elderly population will continue to grow. What problems could this cause? Can you suggest solutions to any of those problems?

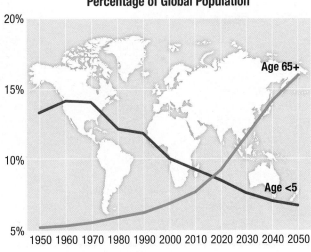

Young Children and Older People as a Percentage of Global Population

Source: United Nations Department of Economic and Social Affairs, Population Division. *World Population Prospects.* The 2004 Revision. New York: United Nations, 2005.

2. What privileges do seniors have in your community? For example, do they enjoy discounts, free medical care, and so on? At what age should a person be considered a "senior"? What privileges do you think should be given to seniors? Explain.

■ ■ ■ ■ ■ ■ ■ ■ ■ ■ ■ ■ ■ ■ *GO TO* MyEnglishLab *TO DISCUSS ONE OF THE ALTERNATIVE TOPICS, WATCH A VIDEO ABOUT LONGEVITY, AND TAKE THE UNIT 5 ACHIEVEMENT TEST.* ■

GIVING TO
Others

1 FOCUS ON THE TOPIC

1. The photo shows volunteers helping to clean up after a disaster. Why do many people do volunteer work? Have you ever volunteered your time?

2. *Philanthropic organizations* (sometimes called not-for-profit or non-governmental organizations) collect money to support different social and political activities. *Charities* collect money to help needy individuals. Why do people donate to philanthropies and charities? Have you ever donated money?

3. What are some things that wealthy people do with money they don't plan to spend while they are alive? What do you think wealthy people should do with their money?

■■■■■■■■■■■■■■■■■■■■■■■■■■■■■■■■■■■■■■ *GO TO* MyEnglishLab *TO CHECK WHAT YOU KNOW.*

VOCABULARY

1 🎧 Read and listen to an article from a news magazine about philanthropists. Notice the words and expressions in **bold**.

A FEW GOOD PEOPLE

Bill and Melinda Gates

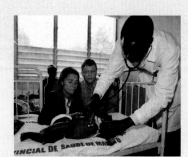

For Bill Gates, founder of Microsoft, giving to others is a personal **requirement**. Believing that every life has equal value, he and his wife created the Bill & Melinda Gates Foundation to improve healthcare, reduce poverty, expand educational opportunities, and provide access to information. This powerful foundation places special **emphasis** on developing countries. It is also involved in granting money to other organizations that are **responsive** to human needs and committed to improving living conditions the world over.

Warren Buffet

He is one of the wealthiest men in the world, but Warren Buffett believes that children should not inherit too much money. So Buffet gave each of his children a gift of $600 million to be used for charity. He always made it clear: If the children ran into financial difficulties and asked him for a loan, he would give them a **definitive** answer: No.

Some people might think that Buffett's position is **debatable**. However, his children are thankful. His son Peter and his wife have established their own **foundation** called NoVo, a non-profit organization dedicated to empowering women and girls around the world. Warren Buffett is also a notable philanthropist, having pledged to give away 99 percent of his fortune to philanthropic causes, primarily via the Gates Foundation.

Karen Pittelman

A growing number of young, wealthy Americans believe in some sort of social **cause**, and one of them is Karen Pittleman. Pittleman says that young people need strong **moral** values. She commented, "So many people work equally hard every day, and yet they're struggling to make ends meet. In the meantime, I was given a fortune just for being born." So she founded the Chahara Foundation, an organization to help low-income women. She hopes her action will **motivate** other wealthy young people to use their money to benefit others. Young philanthropists consult her organization for advice on how to use their wealth to give back to society.

Phoebe Russell

Phoebe Russell is only five years old, but she too wanted to make a **contribution** to others. When she saw a homeless man asking for food, she promised to raise $1,000 for the San Francisco Food Bank. Her teacher tried to persuade Phoebe to set a smaller amount,

more **proportionate** to her age. However, Phoebe was determined. She began collecting soda cans to return for deposit* and asking for small donations so that she could establish a **fund** for hot meals. Before long, her efforts were successful. Phoebe raised $3,736.30, the equivalent of 17,800 heated meals, for homeless people.

Volunteers at a food bank

* **return for deposit:** In some states in the U.S., people who buy drinks in bottles or cans pay a small deposit at the time of purchase. The empty bottles and cans can be returned later, and the deposit is refunded.

2 Work with a partner. Match the words on the left with the definitions on the right.

_____ **1.** cause

_____ **2.** contribution

_____ **3.** debatable

_____ **4.** definitive

_____ **5.** emphasis

_____ **6.** foundation

_____ **7.** funds

_____ **8.** moral

_____ **9.** motivate

_____ **10.** proportionate

_____ **11.** requirement

_____ **12.** response

a. not to be doubted or changed

b. something that is demanded: not voluntary

c. special importance

d. organization that collects money for special purposes

e. reaction or reply

f. money, help, or ideas given to others

g. money kept for a particular purpose

h. having two or more opinions that might be true or right

i. equivalent

j. make someone become very eager to do something

k. related to principles of right or wrong

l. a principle or aim that people support or fight for

GO TO MyEnglishLab FOR MORE VOCABULARY PRACTICE.

PREVIEW

Why do people donate money and volunteer time? The reasons are as varied as the people. You will hear a radio interview by Alex Goodwin, of the program *The Infinite Mind*. He speaks with Stacy Palmer, editor of the *Chronicle of Philanthropy*, a highly regarded publication for people interested in the world of philanthropy.

🎧 How many people volunteer time or donate money to others? First check (✓) your predictions. Then listen to the excerpt to verify your predictions.

1. Percentage of Americans who volunteer their time:

   ❑ 25 percent   ❑ 50 percent   ❑ 75 percent

2. Percentage of Americans who donate money to others:

   ❑ 25 percent   ❑ 50 percent   ❑ 75 percent

MAIN IDEAS

🎧 Read the different reasons people give. Then listen to the whole interview and check (✓) the reasons you hear.

_____ passion for a cause

_____ tax benefits

_____ a desire to repay someone for something

_____ the need to feel useful

_____ moral or religious beliefs

_____ family tradition

_____ legal requirements

_____ school requirements

DETAILS

🎧 Listen to the interview again. Circle the correct answers.

1. Most gestures of everyday generosity _____.

   a. are easy to see   **b.** are spontaneous   **c.** are not recorded

2. When a cause has an enemy or threat, people tend to give _____.

    a. more   **b.** the same as usual   **c.** less

3. Most people seem to feel _____ about giving money than about giving time.

    a. better   **b.** worse   **c.** the same

4. Most cash donations are made to _____.

    a. relatives   **b.** religious organizations   **c.** community projects

5. _____ tend to give anonymously.

    a. Most people   **b.** Wealthy individuals   **c.** Less wealthy people

6. When people are asked about what they give, they _____.

    a. answer accurately   **b.** exaggerate their donations   **c.** find it difficult to respond

7. The group that is most important to educate about giving is _____.

    a. wealthy people   **b.** young people   **c.** influential people

GO TO MyEnglishLab *FOR MORE LISTENING PRACTICE.*

MAKE INFERENCES

UNDERSTANDING DEGREES OF CERTAINTY

Even if speakers do not say something directly, they often communicate their opinions through their pace (speed), word choice, tone of voice, and amount of hesitations. They may sound convinced and sure, or they may sound unsure or doubtful.

🎧 Read and listen to the example. Pay attention to the second speaker's tone of voice.

Example

    Goodwin asks: "What studies have been done on volunteering and charitable giving?"

    Palmer answers: "Actually, we don't know all of that much about what really motivates people to give. We know how often they give."

Palmer sounds very unsure. There are clues in her pace, language, and topic shift. She hesitates, then she uses general and vague language to answer: "we don't know all of that much" and "what really motivates people." Then, she changes the topic to something she is very sure about: "We know . . ."

🎧 Read the questions that Goodwin asks Palmer. Then listen to the excerpts. Mark the degree of certainty of Palmer's responses on the scale. Discuss your answers with a partner. Then listen again.

Excerpt One

Goodwin's question: Do positive appeals work better than negative appeals?

How certain does Palmer feel? What clues do you hear?

very sure	somewhat sure	unsure
1	2	3

Excerpt Two

Goodwin's question: Well, what about the difference between volunteering time and volunteering money?

How certain does Palmer feel? What clues do you hear?

very sure	somewhat sure	unsure
1	2	3

Excerpt Three

Goodwin's question: What about social class? Is that as predictable as it should be?

How certain does Palmer feel? What clues do you hear?

very sure	somewhat sure	unsure
1	2	3

EXPRESS OPINIONS

1 Work in a small group. Take turns reading aloud the comments of donors and volunteers.

A. I'm 26, and I teach elementary school students in the United States. I encourage my students to help those that are less fortunate. So, for example, we all bring cans of food from home to be donated to the local food pantry at Thanksgiving. My school also sponsors toy drives for needy children during the holidays.

B. I'm a project manager for an advertising firm. I'm in my 40's and have three kids. Not many of my co-workers share my view, but I think everyone should contribute a small portion of their income to a good cause. My donations usually go to international relief efforts after a flood, earthquake, or hurricane.

C. I have two young children. I'd like to volunteer in my community, but I really don't have time. I have to take care of my own family and myself before I can think about helping others.

D. I'm 23, and just graduated from college. I work hard to earn my paycheck. I think handing people money gives them the idea that they don't have to work. If people want more money, they should get a better job!

2 Discuss these questions with the class.

- Do you understand these people's points of view? Do you share their views?

- Which person is most like you? Which person is least like you?

■■■■■■■■■■■■■■■■■■■■ *GO TO* MyEnglishLab *TO GIVE YOUR OPINION ABOUT ANOTHER QUESTION.*

LISTENING TWO THE MYSTERY DONOR

VOCABULARY

Some people who donate money want to be publicly noticed and thanked; others prefer to donate quietly and anonymously. This is an informal radio report in which a Mystery Donor explains the reasons why she gives money away.

1 Read the words and phrases in the box aloud. Discuss their meanings with a partner. Use a dictionary if necessary.

fly under the radar	inspiring	think outside the box
have access to	tend to focus on	

2 Complete the sentences below with a word or phrase from Exercise 1. Then take turns reading the sentences aloud.

1. If they want to help others, most people _____ charity organizations in their own community.

2. Eileen and Mary created an organization that helps other people start organizations. These people are so creative; they always _____.

3. The mission of the One Laptop per Child (OLPC) project is to see that children in developing countries _____ computers.

4. Julie always participates in a Secret Santa program at work, where the office staff give gifts anonymously to one another. She finds it _____ to see her co-workers' faces each time they open a small gift.

5. Julie has always liked to give anonymously, and this program allows her to _____ as a secret Christmas donor.

Giving to Others   137

COMPREHENSION

Listen to the interview and circle the correct answers.

1. The Mystery Donor started giving to charity because _____.

   a. she needed to find meaning in her life

   b. she had access to more money than she needed

   c. her family encouraged her to donate money

2. She donates _____ of her income every year.

   a. 10 percent

   b. 25 percent

   c. 50 percent

3. She gives anonymously because she _____.

   a. is worried people will think she didn't give enough

   b. is embarrassed about how much money she has

   c. doesn't want to change her relationship with the receivers

4. One motivation she has for giving to single mothers is that she _____.

   a. was the child of a single mother

   b. was a poor single mother herself for a while

   c. is most interested in children's causes

5. Philanthropists such as the Mystery Donor _____ large foundations.

   a. push their political beliefs on

   b. give most of their donations to

   c. are more flexible and responsive givers than

6. The Mystery Donor _____ if the donation was received.

   a. calls to see

   b. doesn't ask

   c. is always told

■■■■■■■■■■■■■■■■■■■■■■■■■■■ *GO TO* MyEnglishLab *FOR MORE VOCABULARY PRACTICE.*

LISTENING SKILL

IDENTIFYING THE PURPOSE OF EXAMPLES

Radio reports often include examples spoken by different people. These direct quotations have various purposes. For example, they may explain the reporter's statements or engage the listener's emotions. They also offer first-hand evidence.

🎧 Listen to the example. Then answer the question.

Example

The reporter says: "Her career as a benefactor really began after she lost her husband."

Then the reporter includes a quotation from the Mystery Donor: "My husband died about three years ago, and I had access to more money than I needed for expenses. So, it was an opportunity to start giving money away."

Why does the reporter insert the donor's own words instead of reporting the idea herself?

a. To explain the situation to the listener

b. To engage the listener's emotions directly

Answer: a. The reporter states a fact and then includes a direct quote in which the donor gives her unusual reason for becoming a philanthropist.

🎧 Listen to the excerpts. Circle the most important reason the reporter uses the Mystery Donor's own words.

Excerpt One

The reporter says: "These small personal gifts often go to helping single mothers. Their experience echoes her own years ago." Then she inserts the donor's words in her own voice. Why?

    a. To explain the situation to the listener

    b. To engage the listener's emotions directly

Excerpt Two

The reporter says: "The Mystery Donor says she may create a foundation one day, but right now she enjoys the freedom that comes from giving on her own." Then she inserts the donor's words. Why?

    a. To explain the situation to the listener

    b. To engage the listener's emotions directly

GO TO MyEnglishLab *FOR MORE SKILL PRACTICE.*

STEP 1: Organize

Work with a partner or a small group. The chart includes information from Listening One, which describes general information about who gives money, and Listening Two, which describes the specific case of one philanthropist. Fill in the missing information.

	TYPICAL DONORS	THE MYSTERY DONOR
1. Who volunteers or donates money?	• Half of all Americans volunteer. • 75 percent of Americans give money.	•
2. Why do people give?	• • • •	• She heard a story on the radio and wanted to help. • She began to give after she lost her husband. • She had more money than she needed.
3. What background factors cause people to give?	• a worthy need or cause • the amount of money or time they have available • the importance of being recognized for their contributions	•
4. Who receives the money or time?	• • •	• an unknown single mother who had broken her leg
5. How does the giver feel?	• that he or she is doing something important	•
6. Does the donor prefer to be public or anonymous?	• Many people like to have their name attached to their gift.	•

STEP 2: Synthesize

Role-play an interview between a reporter from the *Chronicle of Philanthropy* and the Mystery Donor.

Student A: Chronicle Reporter: Ask the Mystery Donor questions based on the chart on page 140.

Student B: The Mystery Donor: Answer the questions as the real Mystery Donor might. Then switch roles.

Example

REPORTER:	I'd like to interview you about philanthropy. The typical American donates money to charity. How about you?
MYSTERY DONOR:	Yes, I do, too. I actually donate hundreds of thousands of dollars every year.
REPORTER:	Wow! That's really generous. Who do you give it to?
MYSTERY DONOR:	Well, I give it to people who really need my help, but I give anonymously.
REPORTER:	That's amazing. I heard that they called you "The Mystery Donor," and now I see why. Why do you prefer to fly under the radar?

■■■■■■■■■■■■■■■■■■■■■■■■■■■■■ *GO TO* MyEnglishLab *TO CHECK WHAT YOU LEARNED.*

3 FOCUS ON SPEAKING

VOCABULARY

REVIEW

1 Complete the chart with the different forms of the words. Then compare your answers with a partner.

NOUN	VERB	ADJECTIVE	ADVERB
access			
		moral	
requirement			
cause	cause		
	motivate		
contribution			
foundation			
	focus		
	define	definitive	
response			
fund			
		debatable	
emphasis			
		inspiring	

2 On the next page is a speech by the president of the board of directors of a philanthropic organization. Complete the sentences with appropriate forms of words from the box. Then, with a partner, take turns practicing the speech.

access	contribution	moral	requirement
cause	focus	motivate	response

Tsunami Relief Fund

Helping others in times of crisis

Good evening. I'm Ron Prosperi. The film clips you have just seen of tsunami disasters speak for themselves. We all know that people around the world suffer from such terrible events every year. Their future depends on other people's

_____ to their situation.
(1)

Tonight, I'm not here to _____; I'm here to tell you that my
(2)

involvement with the Tsunami Relief Fund has enriched my own life.

You and I are among the fortunate. No one in this room is struggling to survive every day. Each one of us has _____ to wealth, either because we've had work
(3)

that has paid us well or because we inherited it from our parents. So let's be honest: We all have enough to take care of our own families and still be generous to others. No one is

_____ to help others, but there comes a time when we should give back to
(4)

society. Even a small donation will help so many others.

Our staff are working people, using their time and skills to rebuild homes, feed the hungry, and treat the sick. Look, it's easy to _____ on our own problems
(5)

instead of the broader world outside us, but these volunteers are very _____
(6)

to helping the victims. They donate their time far from home at great expense to themselves. But they can't continue without your help.

Let me be brief: Charity work is life-changing. Please make a generous

_____ tonight. Write a check right now. Help with our next volunteer
(7)

project. Your life will be richer for it. Or if you prefer, send in a donation anonymously to

this worthy _____. Either way, I know you won't regret it.
(8)

Thank you.

EXPAND

3 Now read the email written by an audience member who is a friend of the speaker. Complete the email with expressions from the box. (Not all of the expressions will be used.)

a learning curve	pay off
fly under the radar	think outside the box
in a big way	turn (someone) down
make a difference	year round

Subject: Great speech!
From: Joe Lynch
To: Ron Prosperi

Hey Ron,

That was a great speech last night. It affected me _____ (1): I have been thinking all night about what you said. I hope your efforts _____ (2) and that a lot of people will contribute to the fund. You're right: If we all _____ (3), we can come up with some creative solutions to help those in need.

It's the holiday season right now, so maybe people will be generous when they give. But we really need to find a solution _____ (4). If we work together, perhaps we can really _____ (5).

You're a good friend and a great speaker. How can anyone _____ (6)? I've made a contribution on your website. I thought about _____ (7) and making an anonymous contribution—but I decided against it because I want you to know what an impact your words had on me!

See you at the game Friday,

Joe

CREATE

Work with a partner or a small group. You have $1 million to give to a not-for-profit organization. Read the website information about different organizations and discuss each one. Decide which ones to contribute to and how much to give. You can give all the money to one organization or divide it among the organizations.

Each time you use a word from Review or Expand, check it off (✓) in the boxes. Then share with the class how you divided the money and why.

The Nature Conservancy

The mission of The Nature Conservancy is to preserve the plants, animals, and natural environment of life on Earth by protecting the lands and waters. The Nature Conservancy works with corporations, traditional communities, and other partners to develop ways for people to live and work without hurting the natural world around them. The Nature Conservancy also raises money to buy fragile land from developers.

The International Committee of the Red Cross

The ICRC is an independent, non-political organization that protects human life. The ICRC does not support or oppose governments. Instead, it tries to protect the lives of people who are victims of war and internal violence. It gives medical aid and other assistance. Its main office is in Geneva, Switzerland, but the ICRC has offices in 80 countries and has a staff of more than 12,000.

Habitat for Humanity International

Habitat for Humanity International helps reduce poverty and homelessness throughout the world. Habitat invites people of all backgrounds, races, and religions to build houses together with families who need them. Volunteers give money, materials, or their own work to build simple but good houses side by side with the new owners. The new owners buy the homes at no profit, and Habitat provides them with low-cost loans.

Amnesty International

Amnesty International (AI) is a worldwide movement of people who work toward human rights around the world. AI does not support or oppose any government or political system. It tries to work with governments to protect the basic human rights of all individuals by helping to prevent discrimination and physical and mental abuse.

GO TO MyEnglishLab *FOR MORE VOCABULARY PRACTICE.*

GRAMMAR

1 Work with a partner. Read the paragraph aloud and answer the questions.

Sting is a popular British musician **(A.) who is actively involved with humanitarian and environmental causes**. With the support of his wife and a native leader, Sting established the Rainforest Foundation, an organization **(B.) whose goal is to help save the world's rainforests**. Although at first it operated only in Brazil, **(C.) the country where it was founded**, the organization now operates in other countries, too. In fact, a frog **(D.) that is native to Colombia** has been named after Sting to honor his contributions to the environment.

1. Which nouns do the phrases in **bold** describe?

2. Which word in **bold** indicates the noun that is being described?

RELATIVE PRONOUNS IN ADJECTIVE CLAUSES

Adjective clauses (also called relative clauses) are used to add information about nouns. Usually, the adjective clause directly follows the noun it refers to. These clauses are introduced by a relative pronoun, such as *who, that, which, whose, where,* or *when.*

An **identifying adjective clause**, sometimes called a restrictive clause, gives essential information about the noun it refers to. In writing, commas surround the identifying adjective clause.	Sting is the singer **who helped establish the Rainforest Foundation**. The foundation **that Sting established** is involved with conservation.
A **non-identifying adjective clause**, or non-restrictive clause, gives extra information about the noun it refers to. It is set off in a written sentence by commas. Pronunciation note: In speaking, people often pause and lower their tone of voice to say the words in the non-identifying relative clause.	The Rainforest Foundation, **which was founded in 1989**, is working to protect forests around the world.
Who refers to people. It can be the subject or the object of an adjective clause.	Sting is a musician **who** *[subject]* **is concerned about the environment**. Musicians **who are concerned about the environment** sometimes donate their time to raise funds.
In spoken English, *who* is usually used instead of the more formal *whom*, even when it is the object of an adjective clause.	There are many hundreds of young people **who** (or **whom**) *[object]* he has inspired.
That and *which* refer to places and things. They can be the subject or object of an adjective clause.	The Rainforest Foundation is a group **that / which** he founded to protect the world's natural resources.

That cannot be used in a non-identifying adjective clause (sometimes called a non-restrictive clause) or after a preposition. You must use *which*.	The foundation, **which** is working with human rights groups, raises money to protect tropical rainforests.
In identifying adjective clauses (or restrictive clauses), English speakers often delete the relative pronoun when it is the object of the verb.	This is an organization **(that)** many young people are interested in.
Whose refers to people's possessions. It can be the subject or object of an adjective clause.	That's the man **whose** organization I want to work for.
Where refers to a place; *when* refers to a time. They can be the object of an adjective clause.	Brazil is one of the countries **where** the foundation's efforts have been successful. The foundation was started at a time **when** many people were unaware of the environmental problems we face.

2 Work with a partner. Fill in the blanks with **who, that, which, whose, when,** or **where.** Then take turns reading about the projects aloud.

The *Hole in the Wall* is a project _____ began several years ago in New Delhi,
(1)

India. Dr. Sugata Mitra was a computer scientist _____ had the innovative idea of
(2)

helping the children in the neighborhood _____ he worked. In the wall outside his
(3)

office, he installed a computer, _____ was connected to the Internet and available
(4)

for neighborhood children to play with. Within minutes, children began to touch the computer, a

machine _____ many of them had never seen before. Now there are many children,
(5)

both boys and girls, _____ lives have been touched by Mitra's generosity and
(6)

_____ have gained a high level of computer literacy.
(7)

Orbis International, _____ is the name of an innovative humanitarian organization,
(8)

operates out of an airplane. The plane is equipped as a flying eye hospital, a kind of hospital and

training facility _____ flies all over the world to deliver medical assistance and
(9)

(continued on next page)

training to local doctors. Bangladesh, China, Ethiopia, India, and Vietnam, _____
(10)
are the priority nations for the project, employ local health professionals _____
(11)
receive special training and support from the Orbis group. The approximately 30 million people

_____ have been helped in over 70 nations of the world include both adults
(12)
and children. The world surgeons _____ donate their time and the volunteers
(13)
_____ form the backbone of the organization share a single goal: to save people's
(14)
sight worldwide.

CAMFED, _____ stands for the Campaign for Female Education, was launched
(15)
in 1993 with the goal of fighting poverty and disease in rural Africa. That was a time

_____ families _____ could not afford to educate all their children gave
(16)   (17)
priority to boys, but the group's founders knew that women _____ are educated are
(18)
more likely to become leaders in their communities by encouraging others to get jobs and raise

healthy children. Now, over 500,000 young women _____ lives were transformed
(19)
by the campaign are giving back to the organization by making their own contributions. CAMFED,

_____ members include actor Morgan Freeman, has won many international
(20)
awards to continue its work. The small program _____ was first developed has now
(21)
expanded to numerous countries.

3 Work with a partner.

Student A: Ask Student B questions 1 through 4.

Student B: Cover the left column. Answer the questions. Use a variety of adjective clauses in your answers. Then switch roles after question 4.

Example

A: Who is Karen Pittleman?

B: Let me see . . . I think she's a woman who inherited a lot of money when she was young.

Student A	Student B
1. What's a philanthropist?	**1.** Well, a philanthropist is someone who . . .
2. What is Camfed?	**2.** Hmm. I think (that) . . .
3. Who's Phoebe Russell?	**3.** As far as I can remember, . . .
4. Why are holidays important times for philanthropy?	**4.** I'm not sure I remember, but I think . . .
Now switch roles.	
5. What's a charity?	**5.** Well . . .
6. What is Orbis International?	**6.** Oh . . .
7. Who's Sting?	**7.** I think he's . . .
8. Why is it important to teach young people about philanthropy?	**8.** I guess it's because . . .

■■■■■■■■■■■■■■■■■■■■■■■■■■■■■ *GO TO* MyEnglishLab *FOR MORE GRAMMAR PRACTICE.*

PRONUNCIATION

INTONATION IN LISTS

When we list items or talk about a series of items, we use a special intonation depending on whether the list is finished (everything has been listed) or unfinished (there are more items in the list that aren't mentioned).

For the items in a finished list, the speaker's voice rises on every item except the last one. The speaker's voice falls on the last item. Falling intonation tells the listener your list is finished. The word *and* is usually used in finished lists.

The Nature Conservancy works with **corporations**, **communities**, and

non-profit organizations.

For the items in an unfinished list, the speaker's voice rises on every item, including the last one mentioned. This tells your listener that there are other possibilities. The conjunction *and* is not usually used in closed lists (but can be).

People who volunteer with the Nature Conservancy include **students**,

local businesspeople, **nature lovers** . . .

🎧 Listen to the conversation. Then answer the questions.

José: My neighbor said you could help me find some volunteer work. I'd really like to work with people.

Ms. Johnson: Great. We're looking for volunteers at **the Senior Center**, **the library**, and **the after-school program**.

José: What's available in the after-school program? I like working with kids, but I'm taking classes myself, so my schedule is a little tight.

Ms. Johnson: Well, let's see, the teacher of the youngest group needs an assistant on **Monday**, **Tuesday**, and **Friday**.

1. Ms. Johnson mentions positions at the Senior Center, the library, and the after-school program. Do you think Ms. Johnson has other volunteer positions available?

2. Does the teacher of the youngest group in the after-school program need help on Wednesday? How do you know?

1 🎧 Listen to the sentences. Write **F** in the blank if the speaker has finished the items or ideas in the list. Write **U** in the blank if the list is unfinished. Underline the words or ideas that are being listed.

1. The World Wildlife Fund works with governments, local communities, non-profits. _____

2. How can you help? You can help by giving your time, your money, and your ideas. _____

3. I need a vacation—I'm tired of waking up early, spending hours on the road, working at night. _____

4. If you volunteer at the Senior Center, you'll feel good about yourself, meet new people, and learn more English. _____

5. Americans give a lot between Thanksgiving and Christmas: There are food drives, coat drives, toy drives. _____

2 Work with a partner. Read the sentences in Exercise 1 to your partner. Decide whether you want to read the lists as finished lists or unfinished lists. Use appropriate intonation. Your partner will say "finished" or "unfinished." Then switch roles.

3 🎧 Listen to the conversation. Underline the words or ideas in lists and draw intonation lines over those items. Then practice the conversation with a classmate.

A and B are first-year college students who live in the same dormitory. They are discussing the upcoming Thanksgiving Day holiday.

A: Are you having Thanksgiving dinner at your house?

B: Actually, every year we spend Thanksgiving at a homeless shelter. We decorate the shelter, help with the cooking, serve the guests, and talk to them. Would you like to come?

A: Yes, I really would. For a long time, I've been thinking about volunteering somewhere—at a school, the library, a retirement home. This sounds so interesting.

B: Great. We can pick you up here Thursday morning. Just bring your hands, your energy, and a smile. The shelter supplies everything else.

4 Work in small groups. Think of at least three things that ordinary people could do to help your school, your town, or your country. Describe them to members of your group. Speak clearly and use intonation carefully. Remember that speakers usually use "*and*" if their list is finished.

SPEAKING SKILL

Work with a partner. Read the conversation between two students who are working on a project together. Pay attention to the expressions in **bold**.

A: OK, so let's get started and get this philanthropy research paper finished. **Our top priority** is selecting the right topic, don't you think?

B: Yeah. But **it's also important** to make sure we can get the information we need for the research. Then there's the writing and then the editing . . .

A: Well, I think the least important thing right now is the writing. We can only do that when we have everything else we need first.

When people are discussing more than one task or idea, it helps to prioritize or rank them to indicate the most important and the least important. Here are some useful expressions:

PRIORITIZING OR RANKING IDEAS		
Highest Priority	**Also a Priority**	**Lowest Priority**
Our top priority is . . .	But it's also important . . .	The least important thing is . . .
First of all, . . .	In addition, . . .	Of least concern is . . .
First and foremost, . . .	Another consideration is . . .	The lowest priority is . . .
Above all, . . .	Aside from that, . . .	

1 Read the ads for volunteer jobs with non-profit organizations.

WANTED

Part-time worker at neighborhood animal shelter. Help find homes for abandoned animals. Help with feeding, walking, and taking care of animals. Some contact with the public and experience in office work necessary. Volunteers needed at least eight hours per week: daily 8 A.M. to 10 P.M.

POSITION

Volunteer fundraiser for charitable healthcare organization. Responsibilities include helping to find new donors and raising money for yearly budget. Responsible for helping with black-tie fundraising dinner. Handle correspondence and telephone fundraising drive.

VOLUNTEER HELP NEEDED

Hospital worker. Volunteer needed to be a companion to ill patients. Read aloud to patients, take them for walks, offer a shoulder to lean on. Our motto: "A friend when you need one." Call 555-5863 or email us at *www.we-care.org*.

VOLUNTEERS NEEDED

Public radio station needs volunteer telephone representatives for one week during our Phone-a-thon Appeal. Answer calls, encourage donations, and take credit card information for payment. Your time will be spent on a good cause.

Work with a partner. Read the personal qualities listed. Discuss the qualities that are needed for each job (you may also add your own ideas). Then prioritize the qualities. Use the vocabulary and grammar you learned in this unit.

Important qualities for job candidates

be able to:	• finish tasks • work long hours • get along with people	
be:	• flexible • cheerful • clean	• assertive • patient
have:	• good listening skills • good communication skills • good office skills • compassion	• emotional strength • experience (with _____) • a sense of humor • a stylish appearance

Example

STUDENT A: **First and foremost**, volunteers at the animal shelter must love animals.

STUDENT B: Of course. **But it's also important** for them to have good communication skills, don't you think?

STUDENT A: Yes, you're right. And **aside from that**, I think the animal shelter will want **a person who** has good office skills for the administrative work.

■■■■■■■■■■■■■ *GO TO* MyEnglishLab *FOR MORE SKILL PRACTICE AND TO CHECK WHAT YOU LEARNED.*

FINAL SPEAKING TASK

A PSA, or public service announcement, is a short announcement aired on the radio or television that educates people about an important cause or encourages them to donate money or volunteer time.

*In this activity, you will create and present a PSA. Try to use the vocabulary, grammar, pronunciation, and listening and speaking skills that you learned in this unit.**

STEP 1: 🎧 Listen to the PSA. Then answer these questions.

- What is the PSA encouraging people to do?

- Do you think the PSA is persuasive? Why or why not?

---

* For Alternative Speaking Topics, see page 157.

STEP 2: Work with a partner. Select a not-for-profit organization from the following list, find one of your own on the Internet, or use one of the organizations you learned about in this unit.

The Nature Conservancy   Habitat for Humanity International

The Red Cross   The Union of Concerned Scientists

Doctors Without Borders   Amnesty International

UNICEF   World Wildlife Fund

Other: _____

STEP 3: Plan your PSA by completing the chart below.

AUDIENCE:	
Is the PSA for college students? Parents? Middle-income people?	
METHOD:	
Is your ad for radio? TV? Internet?	
REQUEST:	
Exactly what do you want people to do?	

STEP 4: Write your one-minute PSA. Use the vocabulary, grammar, and prioritizing language from the unit. Then perform or record it for the class.

Listening Task

Listen to your classmates' PSAs. Choose one that you would volunteer for or donate money to. Explain your choice.

UNIT PROJECT

Work with a partner. Research and report on a philanthropic organization or a philanthropist.

STEP 1: Choose a non-profit organization or a philanthropist you would like to know more about. Select from the groups or people in this unit, choose from the box below, or think of your own.

Philanthropists

Hasso Plattner

Joan Kroc

John D. and Catherine T. McArthur

Brooke Astor

George Soros

John Kluge

Oveta Culp Hoby

Carol F. Sulzberger

Pierre Toussaint

Tan Tock Seng

Oprah Winfrey

Victor Fu

Zainab Salbi

Charles F. Feeney

David Geffen

Robert Wood Johnson

John D. Rockefeller

Ted Turner

STEP 2: Go online to research your philanthropist or organization. Take notes on origin and background and other interesting information that you find. Answer questions such as these:

- What is the mission of the organization?

- What are some examples of its activities?

- How effective is it?

- Would you donate time or money to this organization?

STEP 3: Prepare a short report on the organization or person you chose. Then present your report to the class and listen to your classmates' reports.

ALTERNATIVE SPEAKING TOPICS

Work in a small group. Read the two different viewpoints about high school students and volunteering. Then discuss the questions.

Student A: "High schools should require community service in order for students to graduate. It's just as important for students to learn to be good citizens as it is for them to learn math, history, and science. Even students who didn't like the idea at first would probably change their minds after they spent some time volunteering."

Student B: "Service opportunities should be available for students who are interested, but they shouldn't be required. Students should have some choice about what they want to do in high school, but I think it would be great if volunteering could be part of that choice. They could get credit for service the same way they do for art, music, or gym classes."

1. Which student's viewpoint is most like your own?

2. For high school students, what are some benefits of volunteering? What are some drawbacks?

3. How many hours a week should students volunteer?

4. Should teenagers be required or encouraged to volunteer when they are not in school? (for example, after school or on weekends, or during vacations)

5. What kinds of organizations would be best suited for teenage volunteers?

■■■■■■■■■■■GO TO MyEnglishLab *TO DISCUSS ONE OF THE ALTERNATIVE TOPICS, WATCH A VIDEO ABOUT A LOCAL TEEN MAKING A DIFFERENCE, AND TAKE THE UNIT 6 ACHIEVEMENT TEST.* ■■■■■■■■■

DO YOUR
Homework!

1 FOCUS ON THE TOPIC

1. Look at the photo. Do you think this student is in the mood to do homework? Why or why not?

2. Describe your homework routine. When do you typically do your assignments? Where do you do them? Do you do anything else at the same time?

GO TO MyEnglishLab *TO CHECK WHAT YOU KNOW.*

LISTENING ONE HOMEWORK ISSUES

VOCABULARY

1 Read and listen to a psychologist's presentation to parents of children in elementary school. Pay attention to the words in **bold**.

Thank you for coming to the meeting. I'm talking this evening about helping your children develop the habits they need to do well in school. The hypothesis we'll work from is that children's choices early in life reflect their later choices. Do you remember that famous marshmallow experiment conducted at Stanford University? Researchers gave little children one marshmallow and left them alone in a room for fifteen minutes. The children were told that if they did not eat that marshmallow, they would be given two marshmallows later on. Alternatively, they could eat the first one, but then they would not get another one later. Some of the children, as you might expect, ate the marshmallow

Fighting the desire to eat a marshmallow

without **hesitation**. However, about one third resisted eating it and were able to wait until they got a second marshmallow. But here's what's **shocking** about the later results of the test. The kids at age 4 who waited then performed better at age 18 on tests of confidence, concentration, and in other areas. The experiment has been repeated a few times, so we now have results from a **sample size** of about 600 children. This means that overall, it's a pretty **rigorous** study.

So **it turns out** that this study tells us a lot about discipline and **motivation**. Students of all ages are tempted to take shortcuts at school. After all, it's easier to just finish your homework quickly and then watch TV or play with friends than to **plow through** a difficult assignment, and some children **figure** that they can do OK in school without putting in too much effort. However, parents often feel **conflicted** when they see their children acting that way, and let me tell you, I've heard plenty of **heated** discussions among frustrated parents and resentful kids.

The challenge is to help children see that doing homework now, working hard now, will pay off with greater rewards later—rewards like higher grades and an easier time in school.

2 Match the words on the left with the definitions on the right.

_____ **1.** conflicted   **a.** very angry and excited

_____ **2.** it turns out   **b.** careful and thorough

_____ **3.** figure   **c.** size of the experiment group

_____ **4.** heated   **d.** work your way through something difficult

_____ **5.** hesitation   **e.** actually; it happens to be

_____ **6.** motivation   **f.** unsure or ambivalent about something

_____ **7.** plow through   **g.** the determination and desire to do something

_____ **8.** rigorous   **h.** pausing because you are uncertain

_____ **9.** sample size   **i.** extremely surprising

_____ **10.** shocking   **j.** have a particular opinion after thinking about something

GO TO MyEnglishLab *FOR MORE VOCABULARY PRACTICE.*

PREVIEW

Geri-Ellen Dow tells an interviewer about an experiment she conducted to help her teenage son with his summer reading of some long, difficult classic literature. She drew inspiration from economist Steven Levitt, whose book *Freakonomics*, written with journalist Stephen Dubner, investigates motivation.

🎧 Listen to the introduction. Kai Ryssdal, the interviewer, refers to an idea that inspired Dow's experiment. Then answer the questions.

According to the interviewer, how did Levitt suggest motivating children to get good grades?

_____

Do you think this method of motivation would help a high school student finish his summer reading? Why or why not? Discuss your ideas with a partner.

MAIN IDEAS

1 Listen to the whole interview. Look again at your answers from Preview. How did your answers help you understand the interview?

2 Circle the correct answers.

1. **Hypothesis** What did Geri-Ellen Dow believe?

    a. Her son had been assigned too much homework to finish.

    b. Her son wasn't motivated to do his homework by himself.

    c. The reading assignment was not worthwhile.

2. **Design** What did she offer her son?

    a. $40 to read two books

    b. $20 to start the reading and another $20 to finish

    c. $50 for good grades on his reading tests

3. **Results** What happened?

    a. Her son finished reading both assigned books.

    b. Her son read only one of the books.

    c. Her son finished one book on time and one book late.

4. **Interpretation** What did Dow conclude?

    a. Her expectations weren't clear enough.

    b. Paying children to study is wrong.

    c. Parents don't need to provide extra motivation.

DETAILS

🎧 Listen again. Circle the correct answers.

1. Which book was NOT assigned to Dow's son for summer reading?

   a. *Great Expectations*

   b. *The Iliad*

   c. *The Odyssey*

2. Why was Dow looking for ways to motivate her son?

   a. Her son had many other things to do that summer.

   b. The teacher had said the homework was optional.

   c. Her son wasn't really excited about school.

3. When did her son start reading the second book?

   a. A few days before school started

   b. On the first day of school

   c. Just after school started

4. Why was Dow hesitant about paying her son?

   a. Although he didn't finish his work, he seemed to be working hard.

   b. He said he'd finished the work, but she didn't believe him.

   c. He finished the reading, but he got poor results on his tests.

5. What did Dow conclude about the reward she offered?

   a. The amount of money was too much.

   b. The amount of money was too little.

   c. The amount of money wasn't important.

6. What does the interviewer think about paying students to do homework?

   a. Schools should forbid parents to pay children to work.

   b. Paying is an easy and effective way to motivate students.

   c. Paying kids is a personal choice for parents.

GO TO MyEnglishLab FOR MORE LISTENING PRACTICE.

MAKE INFERENCES

UNDERSTANDING HUMOR

In this light-hearted interview, a mother describes a homework experiment with her son as if it were a serious scientific experiment. The speakers sometimes use a special form of humor in which they say something they don't really mean (*irony*). You can identify irony from the speaker's tone of voice and, also, by the sense of the words. If the words don't seem logical, or if they seem exaggerated, it's possible the speaker means them to be humorous. The speakers also use *understatement* for humor, a form of exaggeration in which the speaker pretends something is weaker, smaller, or less than it really is.

🎧 Read and listen to the example. Pay attention to the interviewer's tone of voice as he responds to Dow's comment.

Example

Dow: Heh. I'm always looking for ways to motivate the kids because they don't seem to be really excited about school themselves.

Ryssdal: Shocking, shocking!

Although the interviewer says he is "shocked" that kids aren't motivated by school, he really means the opposite—that he is *not* surprised.

🎧 Listen to the excerpts and circle the correct answers.

Excerpt One

How does Dow think her son feels?

a. She is sure that he didn't think $20 was enough.

b. She couldn't tell if he thought $20 was enough or not.

Excerpt Two

What does Dow think the interviewer means?

a. She should repeat the experiment next summer with more children to get more information.

b. Her experience wasn't a scientific experiment from which she could draw general conclusions.

Excerpt Three

What is the interviewer going to do later?

a. Talk to Steven Levitt about improving his theories

b. Not talk to Steven Levitt about improving his theories

EXPRESS OPINIONS

Work in a small group. Discuss the questions.

1. Do you think Geri-Ellen Dow's idea to pay her son to do his homework was a good idea? Explain your reasons.

2. Kai Ryssdal feels that $20 is not enough to read a long, difficult book like *The Odyssey*. Do you agree? If parents give rewards to children for doing homework, should the rewards vary with the assignment?

3. Have you experienced either getting or giving rewards for doing homework? Explain.

■■■■■■■■■■■■■■■ *GO TO* MyEnglishLab *TO GIVE YOUR OPINION ABOUT ANOTHER QUESTION.*

LISTENING TWO TIGER MOM

VOCABULARY

Amy Chua is the author of a book about parenting in which she writes about the strict way she raised her children. Her approach angered many parents, but other parents agreed with her. You will hear an interview with Amy Chua.

Work with a partner. Read the words and phrases in the box aloud. Check any meanings you don't know in a dictionary. Then complete the book summary with the correct word or phrase.

> controversy
> in a nutshell
> measure up to (someone's expectations)
> mindset
> privilege

The recent book *Battle Hymn of the Tiger Mother* has created a lot of _____
(1)
among parents. Amy Chua describes how, as a Chinese mother in the United States, she tried to

teach her children that learning was an obligation and a _____. She expected her
(2)

children to _____ her expectations and do well in school. _____,
(3)   (4)

(continued on next page)

she says parents should be very strict and establish strong rules for their children. Many parents reacted negatively to her _____, saying that she was far too strict. Others pointed

(5)

out that not all immigrants were alike.

COMPREHENSION

🎧 Listen to the interview and answer the questions. Then compare your answers with a partner's answers.

1. The interviewer reads an excerpt that describes activities that Amy Chua did not permit her daughters to do. Check (✓) the things that her daughters were NOT allowed to do.

_____ Have a sleepover (spend the night at a friend's house)

_____ Have a play date (meet a friend after school)

_____ Get tutoring for their homework

_____ Watch TV or play video games

_____ Choose their own extracurricular activities

_____ Get any grade less than B

_____ Play any instruments other than the violin or the piano

_____ Play sports

2. Ms. Chua's book is about her transformation as a mother. With her first daughter, she was a complete "Tiger Mom." However, with her second daughter, she had to soften her methods somewhat. Check (✓) all the reasons Ms. Chua gives for this change.

_____ The second daughter rebelled (refused to obey).

_____ The second daughter's personality is very much like her own.

_____ The two daughters had very different abilities.

_____ Mother and daughter had terrible fights.

_____ The second daughter wanted to play the French horn.

_____ Chua's husband disagreed with her methods.

3. Ms. Chua claims that her values are American, especially those of immigrant families. Check (✓) all the values she mentions.

_____ Working hard

_____ Never giving up

_____ Not fighting with your parents

_____ Not making excuses

_____ Taking responsibility

_____ Earning your own money

_____ Being self-reliant

4. Circle the correct words to complete this conclusion: Ms. Chua suggests that parents need a hybrid, or a balanced, model. In her view, both approaches are extreme: The Tiger Mom approach is overly (*permissive / strict*), while the Western approach is overly (*permissive / strict*).

■■■■■■■■■■■■■■■■■■■■■■■■■■ *GO TO* MyEnglishLab *FOR MORE VOCABULARY PRACTICE.*

LISTENING SKILL

LISTENING FOR CLARIFICATION

In conversations, speakers often clarify what they just said, using signal phrases such as *that is, you know, in other words, in fact, I mean,* and so on. Here, the topic is controversial. Amy Chua feels that her book has been misunderstood, so she's especially eager to clarify her position.

Example

Listen to the example. Then answer the questions.

1. Kiran Chetry is clarifying the phrase "in the Asian culture." What does it really mean here?
   a. Her father is from Nepal.
   b. She wants to promote Asian values.
   c. She is talking about people who visit Nepal.

2. What signal phrase did you hear? _____

Answers: 1. a.   2. I mean

🎧 Listen to the excerpts and answer the questions.

Excerpt One

1. Ms. Chua wants to clarify what she means by saying she is not speaking for all Chinese parents. What does she really mean?

   a. Her comments don't apply to Chinese parents.

   b. Her comments apply to a lot of immigrant parents.

   c. Her comments only apply to Chinese parents living in the United States.

2. What signal phrase did you hear? _____

Excerpt Two

1. What does Ms. Chua want to clarify about Chinese values?

   a. What the values actually are

   b. The fact that the values are not actually Chinese values

   c. The fact that the values are no longer relevant

2. What signal phrase did you hear? _____

■■■■■■■■■■■■■■■■■■■■■■■■■■■■■■■■ GO TO MyEnglishLab *FOR MORE SKILL PRACTICE.*

STEP 1: Organize

How did the interviewees in Listenings One and Two motivate their children? Complete the chart with your notes.

QUESTION	LISTENING ONE GERI-ELLEN DOW	LISTENING TWO AMY CHUA
What methods did you use to motivate your children to do schoolwork?	I offered . . .	I established rules like . . .
How successful were your methods?	Not completely successful because . . .	
Did you have any doubts about your methods?		I might have gone a little too far by . . .

STEP 2: Synthesize

1 Work in groups of three to role-play an interview and discussion with Ms. Dow and Ms. Chua. The interviewer asks the questions in the chart, and Ms. Dow and Ms. Chua answer with information from the chart. Each person can ask follow-up questions, which Ms. Dow and Ms. Chua answer based on information from the listenings.

Example

INTERVIEWER: Both of you are concerned about your children's schoolwork. What methods did you use to motivate them?

Ms. Dow: Well, I tried bribery. Here's what I did: First, I offered my son . . .

Ms. Chua: Don't you think your son should do his homework just because it's his responsibility?

Ms. Dow: Well, schoolwork isn't very exciting, so . . .

2 Ms. Dow and Ms. Chua can ask each other one or two follow-up questions. The interviewer takes notes on what they say.

3 Compare the responses with the class.

■■■■■■■■■■■■■■■■■■■■■■■■■■■■■■■■ *GO TO* MyEnglishLab *TO CHECK WHAT YOU LEARNED.*

VOCABULARY

REVIEW

Read the transcript of a radio show. Complete the transcript with words and expressions from the box.

conflicted	figure	privilege
controversy	heated	reasonable
in a nutshell	hesitation	
it turns out	plow through	

IS HOMEWORK EFFECTIVE?

This is Dr. Clarence, Principal of Roundtop Middle School, responding to the question many of

you have asked: Is homework effective? Well, _____ that this is not an easy
(1)

question to answer: In fact, there is plenty of _____ not only about how
(2)

much homework is optimal, but whether it's necessary at all. Some parents believe that education

is a real _____ and that children need to make the most of the opportunity
(3)

to improve their skills after school. But last week we had some _____
(4)

comments from parents who said their children were being overwhelmed by too much homework.

_____, people don't really agree about it.
(5)

Research shows that children today do about 50% more homework than they did about 30 years

ago. Even if you believe it is _____ for children to study at home, you might
(6)

believe, like many people do, that it is not a good idea to have kids _____
(7)

page after page of work when they are tired and burned out. So what's the solution?

One mother responded with no _____. She said: "I
                                           (8)

_____ that ten minutes per night, per subject, is enough. And no more than
          (9)

two hours!" But another mother who called in was more _____ about her
                                                                    (10)

children's homework. "I don't tell them what to do," she said. "I leave it up to them."

EXPAND

1 Work in groups of three. Read the students' conversation. Pay attention to the words and expressions in **bold**.

ALEX: OK, so we agree, right? We're going to write about different attitudes toward doing homework.

BRUNO: And we need to include more than just personal anecdotes in our paper. The professor might **take issue with** a paper that just talks about ourselves.

CHEN: OK, here's an idea. Check out this website about the four "types" of students when it comes to doing homework. The first type is called the *Procrastinator*. That's someone who keeps putting things off until later. It's someone who doesn't **buckle down** and do the work.

ALEX: That's interesting—let me have a look. OK, the second type is the *Overachiever*. That's someone who does too much homework! It's like that woman in our statistics class. She always **goes over the top** and does about twice as much work as anyone else.

BRUNO: It's true she's always studying. But her hard work might **pay off** in the long run.

ALEX: Well, maybe you're right, Bruno.

CHEN: Here's the next person: the *Refuser*. That's a person who just won't do the work.

ALEX: I have a person like that in my Economics class. He never wants to participate in group projects. I just don't understand that.

BRUNO: Group work is quite difficult to do well. There are always **a few hiccups**.

CHEN: I know what you mean! OK, the last type of person is *Just Right*. This is a person that always **measures up to expectations**.

ALEX: That would be like us, right?

CHEN: Very funny, Alex. Now, let's think about how we can apply those personality types to something . . . perhaps our class?

2 Match the words and expressions on the left with a definition on the right.

_____ **1.** take issue with   **a.** concentrate and do your work

_____ **2.** buckle down   **b.** some minor problems

_____ **3.** goes over the top   **c.** reaches the expected standard

_____ **4.** pay off   **d.** have objections to

_____ **5.** a few hiccups   **e.** works excessively, too much

_____ **6.** measures up to expectations   **f.** lead to good results

CREATE

Work in pairs. Take turns reading the student comments below. As a group, decide who made the comment: a Procrastinator, an Overachiever, a Refuser, or Just Right. Use the vocabulary in parentheses, as well as other vocabulary from the unit in your discussion.

1. **A:** I'm just not in the mood to do that assignment right now. I can do it tomorrow, though, or maybe this weekend would be better.

   B: (point out, pay off)

   Example

   B: This person is obviously a Procrastinator. I would like to <u>point out</u> that the person probably won't do the work tomorrow! He or she is sure to wait until the weekend. But this type of behavior doesn't <u>pay off</u>, in my opinion.

2. **A:** I finished the assignments in the chapter and got everything right, but I think I need to understand the topic better. I'm going to go online and do some additional background research.

   B: (plow through, pay off, measure up to expectations)

3. **A:** I don't think the assignment the teacher gave is that important, so I'm going to skip it and do some other work instead. She probably won't check it anyway.

   B: (heated, hesitation, in a nutshell)

4. **A:** I'm not going to school today because I just don't feel like it.

   B: (reasonable, conflicted, controversy)

5. A: I'm going to ask my friend later to help me with my homework because I don't understand it. But first, I just want to finish watching this TV show.

   B: (take issue, it turns out, figure)

6. A: The other people in my group weren't doing the work for our group project very well, so I did their part for them.

   B: (a few hiccups, buckle down)

■■■■■■■■■■■■■■■■■■■■■■■■■■■■ *GO TO* MyEnglishLab *FOR MORE VOCABULARY PRACTICE.*

GRAMMAR

1 Work with a partner. Read the conversation. Then explain what the phrases in **bold** mean.

A: Hey, want to come over and play some video games after school?

B: I can't. My dad **makes me do** my homework right after school.

A: Oh, too bad! Can't you **get him to change** his mind?

B: No, it's the only time he can **help me do** the math problems, and I really need his help.

MAKE, HAVE, LET, HELP, AND GET

1. Use *make, have,* and *let* + object + base form of the verb to talk about things that someone can **require, cause,** or **allow** another person (or an animal) to do.

   You can also use *make* to mean *cause to / force to.*

   - She **has** her kids **do** their homework immediately after school.
   - She **makes** them **turn off** the TV.
   - She **lets** them **play** computer games later.

2. *Help* can be followed by:

   Object + base form of the verb (more common)

   OR

   Object + infinitive

   The meaning is the same.

   - He **helped** me **do** the homework.
     OR
   - He **helped** me **to do** the homework.

3. *Get* has a similar meaning to **make** and **have,** though it implies a less direct action by the subject of the sentence.

   It is always followed by **object + infinitive,** not the base form of the verb.

   - The teacher **got** us **to do** extra homework.
     NOT
     The teacher got us do extra homework.

Do Your Homework! 173

2 Read the conversation between a mother and father about their child. Complete the sentences using the verbs in parentheses. Use the correct pronouns where necessary.

MOTHER: Andre's teacher told me he isn't doing well in school right now.

FATHER: Not doing well? What exactly is the problem?

M: He's a little lazy. I can't ___get him to do___ his homework without bribing
(1) (get / do)
him to do it.

F: I'll speak to him tonight, but why can't you _____ and do it?
(2) (make / sit down)

M: He has extra study classes two days a week and sports after school the

other three days. When he gets home from school, he's so tired that I

_____ TV or play his music. He's just a kid. You see him at
(3) (let / watch)
8:30. He conks out on the sofa. The poor child is exhausted.

F: Well, he has to do his homework. I guess we'll have to _____
(4) (have / stop)
watching TV.

M: I think we also have to help. He says he doesn't understand the concepts in

science, and the problems in math are hard, too.

F: Well, then we'll help. I can _____ the science. But the math . . .
(5) (help / understand)
you're much better at that.

M: OK, I'll help with the math. And, when he comes home from school, maybe

I'll _____ a short nap. Then studying might be easier for him.
(6) (have / take)

F: Good idea. If all this doesn't work, we'll _____ the sports for
(7) (make / give up)
a while.

M: OK. But if we can _____ his homework, maybe we won't have
(8) (get / do)
to go that far.

3 Work in a small group. Some parents are asking a school counselor for advice about their children's homework problems.

a. Take turns reading the problems aloud.

b. Each group member writes some suggestions from the counselor, using *make, have, let, help,* or *get.* Write the suggestions on slips of paper.

c. One student reads all the suggestions aloud. Then the group votes on the best one.

Example

PARENT: My son rushes through his homework, finishes quickly, and is careless.

COUNSELOR: Have him do one assignment at a time, and then **help him check** his work.

B. My daughter often can't understand her homework assignments. They seem unclear to me, too.

A. My son rushes through his homework, finishes quickly, and is careless.

C. My kids can't seem to concentrate on their homework. They get up every few minutes and are easily distracted. Do you think it's because they eat a lot of candy while they're working?

D. My son plays baseball, practices violin, and then does his homework. By that time, he's very tired.

E. My children listen to music or watch TV while doing their homework. I don't know if they can really concentrate.

F. My son always finishes his homework—but then leaves it at home or brings it to school but forgets to turn it in.

G. My daughter always calls her friends for help with her homework. But I think they spend most of their time chatting about other things.

GO TO MyEnglishLab *FOR MORE GRAMMAR PRACTICE.*

PRONUNCIATION

STRESSED AND UNSTRESSED VOWELS

Stressed Vowels

Stressed vowels in English are longer, louder, and higher in pitch.

abōlish	ādvocates

Unstressed Vowels

- Unstressed vowels are short.
- Unstressed vowels are usually pronounced /ə/, regardless of how they are spelled.
- /ə/ has a special name, *schwa*. It is the sound of the hesitation word native speakers use when they need time to think: *uh . . . uh*.
- Schwa (/ə/) is the most common vowel sound in English.

ago (əgō)   office (ōffəs)   minute (mīnət)

- Unstressed vowels spelled with the letters *i* or *e* can be pronounced /ə/ or /ɪ/.

dəcīde *or* dɪcīde (decide)

- The unstressed endings –*ow* and –*y* are not pronounced /ə/

wīndow   būsy

---

1 🎧 Listen to the words and put a line over the stressed vowels. Then practice the words with a partner. Make the stressed vowels longer, louder, and higher in pitch.

1. message
2. optional
3. distraught
4. promotions
5. social

6. abolish
7. heritage
8. tangible
9. decision
10. responsible

2 🎧 Listen to the words and repeat them. The spellings show how the unstressed vowels are pronounced. Write the normal spelling of the words on the line. Then check your answers with a partner and practice saying the words. Use the phonetic spellings to guide your pronunciation.

1. mīnəməl

    minimal

2. əcōūntəbəl

_____

3. əchīēvemənt

_____

4. ēksələnt

_____

5. kəmplēte

_____

6. əsīgnmənts

_____

7. mōnətər

_____

8. dəmānding

_____

9. əgrēē

_____

10. rədīkyələs

_____

11. əpīnyən

_____

12. əbōləsht

_____

3 🎧 Listen to the questions and repeat them. The spellings in **bold** show the pronunciation. Then work with a partner. Ask and answer the questions.

1. Do you **əgrēē** that kids today do too much homework?

2. Did your parents **mōnətər** your homework?

3. Did you have **dəmānding** homework **əssīgnmənts** in school?

4. Do you think homework should be **əbōləsht** in elementary school?

SPEAKING SKILL

ASKING FOR AND OFFERING CLARIFICATION

For many reasons, speakers need to use and listeners need to ask for clarification. The content may be difficult, pronunciation or listening skills may pose a problem, or there might be unexpected noise in the environment. If something is not clear, ask for clarification. If someone asks you for clarification, explain your idea again or in another way.

If you don't understand or need clarification:	To restate and clarify your idea:
Can you explain what you just said?	In other words, . . .
I'm not sure I understand.	To put it another way, . . .
Could you repeat what you said?	I mean that . . . / You know, . . .
Could you clarify that for me?	What I'm saying is . . .
	What that means is . . .

1 Divide the class into two groups, A and B. Group A looks at the statements below. Group B looks at the statements on the next page.

2 Read the sentences assigned to your group and work together to explain them in your own words.

3 Work in pairs, with one student from Group A and one from Group B. Take turns reading your sentences and asking each other for clarification, using the phrases to help you. Student A should read the first comment in a way that makes it difficult to understand: For example, read it too fast, cough, or mumble so that Student B has to ask for clarification.

Example

STUDENT A: Some of the children in that experiment had trouble delaying gratification.

STUDENT B: Hmmm, I'm not sure I understand.

STUDENT A: What I'm saying is that they ate the marshmallow right away. They couldn't wait for their reward. They had to have it immediately.

Student A

1. Schools should give students who do well special incentives, like money or prizes. This will motivate students to work harder both in and out of school.

2. The best way for parents to enforce rules about homework is through strict consequences, such as loss of privileges.

3. A study by the Public Agenda Foundation found that 25 percent of parents want more homework for their children, and only 10 percent want less.

Student B

1. Some people believe that too much studying and reading is very unhealthy for children, and that more time should be spent doing some kind of physical activity.

2. Teachers should be rewarded when their students do well on standardized tests, and teachers should have consequences, such as loss of promotions or salary raises, if their students do poorly.

3. Some schools have a "10-minute rule," which says that teachers should give no more than ten minutes of homework per subject every day.

■■■■■■■■■■■■■■■■■■■■■■■■■■■■■ *GO TO* MyEnglishLab *TO CHECK WHAT YOU LEARNED.*

FINAL SPEAKING TASK

In this activity, you will role-play a public school board meeting in which you exchange viewpoints about homework and reach a policy decision for high school students. Try to use the vocabulary, grammar, pronunciation, and language for asking for clarification that you learned in this unit.*

STEP 1: Read about this challenge faced by a school district. Make sure you understand the situation. Ask your classmates or instructor for clarification if necessary.

The School Board of Wallsdale is made up of residents who have been elected to make decisions about school policy. Tonight, the Board is meeting to consider how to raise test scores, which have been dropping in recent years. The policy debate focuses on homework at the high school level. Some parents have complained that their children don't have enough free time for activities and family, and that the homework they get isn't useful. Others feel that homework is an essential part of learning. So the Board will come up with a policy about how much homework should be given and the types of assignments that are most appropriate.

---

* For Alternative Speaking Topics, see page 181.

STEP 2: Divide into three groups as below. Discuss your ideas for that group's point of view and take notes. Use the ideas in the chart and your own ideas.

SCHOOL BOARD MEMBERS	ANTI-HOMEWORK PARENTS	PRO-HOMEWORK PARENTS
• You will finalize the homework policy for the local high school. • You want students to learn effectively. • You want parents to be satisfied with their children's education. • You want to make a decision in a reasonable way, that will be most likely to raise test scores and that will please the most people in the community.	• You think students currently have too much homework. • Students get homework from many teachers. The total amount of homework increases very quickly. • Students don't have enough time for extracurricular activities, such as sports and music, or part-time jobs. • Students who spend hours on homework have little social life and do not spend enough time with their families. • The types of homework students are being assigned now aren't useful.	• Your members think homework is essential for success in high school and beyond. • Students need to review what they learn in school. • By doing homework, students learn to be more responsible and develop a sense of discipline. • It is impossible for teachers to cover all the material students have to learn. Students must also learn to work by themselves. • Teachers should be allowed to make their own decisions about what kind of homework to assign.

STEP 3: Meet in new groups of three: one school board member, one pro-homework parent, and one anti-homework parent. Use your notes and hold a meeting. Present your points of view, and ask for and offer clarification as necessary. Use the new vocabulary to make your points more precise and powerful. The school board member will make notes about the final decision.

Listening Task

Listen to the final decision from each group. What similarities do they have? What differences? Then vote as a whole class on which solution seems the most effective and fair.

UNIT PROJECT

Research homework in different countries. Choose at least two to compare and contrast. One of the countries may be your own.

STEP 1: Look at the research areas in the chart on the next page. You may also add your own ideas. Then select two or more countries to compare by researching online (you can look for official reports and also informal accounts from individuals) and by interviewing people you know. Take notes on what you find.

	AMOUNT OF HOMEWORK TYPICALLY ASSIGNED	COMMON TYPES OF HOMEWORK ASSIGNMENTS	STUDENTS' ATTITUDES TO HOMEWORK	TEACHERS' ATTITUDES TO HOMEWORK	PARENTS' ATTITUDES TO HOMEWORK
COUNTRY #1: _____					
COUNTRY #2: _____					

STEP 2: Prepare a report to present in class. Discuss similarities and differences in the countries you researched. Do the homework policies and systems seem to be working in each country? Do you think they could be improved?

ALTERNATIVE SPEAKING TOPICS

1 Read the quotes about homework. Work in a small group and discuss what they mean, asking for and giving clarification as needed.

The worst thing a kid can say about homework is that it is too hard. The worst thing a kid can say about a game is it's too easy.
  Henry Jenkins, Associate Professor of Literature and Director of the Comparative Media Studies Program at the Massachusetts Institute of Technology

Homework, I have discovered, involves a sharp pencil and thick books and long sighs.
  Katherine Applegate, award-winning author

One of life's most painful moments comes when we must admit that we didn't do our homework, that we are not prepared.
  Merlin Olsen, athlete, radio commentator, and actor

Rewards and punishments are not opposites at all; they are two sides of the same coin. And it is a coin that does not buy very much.
  Alfie Kohn, author and lecturer on topics in education, parenting, and human behavior

2 As a class, discuss your reaction to the quotes. Do you agree or disagree? How have your experiences with homework been similar or different?

■■■■■■■■■■■■■■■*GO TO* MyEnglishLab *TO DISCUSS ONE OF THE ALTERNATIVE TOPICS, WATCH A VIDEO ABOUT A HOLIDAY FROM HOMEWORK, AND TAKE THE UNIT 7 ACHIEVEMENT TEST.* ■■■■■■■■■■■■■

PROS AND CONS OF
Gaming

1 FOCUS ON THE TOPIC

1. Do you regularly play any video games? If so, how much time do you spend playing? Briefly describe one game you enjoy. If not, explain why they aren't interesting to you.

2. What are some benefits and drawbacks of playing video games?

3. What is a reasonable amount of time per day to spend online? How much time do you spend online? What sorts of activities do you do?

GO TO MyEnglishLab *TO CHECK WHAT YOU KNOW.*

VOCABULARY

1 🎧 Read and listen to an interview in an in-flight magazine for those thinking about investing money in video game companies. Notice the words and expressions in **bold**.

THE ETHICAL INVESTOR
Investing in Game Companies: Should you?

Interviewer: Computer gaming has become wildly popular in recent years with global sales reaching $10.5 billion. I spoke recently to Todd Rudamill, an investment specialist.

Todd, I remember when video gaming was played only by nerds, the kids who were not popular or athletic. We thought these children played video games as a **substitute** for playing with other kids. But now computer gaming has totally **shed its nerdy image** and become cool.

Rudamill: That's right: Both kids and adults are big gamers now. Worldwide, people spend three billion hours per week playing online games. Games are **interactive**, and people play against others around the world; not just people they already know, but people they meet **randomly** through logging on and playing the game. This industry offers tempting investment opportunities and huge profits.

Interviewer: But there must be a downside. What do new investors need to consider?

Rudamill: Well, the gaming industry is controversial. In some cases, too much gaming can be dangerous for users, you know: It's addictive. In fact, some **features** of online games use **reinforcements** to keep players playing—for example, they reward players for the number of hours they spend playing, or the number of games they complete.

Interviewer: Would you really call it an addiction, though?

Rudamill: Oh, yes. Gaming addicts display all the symptoms of other addicts: They have **lost contact with** family and friends, lost sleep, missed school, and lost jobs. Some can quit by going **cold turkey**, but others are **obsessive** about playing video games and actually **go berserk** when their games are taken away. This might scare some investors away.

Interviewer: That all sounds terrible. Why would anyone want to invest in gaming?

Rudamill: Well, gaming isn't a **compulsion** for all players. There are many positive opportunities for gaming, too. Games can be used educationally. Think about games to get kids to take their medicine, or to teach young parents how to care for their babies, or help older adults learn to read. The possibilities are endless!

Interviewer: So, potential investors: **Keep an extra close eye on** this industry. Gaming is in its infancy. There's plenty of room for creative growth.

2 Match the words and expressions in bold with their definitions.

_____ **1.** substitute

_____ **2.** shed its nerdy image

_____ **3.** interactive

_____ **4.** features

_____ **5.** reinforcements

_____ **6.** randomly

_____ **7.** lose contact with

_____ **8.** (go) cold turkey

_____ **9.** go berserk

_____ **10.** obsessive

_____ **11.** compulsion

_____ **12.** keep an extra close eye on

a. thinking so much about something that you don't think about other things enough

b. something new or different used in place of something else

c. involving people working or talking together

d. a strong desire to do something that is wrong

e. pay very close attention to

f. stop appearing unfashionable or lacking in social skills

g. become very angry and violent in a crazy way

h. rewards designed to encourage certain behavior

i. suddenly stop an activity or give up a substance that you are addicted to

j. stop communicating with

k. important, interesting, or typical parts of something

l. without any definite plan, aim, or pattern

GO TO MyEnglishLab **FOR MORE VOCABULARY PRACTICE.**

You will hear an excerpt from a BBC program on gaming addiction, a growing problem around the world. Before you listen, circle your predictions below.

In the United Kingdom, people spend (*more* / *less*) money on video gaming than they do on film and (*more* / *less*) money than they do on music. In fact, they spend more than (*one* / *three* / *five*) billion pounds a year.

🎧 Now listen to the excerpt to check your predictions.

MAIN IDEAS

PART 1

🎧 Listen to interviews with two gamers, Leo and Chris, and also Chris' mother. Check (✓) the statements that are true about each gamer.

LEO:

_____ is a high school student

_____ just started playing video games recently

_____ believes video games are harmful to him

_____ is going to quit playing video games

_____ believes some games are more beneficial than others

CHRIS:

_____ played only nights and weekends

_____ skipped school because he was playing too much

_____ believes video games are harmful to him

_____ solved his problem by not playing online

_____ believes that playing games in moderation is OK

_____ had physical reactions to restrictions on his game playing

PART 2

🎧 Listen to comments by a world authority on gaming, Professor Mark Griffiths, and Adrian Hon, an award-winning games designer. Circle the correct answers.

1. Video games are harmful for _____.

    a. only a few people

    b. about half of all players

    c. almost everybody

2. It's difficult to know how serious gaming addiction is because _____.

    a. it doesn't cause many physical problems

    b. gamers prefer not to talk about their problems

    c. there hasn't been enough research

3. The best way to get people to play video games more is to reward them _____.

    a. frequently

    b. at predictable times

    c. randomly

DETAILS

🎧 Listen again. Circle the correct answers.

1. How much time has Leo been playing games each day?

    a. 2 hours

    b. 12 hours

    c. 20 hours

2. Which was NOT an effect of Leo's gaming?

    a. His schoolwork suffered.

    b. He lost contact with friends.

    c. He didn't get enough sleep.

(continued on next page)

3. Leo compares video games to _____.

    a. a disease

    b. gambling

    c. surfing the Internet

4. Where did the teenagers in Chris's family play computer games?

    a. at their friends' houses

    b. in their bedrooms

    c. both at school and at home

5. What sent Chris into a violent rage?

    a. He lost an important game.

    b. His parents told him to stop playing.

    c. He temporarily lost Internet service.

6. According to Professor Griffiths, how does gaming compare to other addictions?

    a. Gaming is more addictive than tobacco or alcohol.

    b. There are fewer addicts of gaming than of gambling.

    c. Gaming addicts have the same symptoms as other addicts.

7. Research suggests that _____ games cause the most problems.

    a. interactive

    b. online

    c. violent

8. The variable rate of reinforcement theory was first developed from studies on _____.

    a. rats and food

    b. athletes and sports

    c. people and gambling

GO TO MyEnglishLab *FOR MORE LISTENING PRACTICE.*

MAKE INFERENCES

LISTENING FOR EMPHASIS

Speakers emphasize words in different ways. They can say them louder or with a higher pitch, so they're heard more clearly. They can also pause after the word, which signals to listeners that what they just heard was something important. Noticing the speaker's emphasis helps listeners know what to focus on.

🎧 Listen to the example. Notice the word to which the speaker gives special emphasis.

Example

Interviewer: The good news is that for the vast majority of people, video games are something that's very positive in their lives, but we have to take on board that there is a growing literature that suggests for a small but significant minority, things like gaming can be potentially problematic.

1. Which word received special emphasis? Circle the correct answer
   _____ a. good (*The good news is that*)
   _____ b. but (*but we have to take on board*)
   _____ c. potentially (*can be potentially problematic*)
2. The speaker emphasizes
   a. an important contrast
   b. a surprising addition

Answers: 1. b. The word "but" is said both louder and at a higher pitch. 2. a. The stress on the word "but" emphasizes the importance of the contrast.

🎧 Listen to the excerpts and circle the correct answers. Pay attention to the speakers' intonation and attitude.

Excerpt One

1. Which word receives special emphasis?

   a. just (*This game is just a disease.*)

   b. very (*It's very hard to explain properly.*)

   c. really (*one of those things you really have to experience*)

2. What does speaker want to emphasize?

   a. that a problem is insignificant

   b. that the listener must take some action

(continued on next page)

Excerpt Two

1. Which word receives special emphasis?

   _____ **a.** almost (*my dad almost had to pin me down*)

   _____ **b.** That (*That was the point*)

   _____ **c.** really (*we started to really understand*)

2. What does the speaker want to emphasize?

   a. his or her own opinion

   b. something the other speaker said

EXPRESS OPINIONS

Work in a small group. Discuss the questions.

1. Do you know anyone like Leo or Chris? What solutions could help people like them?

2. Do you think online gaming is more likely to cause problems with addiction than other online activities? Why or why not?

3. Who is responsible for controlling game addiction? Gamers? Parents? Teachers? Game developers? Others?

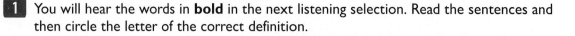 *GO TO* MyEnglishLab *TO GIVE YOUR OPINION ABOUT ANOTHER QUESTION.*

LISTENING TWO TRUTHS AND MYTHS IN GAMING

VOCABULARY

1 You will hear the words in **bold** in the next listening selection. Read the sentences and then circle the letter of the correct definition.

1. I'm not **capable of** winning this video game. I just can't do it!

   a. able to (do something)   **b.** motivated to (do something)

2. Video games where players work together can teach the valuable skill of **cooperation**.

   a. working with other people   **b.** solving problems alone

3. Gamers **crave** rewards when they play games, such as earning points.

   a. lose interest in   **b.** want very badly

4. Movies and books can provide **escapist** opportunities to enter an imaginary world.

   a. avoiding reality through fantasy   **b.** practical and realistic

5. Games often involve using a **strategy** to solve a complex problem.

   a. luck or chance   **b.** a plan or method to achieve results

2 Complete the conversation with a word or phrase from the box. Then take turns reading the conversation aloud.

capable of	cooperation	crave	escapist	strategy

SHEILA: Hi, Dr. Marsden. Listen, I'm worried about my son. He spends hours

and hours playing games online. He seems to _____ the
                                                        (1)

stimulation.

DR. MARSDEN: Well, I wouldn't worry too much. He's a teenager, right? Does he have

any other problems? Are you worried about things like discipline or

_____ with you on daily chores, like cleaning the house
        (2)

or helping with meals?

SHEILA: No, not really. He's a great kid. I'm just concerned that he's wasting

his time. He's _____ doing so well in school, but
                        (3)

his grades have slipped. Is he avoiding schoolwork or something?

Shouldn't he be hanging out with his friends instead? Aren't games just

_____ —I mean, a way to avoid facing reality?
        (4)

DR. MARSDEN: Well, kids who play these games are often interacting with other

kids who are online, sometimes even in other countries. It's a great

_____ for communicating with others, actually, and
        (5)

(continued on next page)

for improving his computer skills, and that, in turn, can help with his schoolwork.

Keep paying attention, though, and let me know if he displays signs of actual

addiction.

COMPREHENSION

Jane McGonigal is an award-winning game designer and researcher. When faced with a brain injury that was not healing, she made a video game. She says that this game not only restored her health, but also left her stronger in several ways than she was before her accident.

🎧 Listen to the interview with Jane McGonigal and circle the correct answers.

1. McGonigal admits that video games can be addictive because _____.

   a. many games are poorly designed

   b. they provide the things we crave the most

   c. many gamers have poor self-control

2. According to McGonigal, games allow us to _____.

   a. learn something important about ourselves

   b. apply skills learned online to our daily lives

   c. start out bad at something and then improve

3. McGonigal argues that playing games _____.

   a. reduces violent tendencies because gamers solve problems together

   b. can make players more violent because they see violence onscreen

   c. doesn't make players more or less violent; there's no connection

4. McGonigal says that games are escapist, _____.

   a. and they are therefore dangerous to play too long

   b. but players return to their real lives with improved skills

   c. so they're important ways for stressed people to relax

5. Her conclusion is that playing games _____.

   a. can help people solve problems and world issues

   b. is a harmless way to relax and have fun

   c. can potentially cause problems, so should be monitored

■■■■■■■■■■■■■■■■■■■■■■■■■ *GO TO* MyEnglishLab *FOR MORE VOCABULARY PRACTICE.*

LISTENING SKILL

LISTENING FOR COUNTERARGUMENTS

When speakers want to persuade others, they sometimes first point out an opposing argument. Then they explain why they do not agree with this argument. This strategy is called offering a counterargument.

🎧 Read and listen to the example. What argument is she making?

Example
There are a couple of concerns that come up often when we talk about video games. The first is addiction, and that's definitely a real problem. What I've discovered is that games do a better job, in many ways, of providing the things that we crave most.

McGonigal first concedes that addiction is a problem. She then uses the phrase *What I've discovered is* to make her counterargument—that games do a better job of providing people the things they crave.

🎧 Listen to the excerpts and then answer the questions.

Excerpt One

1. The speaker says that violence in video games is a big concern, and then she offers a counterargument. What does she think?

   _____

2. What words or phrases does she use to introduce the counterargument?

   _____

(continued on next page)

Excerpt Two

1. The speaker says that games are escapist, and then she offers a counterargument. What does she think?

_____

2. What word or phrase does she use to introduce the counterargument?

_____

■■■ **GO TO** MyEnglishLab **FOR MORE SKILL PRACTICE.**

CONNECT THE LISTENINGS

STEP 1: Organize

What are the benefits and drawbacks of gaming? Complete the chart with information from Listenings One and Two.

	BENEFITS OF GAMING	**DRAWBACKS OF GAMING**
L1: BBC REPORTER RAFAEL ROSE	• Gaming is an immersive, interactive experience. •	• Gaming can be addictive. • •
L2: JANE MCGONIGAL	• Games provide a sense of hands-on work. • • •	• Games can be addictive and escapist.

Work with a partner. Role-play a debate between Rafael Rose (L1) and Jane McGonigal (L2), using information from the chart.

> Example
>
> RAFAEL: Games may be really popular, but they can cause problems. A lot of players are addicted. They stop studying, they don't sleep. . . .
>
> JANE: I know, I know. You always hear about gaming addicts, but that's only a few people. For most people, games provide a sense of hands-on work. For example, . . .

■■■■■■■■■■■■■■■■■■■■■■■■■■ *GO TO* MyEnglishLab *TO CHECK WHAT YOU LEARNED.*

3 FOCUS ON SPEAKING

VOCABULARY

REVIEW

Games aren't just for entertainment. Increasingly, they are being used in healthcare settings. Read the questions and answers between a panel moderator and one of the panelists at a health management conference. The panel is discussing ways that health managers can improve results at their hospitals. Choose words from the box to complete the sentences.

capable of	interact	reinforce	substitute
escape	obsessively	strategies	

MODERATOR: Thanks for participating on our panel. So what are some health benefits of gaming for medical patients?

PANELIST: First, it seems that video games can provide relief from pain by allowing patients to _____ a virtual world for their real world of
(1)
pain. Seriously injured soldiers who played games required less medication than those who didn't play.

(continued on next page)

M: Interesting. Now, some of the research also relates to stress.

P: That's right. Stress levels and levels of depression improved for those who played. We believe that games provide a(n) _____ from (2) worry and give patients time to relax.

M: Earlier, we spoke about the elderly playing online games.

P: Yes. Interesting findings there. Elderly patients showed improved vision when the games they played required shooting. Also, seniors who play video games report higher degrees of happiness than those who don't play. And they weren't playing _____, only occasionally. (3)

M: And what about young children? I understand there are specific benefits for them.

P: Right. Studies show that chronically ill children who play games have better attitudes. We believe the _____ they practice in the games (4) _____ their feelings of control. They're more emotionally (5) flexible and have a stronger spirit to get better. It seems gaming helps the brain produce positive emotions.

M: Are there other benefits for young patients?

P: Yes, we found that young children who play video games are _____ performing better on tests of motor skills than (6) non-gamers. Of course, it's possible that kids with better motor skills are just more attracted to games.

M: And what about meeting other players online? Does that help patients?

P: Yes, of course. It's normal for patients to feel a little lonely. But when they _____ with other people, they feel much better. (7)

M: Seems that video gaming would be helpful for our doctors and health workers, as well as our patients.

P: I fully agree, yes.

Read the discussion between the moderator and another panel presenter about how video games can develop useful skills. Use words from the box to fill the blanks.

compulsion	crave	go cold turkey	randomly
cooperative	features	lost contact with	

MODERATOR: Now let's turn to some of the reasons why gaming seems to help people. What is it about video games that makes them so compelling?

PANELIST: Well, the most obvious benefit is that when people are playing, they're focusing on the tasks in the game, not on their illness. The games stop them from worrying so much. Many of the games have _____
(8)
like bright colors and beautiful scenes that make people feel happier. Perhaps that's why people _____ playing these games so much.
(9)
They're fun!

M: Yes, I can see that.

P: And this focus keeps people's minds sharp. For example, gamers can detect new information more easily than non-gamers. For instance, say you're playing a game and a new obstacle _____ appears. You will use
(10)
all your skills to try to overcome it, and, when you do, that brings a sense of satisfaction.

M: We all need that feeling, and I can see how it can help people in the hospital, where it's easy to feel quite isolated.

P: Exactly. I work with patients all the time, and it's common for them to feel a little depressed. They sometimes think they have _____
(11)
the outside world. But look at the benefits of playing online. Suddenly you're in a _____ relationship with other players. They may not be
(12)
in the same room as you, but you're working together toward a goal, and that feels good.

(continued on next page)

M: This all sounds wonderful, but isn't gaming just as risky for patients as it is for everyone else? We know people can become addicted to gaming. They develop a _____ to play.
(13)

P: Well, of course that's true. I guess that if that happens and they need to stop playing, they have to _____, like other players! But that (14) risk is small compared to the great benefits and happiness that gaming has brought to patients.

EXPAND

1 Complete the chart with the different forms of the words. Then compare your answers with a partner.

NOUN	VERB	ADJECTIVE	ADVERB
		interactive	
substitute / substitution			
			initially
		obsessive	
reinforcement			
			randomly
	crave		
		escapist	
strategy			
cooperation			
moderation			
compulsion			
		flexible	
	adapt		
harm			
anxiety			
		powerful	
		playful	

2 Read the speeches that some high school students prepared for their class. Change each word in **bold** so that it is in the correct form. Then practice reading the speeches aloud with a partner.

I'm Sebastian, I'm 17, and I'm a gamer. For years, I've heard people tell me that gaming is

_____ **(harm)**. Games will make me _____ **(anxiety)**!
         (1)   (2)

They are _____ **(powerful)** addictive! Well, I've been playing games all
                (3)

through high school, and I disagree. I have first-hand evidence—myself. I'm an honors student,

I have an active social life and belong to two clubs, plus I'm on the track team. I think video

games have helped make me a better student. I'm more _____ **(flexibility)**
                                                  (4)

with problem-solving, because I'm used to figuring things out quickly. My social life has

improved because I play games with other friends. In fact, my level of _____
                                                            (5)

(playful) has increased from my middle school years.

My name's Nancy, and I love the _____ **(interact)** of video
                                                  (6)

games. After all, when you're playing online, you're never alone. In fact, you're talking to

_____ **(randomly)** people from all over the world! My mother says that I'm
          (7)

using games as a _____ **(substitution)** for quality time with my family. My
                      (8)

father's also worried that I'm using games as a form of _____ **(escape)**, and I
                                                (9)

understand their concern because my friend became totally addicted to gaming, and she felt a

_____ **(compulsive)** to play all day long. But I'm not like that. Gaming is a
          (10)

great activity for teenagers.

I'm Sean, and I also want to stress the way that games teach people to _____
                                                          (11)

(cooperation) with each other. Of course, like anything else, you have to play in

_____ **(moderate)**—you can't be on the computer all day. But the joy of
          (12)

online games is that you can play at any time, so you have a lot of _____
                                                        (13)

(flexible). I also think that games teach people useful skills, like how to strategize and how to

_____ **(adaptation)** to new scenarios.
          (14)

CREATE

Work in pairs. Ask and answer the questions about how gaming can help develop skills for different jobs, using the words in parentheses. Then switch roles.

Student A	Student B
1. Do you really think gamers learn anything useful?	Sure. (*strategy, cooperation, capable of*) Gamers learn **strategy** and **cooperation** from all those hours of play. In addition, they're **capable of** . . .
2. I've heard that pilots train with games. Is that true?	Absolutely. (*substitute, features*)
3. How can playing video games help surgeons become better at what they do?	Oh, they help in several ways. (*capable of, keep a close eye on*)

Now switch roles.

4. Engineering students are often trained using games. What skills do they learn that help them become better engineers?	Well, there are several different skills they learn . . . (*interactive, reinforcement*)
5. I've read that even air traffic controllers are trained to do their jobs well using video games. Why do you think that happens?	Think about it. They have to deal with all kinds of different situations . . . (*randomly, escape*)
6. How could playing games help truck drivers deal with their long hours on the job?	Driving a truck is a hard job because you have to maintain your concentration. . . . (*obsessive, crave*)

■■■■■■■■■■■■■■■■■■■■■■■■ GO TO MyEnglishLab *FOR MORE VOCABULARY PRACTICE.*

GRAMMAR

1 🎧 Read and listen to a conversation about video games. Pay attention to the intonation of the words in **bold**. Then read the conversation aloud with a partner. Use the same intonation.

A: You heard about the new video games they just released on the market, **didn't you?**

B: Yes, those games sound amazing, **don't they?**

TAG QUESTIONS

In spoken English, people commonly end sentences with **tag questions**.

There are two types of tag questions:

- **question type**
- **comment type**

Question Type

- Asks for information or seeks to confirm information the questioner is not sure about.
- Uses rising intonation.

Examples

A: Video games don't make teenagers violent, **do they?**

B: No, I don't think so.

A: *Towers of Strength* is a new game on the market, **isn't it?**

B: Yes, that's right.

Comment Type

- Makes a comment.
- Assumes the listener agrees.
- Uses falling intonation.

Examples

A: That was an interesting report about gaming, **wasn't it?**

B: Yes, it was.

A: You didn't play a lot of games as a teenager, **did you?**

B: No, I didn't.

(continued on next page)

Tag questions have two parts: a **statement** and the **tag**, an added question.

- If the verb in the statement is affirmative, the tag is negative:

  The game is popular among high school students, **isn't it?**

- If the verb in the statement is negative, the tag is affirmative:

  He **didn't** *have a partner for the game,* **did** *he?*

- Tags always use a form of **be**, the auxiliary verbs **do, have,** or **will,** or a modal verb such as **can, could, should,** or **would.** Like a verb, the tag must agree with the subject.

  You're going to the gaming presentation, ~~isn't you?~~ **aren't you?**

  They wouldn't enjoy this game, **would they?**

Answering Tag Questions

Answer tag questions the same way you answer *yes / no* questions. You can agree with a tag question (comment type), or you can answer a tag question (question type) by giving the correct information.

Examples

A: The graphics made a big impact, didn't they? (comment type)

B: **Yes, they certainly did.**

A: The game doesn't require special equipment, does it? (question type)

B: **No, it doesn't. Players just use their regular equipment.**

---

2 ⊙ Complete the conversation with the appropriate tags. Then listen to the conversation. Check your work and mark each tag question as rising or falling. Finally, work with a partner and take turns reading the conversation, using correct intonation.

A: Video games are really popular, _____aren't they_____?
  (1)

B: Yes, right. I heard there are more game stores than bookstores in most cities. That's

  amazing, _____?
    (2)

A: Gaming isn't really popular in other countries, _____?
    (3)

B: Of course it is. You've heard about the reasons why people love video games,

  _____?
    (4)

A: Not really. What are they?

B: Well, first of all, they give players the chance to be a hero. Let's face it, you never

  get to drive fast cars in real life or rescue people from the tops of mountains,

  _____? But games allow you to play those roles.
    (5)

A: Yes, a lot of video games are very exciting, _____?
    (6)

B: And then, video games have really improved in recent years, _____?

(7)

A: You're not doing anything right now, _____? Do you want to go and

(8)

check out that new mystery game?

B: Sure.

A: You were hoping I was going to suggest that, _____?

(9)

B: Right. You really know me well, _____?

(10)

3 Work with a partner and read the statements below. Some are true, and others are false (the correct answers are at the bottom of the page). Make tag questions with the statements. If you think the statements are incorrect, use rising intonation. If you think they are correct, use falling intonation.

Example

Statement: The average age of a gamer is 34.

A: [*A thinks this is false, and uses rising intonation*] The average age of a gamer isn't 34, is it? I think that sounds too old.

B: Well, you're wrong! The average age of a gamer really is 34. That's interesting!

1. Women don't play video games as often as men.

2. People in most households in the United States play video games.

3. Most parents don't limit the video games their children play.

4. Most gamers spend eight hours a week playing video games.

5. Video games have never been linked to relaxation.

6. Players interact with each other as they play.

■ *GO TO* MyEnglishLab *FOR MORE GRAMMAR PRACTICE.*

Statements 2, 4, and 6 are correct. The other statements are incorrect.

PRONUNCIATION

🎧 Listen to the pairs of sentences. In which sentence is the word in **bold** stressed?

Hand the paper **in** to the teacher.
The chair is **in** the corner.

Let's go shopping **on** Sunday.
Do you like this jacket? Then try it **on**.

She lives **up** the block.
I'll pick you **up** at 4:00.

ADVERBIAL PARTICLES

Adverbial particles (part of phrasal verbs) such as *up*, *down*, *off*, *on*, *back*, and *out* are usually stressed.
  I'm fed UP.

- Stress these particles when they are used as adverbs after verbs.
  Log OFF.

- Stress them when they are part of separable two-word verbs.
Turn it DOWN.

- Do not stress these words when they are used as prepositions or as part of an infinitive.
Turn left <u>on</u> the next street.
I want <u>to</u> move!

- Adverbial particles that begin with vowel sounds, like *up*, *on*, *in*, *out*, and *off*, are linked to the consonant sound of the preceding word.
  Come ON.   Hurry UP.   Get OUT.

---

1 🎧 Listen to the sentences. The prepositions and particles are in **bold**. Circle the words in **bold** that are stressed.

1. I tried **to** follow the instructions, but then I gave **up**.

2. I asked him **to** turn it **down**, but he said he didn't want **to**.

3. Come **in** and sit **down**. You look really worn **out**.

4. I want **to** buy a joy stick. This one keeps breaking **down**.

5. I'm taking this new tablet **back**. I can't get it **to** work right, and I'm really fed **up**.

2 Work with a partner. Match the comments on the left with the responses on the right. Then practice the dialogues. Stress the particles and link words together smoothly when appropriate.

_____ **1.** When did your friend show up?

_____ **2.** Do you want to go out tonight?

_____ **3.** I got the new download of that game, but it keeps shutting down.

_____ **4.** I'm fed up with this new monitor.

_____ **5.** Ugh! I have six new messages and no time to reply.

a. I can't. I have to get up early.

b. The same thing happened to me. The new version is always freezing up.

c. Why don't you take it back to the store?

d. But they're probably new customers. You have to text them back.

e. Forty minutes after I called him up.

SPEAKING SKILL

Sophisticated speakers use various techniques to persuade others. One technique is to make concessions before they present their counterargument. This means they agree with or admit to part of the other person's point. Then they offer their own point. Sometimes this is called the "Yes, but no" technique.

USING CONCESSIONS	
To introduce a concession:	To present the counterargument:
It's true that I agree that You're correct in saying that Although / Even though	But / However, On the other hand, Nevertheless, (Note that if you begin the sentence with _Although_ or _Even though_, you should not include any of the expressions above.)

It's true that teenagers spend a lot of time texting. But some of that is valuable communication.

I agree that many video games are violent. Nevertheless, research hasn't shown a link between playing violent games and actual violent behavior.

Even though some video games cost a lot of money, they can be played many times.

Work with a partner. Read the situations. Then have conversations using the concession and counterargument in parentheses.

SITUATION 1

STUDENT A: A video training game vendor (salesperson)

STUDENT B: An airline company manager

The vendor wants to sell a new training game to a small airline to train pilots to navigate in poor weather. The manager is concerned about the expense.

GAME VENDOR: This is one of our most effective training games. Your trainees will learn quickly using it.

MANAGER: (Concession: The game seems effective. Counterargument: The company can't spend extra money on games.)

VENDOR: (Concession: The game is expensive. Counterargument: You can save the money you now pay to trainers.)

Example

GAME VENDOR: This is one of our most effective training games. Your trainees will learn quickly using it.

MANAGER: Although your game is effective for training, we can't spend the extra money.

VENDOR: It's true that this game is expensive; however, you'll save the money you now pay to trainers.

SITUATION 2

STUDENT A: A statistics professor

STUDENT B: The Statistics Department dean

The professor wants to use gaming in the classroom to get students engaged in learning. The dean is concerned that computers will replace good professors.

PROFESSOR: We should introduce some games in class. They can be very effective, and our students are having difficulty with math.

DEAN: (Concession: The students are having difficulty with math. Counterargument: Games can't replace a good professor's knowledge.)

PROFESSOR: (Concession: Games can't replace a good professor's knowledge. Counterargument: Professors can use games as an additional tool.)

SITUATION 3

Student A: A video game salesperson

Student B: An instructor from a driving school

The salesperson is trying to persuade the driver's education school to purchase a video game to help teens learn to drive. However, a parent is concerned: Will teenagers take responsibility for driving safely?

Salesperson: It's very motivating. Kids love playing games!

Instructor: (Concession: All kids love video games. Counterargument: Teens might not drive responsibly if they learn on a game.)

Salesperson: (Concession: Games cannot force teens to drive responsibly. Counterargument: Teens can learn to drive more safely on a game than on the road.)

SITUATION 4:

Two heart surgeons, A and B, are discussing a new computer game for training in new surgical techniques.

Surgeon A likes the game-training idea because it's safer for patients. Surgeon B is not enthusiastic about the game because the only way to get better at surgery is to work on real patients.

Surgeon A: Practicing on a game is safer than practicing on real patients.

Surgeon B: (Concession: Yes, it's safer. Counterargument: The only way to learn correctly is to practice on real patients.)

Surgeon A: (Concession: Practicing on real patients is more effective. Counterargument: It's also more dangerous. New doctors can use the game first, and then practice on real patients later.)

■■■■■■■■■■■■■■■■■■■■■■■■■■■ *GO TO* MyEnglishLab *TO CHECK WHAT YOU LEARNED.*

FINAL SPEAKING TASK

In this activity, you will hold a small-group debate about whether playing violent video games can cause violent behavior. Try to use the vocabulary, grammar, pronunciation, and listening and speaking skills that you learned in this unit.*

STEP 1: Work in groups of four. Each group of four divides into pairs. One pair will argue that violent games are harmful, and one pair will argue that they are not.

STEP 2: Work in your group. Use the information in the box below, from this unit, and your own ideas to make notes to support your side. Practice presenting your arguments out loud with your partner. Imagine what points the other side will make and plan how to respond to them.

YES: VIOLENT VIDEO GAMES . . .	NO: VIOLENT VIDEO GAMES . . .
• teach young people that violence is a good way to solve problems and reach goals. • contribute to bullying. In one study, 60% of middle school boys who played mature-rated games hit or had fights with other boys, compared to 39% of boys who did not play mature-rated games. • reward players for simulated violence, which increases aggressive behavior and thinking. • make children of all ages less sensitive to the problem of violence in society. • [Other reasons]	• have not led to an increase in crime and have not been shown to cause violent behavior. • , like violent movies or books, don't cause violence, although they may have more appeal for young people who are already violent. • are a safe way for people to get rid of the angry or violent feelings that they experience. • have lots of benefits for the brain and teach valuable skills and strategies that can be applied to real life. • [Other reasons]

---

* For Alternative Speaking Topics, see page 210.

STEP 3: Work with the whole class. Groups take turns presenting their debates. A non-debating student should act as timekeeper. Follow this pattern:

Side 1: Two minutes to present arguments

Side 2: Two minutes to present arguments

Side 1: Three minutes to respond to Side 2's arguments and make a conclusion

Side 2: Three minutes to respond to Side 1's arguments and make a conclusion

Listening Task

Watch your classmates' debates, and then discuss the process with the whole class. Did you change your initial opinion? Which arguments for each side were the most convincing? Why?

UNIT PROJECT

Work with a partner or small group. Investigate and report on a popular online game.

STEP 1: Spend some time playing the game and comparing your reactions. Take notes to help you remember what you thought about playing the game.

STEP 2: Make a chart or graphic organizer that shows how the game rewards players (by giving points, by advancing the player to the next level, etc.). Are the rewards predictable or random?

STEP 3: On the Internet, research and categorize reviews from players of the game. What do players enjoy about the game? What do they find frustrating? What are some typical comments that show why the game is so engaging?

STEP 4: Prepare notes and make a short presentation to your group or class.

1. Summarize the object and basic rules of the game.

2. Say what you liked and disliked. Discuss your experience.

3. Relate what reviewers and other players have said about the game.

4. Make a recommendation about the game. Is it addictive? Is it educational? Does it have any benefits? Would you recommend it to a friend? Would you recommend it to a parent or teacher?

ALTERNATIVE SPEAKING TOPICS

 1 Explain the meaning of the following saying and why you agree or disagree with it. In what other ways is learning a language like playing a video game?

Learning a foreign language is like playing a video game. You can never win, but you can keep losing at higher levels.

2 Work in groups of three. Read the advertisement for a historical computer game. Then role-play a discussion between a professor who wants to use the game in class, a student who doesn't, and an administrator who isn't sure. Use the ideas below and your own ideas.

Addict students to learning—play *Civilizations through the Ages*! In this highly interactive game, different players choose and build a civilization. They make choices about whether to develop agriculture or manufacturing or commerce, how many cities to build and where, and whether to invade neighboring countries. The computer program gives them information about the historical times, and they react to that information. Can be played individually or cooperatively.

Professor (in favor)	Student (opposed)	Administrator (not sure)
• highly motivating • gives students experience making decisions • can compare students' decisions to actual historical events • students will understand better why historical events happened the way they did • •	• can play games at home; come to class for something different • games aren't real life • professor should be teaching information directly • • •	• Games are fun, but do students really learn anything? • What does research show about using games in class? • How can games be used effectively? • Best method to use in class is one that gets results. • •

■ ■ ■ ■ ■ ■ ■ ■ ■ ■ ■ ■ ■ ■ *GO TO* MyEnglishLab *TO DISCUSS ONE OF THE ALTERNATIVE TOPICS, WATCH A VIDEO ABOUT DISCONNECTING FROM WORK EMAIL AFTER HOURS, AND TAKE THE UNIT 8 ACHIEVEMENT TEST.* ■ ■ ■ ■ ■ ■ ■ ■

UNIT WORD LIST

The Unit Word List is a summary of key vocabulary from the Student Book. Words followed by an asterisk (*) are on the Academic World List (AWL).

UNIT 1

achievements*
at the speed of light
before our very eyes
confidence
fascinated
interact*
involuntary
myth

objective*
put down on paper
renowned
revise*
trait
unconscious
unfamiliar
versus

UNIT 2

average
buckle down
devastated
diagnosis
get going
go far beyond
grief
hardships
inspirational
make something
  look cool

no small task*
overcome great
  odds*
persevere
stereotypical
that was it
tough
what keeps me going

UNIT 3

accumulate*
consistency*
fatigue
get cranky
have a tendency to
intrinsic*
maintain*
over the course of
pretty well

priority*
proven clinically
recover*
reset
sleep deprivation
tolerate
that being said
touch on

UNIT 4

anticipate*
context*
controversy
end up
figure out
give the floor to
manipulate*
off the top of your
  head

transfer*
just doesn't get it
spontaneous
intriguing
rote
socialized
take advantage of
turns out

(continued on next page)

UNIT 5

ameliorate the risk
back on your feet
catch on
dos and don'ts
encounter*
facing a short term
   crisis
happy go lucky
improve the odds

myth
never look back
radically*
recruit
set the parameters*
straightforward*
sufficient*
thriving
tugging at me

UNIT 6

cause
contribution*
debatable*
definitive*
emphasis*
foundation*
fly under the radar
funds*
have access to*

inspiring
moral
motivate*
proportionate*
requirement*
response*
tend to focus on*
think outside the box

UNIT 7

conflicted*
controversy*
figure
heated
hesitation
in a nutshell
it turns out
measure up to
   expectations

mirror image*
motivate
plow through
privilege
reasonable
rigorous
sample size
shocking

UNIT 8

be capable of*
cooperation*
compulsion
crave
escapist
features*
go berserk
go cold turkey
interactive*

keep a close eye on
lose contact with*
obsessive
randomly*
reinforcement*
shed its nerdy image
strategy*
substitute

GRAMMAR BOOK REFERENCES

NorthStar: Listening & Speaking Level 4, Fourth Edition	Focus on Grammar, Level 4, Fourth Edition	Azar's Understanding and Using English Grammar, Fourth Edition
Unit 1 Passive Voice	**Unit 18** The Passive: Overview	**Chapter 11** The Passive: 11–1, 11–2, 11–3
Unit 2 Gerunds and Infinitives	**Unit 9** Gerunds and Infinitives: Review and Expansion	**Chapter 14** Gerunds and Infinitives, Part 1 **Chapter 15** Gerunds and Infinitives, Part 2 15–2
Unit 3 Present Unreal Conditionals	**Unit 23** Present and Future Unreal Conditionals	**Chapter 20** Conditional Sentences and Wishes 20–1, 20–2, 20–3
Unit 4 Reported Speech	**Unit 25** Direct and Indirect Speech **Unit 26** Indirect Speech: Tense Changes	**Chapter 12** Noun Clauses 12–6, 12–7
Unit 5 Contrasting Simple, Progressive, and Perfect Verbs	**Unit 1** Simple Present and Present Progressive **Unit 2** Simple Past and Past Progressive **Unit 3** Simple Past, Present Perfect, and Present Perfect Progressive **Unit 4** Past Perfect and Past Perfect Progressive	**Chapter 2** Present and Past; Simple and Progressive 2–1, 2–2, 2–5, 2–7, 2–8 **Chapter 3** Perfect and Perfect Progressive Tenses: 3–1, 3–4, 3–7

(continued on next page)

NorthStar: Listening & Speaking Level 4, Fourth Edition	*Focus on Grammar, Level 4, Fourth Edition*	*Azar's Understanding and Using English Grammar, Fourth Edition*
Unit 6 Relative Pronouns in Adjective Clauses	**Unit 13** Adjective Clauses with Subject Relative Pronouns **Unit 14** Adjective Clauses with Object Relative Pronouns or *When* and *Where*	**Unit 13** Adjective Clauses
Unit 7 *Make, Have, Let, Help,* and *Get*	**Unit 10** *Make, Have, Let, Help,* and *Get*	**Chapter 15** Gerunds and Infinitives, Part 2: 15–7, 15–8
Unit 8 Tag Questions	**Unit 7** Negative *Yes/No* Questions and Tag Questions	**Appendix B** Questions: B–5

AUDIOSCRIPT

Listening One, page 6, Preview

There is a composer studying at New York's renowned Juilliard School who some say is the greatest talent to come along in 200 years. He's written five full-length symphonies, and listen to this—he's 12 years old.

page 6, Main Ideas

SCOTT PELLEY: There is a composer studying at New York's renowned Juilliard School who some say is the greatest talent to come along in 200 years. He's written five full-length symphonies, and listen to this—he's 12 years old.

He's a kid named Jay Greenberg, although he likes to sign his work "Bluejay" because, as he told us, blue jays are small and make a lot of noise.

Jay says that the music just fills his head and he has to write it down to get it out. What's going on in Bluejay's head? Have a listen: (*music plays*)

A 12-year-old wrote this. He wrote every note for each and every instrument, and the amazing part is, he wrote it in just a few hours.

And when the last note sailed into the night, Jay Greenberg navigated an unfamiliar stage, past musicians who'd been playing longer than he'd been alive. And Bluejay took his bow.

We haven't seen his like in how long?

SAM ZYMAN: Hundreds of years, probably 200 years. We are talking about a prodigy of the level of the greatest prodigies in history when it comes to composition.

SP: Sam Zyman is a composer. He teaches music theory to Jay at Juilliard in New York City, where he's been teaching for 17 years.

SZ: This is an absolute fact. This is objective. This is not a subjective opinion. Jay could be sitting right here, and he could be composing right now. He could finish a piano sonata before our very eyes in probably 25 minutes. And it would be a great piece.

SP: How is that possible? Well, Jay told us that he doesn't know where the music comes from, but it comes fully written—playing like an orchestra in his head.

As you hear it playing, can you change it as it goes along? Can you say to yourself, "Oh, let's bring the oboes in here or let's bring the string section in here?

JAY GREENBERG: No, they seem to come in by themselves if they need to.

SP: It's not something you're trying to do.

JG: Yes, because, it's like the unconscious mind is giving orders at the speed of light. You know, I mean, so I just hear it as if it were a smooth performance of a work already written, when it isn't.

SP: It's involuntary . . .

JG: I suppose so, yeah.

SP: Like the beating of the heart. You don't have to think about it.

JG: (*pause*) Uh-huh.

SP: It seems all the kids are downloading music these days, it's just that Jay, with his composing program, is downloading it from his mind.

The program records his notes and plays them back; that is, when the computer is up and running. Jay composes so rapidly that he often crashes his computer.

SZ: It is as if he's looking at a picture of the score, and he's just taking it from the picture, basically.

SP: Jay's parents are as surprised as anyone. Neither is a professional musician. His father, Robert, is a linguist, a scholar in Slavic language who lost his sight at 36 to retinitis pigmentosa. His mother, Orna, is an Israeli-born painter.

ORNA GREENBERG: I think, around 2, when he started writing, and actually drawing instruments, we knew that he was fascinated with it.

SP: Started writing? At the age of 2?

OG: Yeah, I'm afraid so. He managed to draw a cello and ask for a cello, and wrote the word cello. And I was surprised, because neither of us has anything to do with string instruments. And I didn't expect him to know what it was.

SP: What a cello was? You didn't have a cello?

OG: No, we had no cello in the house.

SP: Had he seen a cello?

OG: No.

SP: But he knew he wanted one, so his mother brought him to a music store where he was shown a miniature cello.

OG: And he just sat there. He put the cello, and he started playing on it. And I was like, "How do you know how to do this?"

SP: By age 3, Jay was still drawing cellos, but he had turned them into notes on a scale. He was beginning to compose. Jay's parents watched the notes come faster and faster. He was writing anytime, anywhere. By elementary school, his teachers had no idea how to handle a boy whose hero wasn't Batman, but Beethoven.

There's one thing about Jay: When the music comes up in his head, he has a lot of confidence about what he puts down on paper. Do you ever go back and say no, no, that's not right. This should be this way instead of that way?

JG: No, I don't really ever do that.

SP: You don't go back and edit and revise?

JG: No. Don't need to.

SP: Why not?

JG: Because, usually it just comes, it comes right the first time.

page 8, Make Inferences

Example

SAM ZYMAN: A 12-year-old wrote this. He wrote every note for each and every instrument, and the really amazing part is, he wrote it in just a few hours.

Excerpt 1

INTERVIEWER: We haven't seen his like in how long?

SZ: Hundreds of years, probably 200 years. We are talking about a prodigy of the level of the greatest prodigies in history when it comes to composition.

Excerpt 2

OG: He managed to draw a cello and ask for a cello, and wrote the word cello. And I was surprised, because neither of us has anything to do with string instruments. And I didn't expect him to know what a cello was.

Listening Two, page 10, Comprehension

NARRATOR: What is genius?

DAVID Shenk: Well genius is an amorphous term, to be sure, and I actually try to stay away from it in the book. What I talk about in the book mostly is this idea of high achievement, so people becoming great at stuff, becoming really, really good at stuff. I don't think it's really important to make a dividing line to try to figure out, you know, when you've crossed over into genius. The point is gathering your resources, doing the best you can, pursuing whatever it is you love to do with an intensity and a resilience and a passion, and just going as far as you can possibly go.

NARRATOR: What's the new thinking about the relationship between nature and nurture—that is, between the genes we're born with and what we learn from the environment?

DS: We've been living with this myth for about a hundred, hundred and fifty years, going back to the time of Darwin, although I'm not blaming Darwin

for this. Umm, so the idea is that we think that it's nature versus nurture, that there is genes that have all this information that kind of want to push us in a certain direction, and then there is the environment, which is nurture, which is obviously different, and kind of an opposing force and it's kind of either/or and there are all these studies that are constantly trying to figure out well how much is nature and then add onto the nurture. You know is it 60% nature, 40% nurture depending on what trait you're talking about? Well it turns out that genes don't work that way. Genes don't get you part of the way there you know to the point you're born or the point shortly after that or before that. Genes are always interacting with the environment, so the new way to think about this is that it's not nature plus nurture or nature versus nurture. If anything, it's nature interacting with nurture if you have to use those words, so one of the phrases that scientists are using now is G Times E, that is genetics times environment, as opposed to G plus E. They call it an additive model. The additive model is, well, you have so much inborn intelligence and then plus what you get in the environment. That would be the, you know, nature plus nurture. The new model is you can't separate them. You just absolutely cannot separate the effects of genes from the effects of the environment, so all we can do of course is to identify the resources that we have in our environments and maximize them as best we can.

page 11, Listening Skill

Excerpt 1

DAVID SHENK: Is it 60% nature, 40% nurture, depending on what trait you're talking about?

Excerpt 2

DS: The additive model is well, you have so much inborn intelligence and then plus what you get in the environment: that would be, you know, nature plus nurture.

page 20, Pronunciation

Australian painting prodigy Aelita Andre has captured the world's attention with her colorful work. However, people are often surprised when they hear that she is only four years old. The media have called her the "youngest professional painter in the world." Aelita's parents are artists themselves, and they have always encouraged their daughter to paint. They say she can spend hours working on a canvas. The public has responded enthusiastically to Aelita's work—in fact, one of her paintings sold for $30,000. Some critics have called Aelita's work "surrealist abstract expressionism."

UNIT 2: The Achilles Heel

Listening One, page 30, Preview

CAROL SAYLOR: . . . My name is Carol Saylor. I'm 73 years old. I am a sculptor and an art teacher. Slam it down! Punch it some more . . . And I happen to be blind and deaf.

page 31, Main Ideas

CAROL SAYLOR: . . . My name is Carol Saylor. I am 73 years old. I am a sculptor and an art teacher. Slam it down! Punch it some more . . . And I happen to be blind and deaf. When I first got the diagnosis, I was devastated. I thought that this was it. I had this stereotypical picture of blindness that the sighted world has. One of the misconceptions is that you see black, which I don't. I see all kinds of colors and shapes and vibrating spots, and it's quite beautiful.

KATE WHITMAN: Sammy is over here, right to your right . . . My name is Kate Whitman, and I teach art at Heritan high school. Today I brought my 3D multimedia sculpture class to see Carol Saylor's work. For me, her story is just as important as the work itself. She's been through so much hardship, and she's found a way to always overcome and find a way to be positive and keep persevering.

CS: Today we're talking to about 12 students, and I want them to close their eyes and touch my work. Do you have your eyes closed? Yeah. I want them to think about their mind's eye. I want them not to be afraid of blindness.

BOY: I didn't really think about what it would be like to be an artist while being blind and deaf. It's a crazy thing to think about. She's really good with touching things and she can really make the form of the body look cool when she can't even see it.

CS: My favorite subject is the female form. And I like sensuous shapes, and I like faces. The things that I have learned about art go far beyond, I think, what the average sighted person knows. And that's really what my art is all about. I'm trying to demonstrate to the sighted community that there is another level to art.

OPHELIA CASTALITO: My name's Ophelia Castalito, and I'm in 9th grade, and I'm here on a field trip with my school. I thought that she was an amazing artist. She opened my eyes. . . that everything isn't only about what you see, it's also about what you feel.

CS: My art expresses these feelings of grief and loss and also hope. But it is definitely not art therapy. It is way beyond art therapy: It is . . . it's an expression of my inner "gut" (laughs). . . . It's just . . . um . . . it's part of me. I would hate to not be able to do it, because that's what keeps me going, I think.

page 32, Make Inferences

Excerpt One

CS: She opened my eyes . . . that everything isn't only about what you see, it's also about what you feel.

Excerpt Two

CAROL SAYLOR: The things that I have learned about art go far beyond, I think, what the average sighted person knows. And that is really what my art is all about.

Excerpt Three

CS: It is definitely not art therapy. It is way beyond art therapy: It's . . . it's an expression of my inner "gut."

Listening Two, page 35, Comprehension

NARRATOR: They climbed one of the world's tallest mountains—a group of disabled climbers from the New York area. It's a story of reaching new heights and overcoming great odds. Monica Pellegrini introduces us to those inspirational athletes.

CLIMBER 1: I thought a few times going up that I wouldn't make it. . . . um . . . I almost turned back around twice.

MONICA PELLEGRINI: Mount Kilimanjaro, in the northern part of the African nation of Tanzania. Scaling it is no small task for your average climber, but for a group of seven from New York's Achilles Track Club, it was a much greater challenge. They are all disabled in some way. Five are blind. One is deaf and asthmatic. The other, a cancer survivor and amputee.

CLIMBER 2: It was a lot more difficult than I had expected. Er . . . a difficult climb, and the altitude really did affect a lot of us. But we persevered, and the majority of the athletes were able to make it.

MP: The accomplishment makes the group the largest of disabled athletes to ever climb Mount Kilimanjaro—an expedition they call a testament to the human spirit and a chance to empower themselves and others.

CLIMBER 3: I just wanted to reach deep down and grab all the energy I had, and keep on going. Because behind accomplishing this physical challenge for myself, I knew there was a greater message we were all carrying.

MP: The group kept a diary of their travels online, and even when the going got tough, they buckled down, turning to each other for inspiration as they continued on the trail to the peak.

CLIMBER 4: I heard it was going to be hard. I just didn't imagine it was going to be so tough.

MP: Tough, yes, but an experience that will not be forgotten any time soon.

C1: When you're experiencing this wide open space, wind, the sunshine, the strength of the sun like you've never felt before . . .

MP: The adventure began on August 28th and ended this past Sunday when the group, along with their 18 volunteer guides from the Achilles Track Club, reached the summit.

C1: Getting to the top was definitely the high point.

MP: Monica Pellegrini, UPN 9 news.

page 35, Listening Skill

Excerpt 1

CLIMBER 2: It was a lot more difficult than I had expected. Er . . . a difficult climb, and the altitude really did affect a lot of us. But we persevered, and the majority of the athletes were able to make it.

Excerpt 2

CLIMBER 3: I just wanted to reach deep down and grab all the energy I had, and keep on going. Because behind accomplishing this physical challenge for myself, I knew there was a greater message we were all carrying.

UNIT 3: Early to Bed, Early to Rise

Listening One, page 55, Preview

DR. HOWELL: A couple of things to think about when you're dealing with adolescents and sleep issues is that adolescents have a tendency to be a bit of night owls. They tend to want to go to bed later and sleep in later and this is more than just a behavioral choice on their part. Their brains actually act differently. This has been noticed not only in human adolescents but in animal models of adolescents, you'll see they actually like to stay up later and go to bed later. This is particularly troublesome in middle school and high school, when at the same time this is happening in their brains, the school times actually start earlier, sot they both like to go to bed later, but then they're forced to wake up earlier and it often leads to sleep deprivation.

page 56, Main Ideas

DR. HOWELL: A couple of things to think about when you're dealing with adolescents and sleep issues is that adolescents have a tendency to be a bit of night owls. They tend to want to go to bed later and sleep in later and this is more than just a behavioral choice on their part. Their brains actually act differently. This has been noticed not only in human adolescents but in animal models of adolescents, you'll see they actually like to stay up later and go to bed later. This is particularly troublesome in middle school and high school, when at the same time this is happening in their brains, the school times actually start earlier, so they both like to go to bed later, but then they're forced to wake up earlier and it often leads to sleep deprivation.

The only way that you're able to consistently reset your circadian rhythm so that adolescents are able to go to sleep at an earlier time and wake up earlier is One, through consistency, Two, with sunlight for about twenty to thirty minutes first thing in the morning, helps reset the circadian rhythm, and Three, you can use a little bit of low-dose melatonin, which is just an over-the-counter vitamin supplement, about six hours prior to bedtime. Those are the only things that have been proven clinically to help people fall asleep earlier.

What most studies have demonstrated is that you need to recover typically about half of the sleep that is lost. So in an adolescent who could otherwise sleep two more hours a day during the week, that'll add up over five days to ten hours. So over the course of a Saturday and Sunday, if that's the time that they'll have in the morning to the sleep in, they'll need to catch up five hours.

I think one of the first things we need to recognize is that sleepiness is not laziness. There's often time when we think of children or adolescents who are sleeping in class. It is not typically due to slothfulness or just laziness or disinterest. It is actually an intrinsic loss of sleep. I mean, there are perfectly good examples of kids who are lazy and don't want to do anything, but that is different from kids who are not able to maintain wakefulness. So, it's not only school start times, but it's also activity start times. It's not unusual for an adolescent who is both a swimmer as well as in orchestra to have to be at school to start at six o'clock in the morning. This can be extremely devastating to one's wakefulness. Now that being said, most adolescents are able to tolerate it pretty well, but for some it can be just quite devastating.

page 57, Make Inferences

Excerpt 1

DR. HOWELL: I mean, there are perfectly good examples of kids who are lazy and won't do anything, but that is different from kids who are actually not able to maintain wakefulness.

Excerpt 2

DR. HOWELL: It's not only school start times, but it's also activity start times. It's not unusual for an adolescent who is both a swimmer as well as in orchestra to have to be at school to start at six o'clock in the morning. This can be extremely devastating to one's wakefulness.

Listening Two, page 60, Comprehension

LIAN: This is Lian, and, like many of our listeners out there, I'm tired. I'm tired in the morning, I'm tired in the afternoon, and I'm really tired at night. And, frankly, I'm tired of being tired. My excuse is that I have two small children who sleep a little and wake up a lot. Dr. Walsleben, why are we all so tired?

DR. JOYCE WALSLEBEN: We're probably tired because we don't make sleep a priority. And I think, as a young mother and a career woman, your days are pretty well filled, and I would suspect that you probably think you can do without sleep or at least cut your sleep short, and one of the things that happens is we forget that sleep loss accumulates, so even one bad night, teamed with another will make an effect on our performance the following day. The other aspect, which you did touch on, is that even though we may sleep long periods of time, the sleep may not be really of good quality.

L: How serious a problem is sleep deprivation?

JW: Well, it can be very serious, because lack of sleep can affect our performance. It's not . . . We can get cranky and all of that, but if our performance is poor, and we are in a very critical job, we can have a major incident. And there have been many across society in which sleep and fatigue were issues. The Exxon Valdez was one in which the captain got a lot of attention, but the mate who was driving the ship had been on duty for 36 hours. . . . But you can read your local papers; every weekend, you'll see a car crash with probably a single driver, around 2 or 3 A.M., no reason why they would happen to drive off the road, and we all believe that that's probably a short sleep event that occurred when they weren't looking for it.

L: Dr. Walsleben, I know how this sleep deprivation affects me. By the end of the day, with my children, I'm tired and cranky, I'm not making good parenting decisions, I don't have a lot to give my husband when he comes home, and then I just feel too tired to exercise. So I think, "Oh, I'll eat or I'll have a big cup of coffee, and that will give me the energy that I don't have naturally." Are these pretty common effects of sleep deprivation amongst your patients?

JW: They're very common, and so many people accept them . . .

L: I would even say by Friday afternoon, I'm afraid to get behind the wheel of a car, because I just feel like I am not a safe driver on the road. That's how tired I am by Fridays.

JW: I think it's great of you to have recognized that . . . and that's a real, major concern for most of America's workers. By Friday, everyone seems to be missing, probably, five hours of sleep.

page 61, Listening Skill

Excerpt 1

The *Exxon Valdez* was one in which the captain got a lot of attention, but the mate who was driving the ship had been on duty for thirty-six hours. . . . But you can read your local papers; every weekend, you'll see a car crash with probably a single driver, around two or three A.M., no reason why they would happen to drive off the road, and we all believe that that's probably a short sleep event that occurred when they weren't looking for it.

Excerpt 2

DR. WALSLEBEN, I know how this sleep deprivation affects me. By the end of the day, with my children, I'm tired and cranky, I'm not making good parenting decisions, I don't have a lot to give my husband when he comes home, and then I just feel too tired to exercise.

UNIT 4: Animal Intelligence

Listening One, page 82, Preview

(INTERVIEWER) GOODWIN: We've assembled a fascinating group of scientists who make a living working with smart birds, smart chimps, and smart dolphins. All three of them are pushing the edge of the envelope in the animal intelligence field, and they're here to share what they've learned.

page 82, Main Ideas

ALEX GOODWIN: Welcome, all three of you, to The Infinite Mind.

DR. PEPPERBERG: Hi.

DR. STAN KUCZAJ: Hi.

DR. SALLY BOYSEN: Thank you.

AG: Glad to have you. Now let me start with a quick question for each of you. Off the top of your head, what's the smartest thing you've ever seen one of your animals do, thing—you know, something that made you step out and say, "Wow, that's amazing." Dr. Boysen, what about you?

DR. BOYSEN: Oh, you would start with me. I—I guess probably the most remarkable thing I've seen lately is an older chimpanzee that we have in the colony who's now 40. We had a—an arrival of an ex-pet chimp who'd been living in a home for 20 years, and she really has difficulty kind of getting around the lab. She has some retinal damage from diabetes. And, quite literally, I—I think that Sara, the older chimp, recognizes that this other chimpanzee, Abigail, kind of just doesn't get it. And we've seen her literally move through the facility, put her arms around Abigail and lead her down to the right door, for example, in the evening when she's supposed to come in for dinner. This is very remarkable behavior for—for a chimp that was born—raised in captivity, who has not socialized with chimps, and yet she really seemed to understand that Abigail needed her assistance. So I think it's—it's—was a pretty remarkable thing to observe.

AG: Dr. Pepperberg, what about you?

DR. PEPPERBERG: Ours is very different. I believe one of the things that we found that is—that's really very exciting is Alex's ability to use information that he's learned in one context and transfer that to a completely different context. So, for example, he was trained to respond color, shape, matter or none when objects were shown to him and he was asked, "What's same?" or "What's different?" And then we trained him on a task on relative size. So we'd ask him, "What color bigger?" or, "What color smaller?" And the very first time we showed him two objects of the same size and asked him, "What color bigger?" he looks at us and he says, "What same?"

AG: OK.

DR. PEPPERBERG: And—yeah. And then we asked him, "OK. Now you tell us, you know, what color bigger." And he said, "None." And he had never been trained on this.

AG: That is amazing. Dr. Kuczaj, what about you?

DR. KUCZAJ: Well, I have two examples that I'd like to mention. Both of these are spontaneous behaviors involving killer whales. In one example, a young whale was playing with a large disk, which ended up on the bottom of a pool, and it couldn't figure out how to get the disk off the bottom of the pool. And, spontaneously, it blew air bubbles out of its blow hole, which raised the disk off the floor so it could grab it. Another thing that we've observed is—with a number of killer whales is they'll use fish to bait seagulls. As the—the seagulls will get close enough so that then they can try and catch and often succeed in catching the gulls.

AG: OK. Now, Dr. Pepperberg, it's—parrots are particularly intriguing, of course, because they actually vocalize to some extent a kind of communication. Can you really talk to them like you talk to a human? I mean, what's—what's it like?

DR. PEPPERBERG: Well, you can talk to the birds the way you talk to a very young human. They don't speak to us in complete sentences. They don't have the same type of language as we do. We don't even call it language. We just call it two-way communication. But you can come into the lab, you can ask Alex what he'd like to eat, where he wants to go. And he answers numerous questions about colors, shapes, materials,

categories, similarity, difference, numbers. So it's—it's like working with a small child.

AG: And you gave us one example. What else has—has Alex learned to do?

DR. PEPPERBERG: Well, one—one thing he can do is to answer multiple questions about the same objects, and that's important because it shows that he understands the questions themselves. He's not simply responding in a rote manner to the particular objects.

ALEX: Some water.

AG: I think Alex is trying to butt in here. Dr. Pepperberg . . .

DR. KUCZAJ: Good.

AG: . . . do you wanna give Alex the floor here?

DR. PEPPERBERG: Alex, do you wanna do some work huh? Here. Listen. What's here?

ALEX: Beeper.

DR. PEPPERBERG: Very good. It's a little toy telephone beeper. Good birdie. OK. Let's go back to this other thing. What's here? How many?

ALEX: Two.

DR. PEPPERBERG: Good. Can you tell me what's different? What's different?

ALEX: Color.

DR. PEPPERBERG: Color, very good. And what color bigger? What color bigger?

ALEX: Green.

DR. PEPPERBERG: That's right. Saw two keys. One was blue and one was green, and they were the same shape and different color and different size. Very good. He's been asking for water, grapes, go shoulder, all sorts of things while we've been doing this.

ALEX: Some water.

AG: At any rate, we really appreciate all of you appearing on The Infinite Mind, and we'll—we're gonna be coming back to this issue. So thank you all very much.

DR. PEPPERBERG: You're w—very welcome.

DR. KUCZAJ: Thank you.

DR. BOYSEN: Thank you.

AG: Alex, thank you, too.

page 84, Make Inferences

Excerpt 1

DR. BOYSEN: And, quite literally, I—I think that Sara, the older chimp, recognizes that this other chimpanzee, Abigail, kind of just doesn't get it. And we've seen her literally move through the facility, put her arms around Abigail and lead her down to the right door, for example, in the evening when she's supposed to come in for dinner. This is very remarkable behavior for—for a chimp that was born—raised in captivity, who has not socialized with chimps, and yet she really seemed to understand that Abigail needed her assistance.

Excerpt 2

DR. PEPPERBERG: So we'd ask him, "What color bigger?' or, "What color smaller?' And the very first time we showed him two objects of the same size and asked him, "What color bigger?' he looks at us and he says, "What same?' Goodwin: That is amazing.

Listening Two, page 87, Comprehension

Controversy surrounded the disappearance of some crabs at an aquarium in Oregon a few years ago. One morning, workers found crabs missing from their tank and empty crab shells on the floor. New crabs were brought in to replace the dead ones, but the same thing happened several more times. Who was guilty? They installed an overnight camera to find out.

It turns out that a sneaky octopus had learned to take advantage of his night-time privacy. Did he anticipate a midnight snack? It looks that way. He waited all day until workers went home. Then he was able to manipulate his body, lengthening and narrowing himself to fit into an air tube that led out of his covered tank. He moved across the floor into the crab tank. After enjoying a midnight crab meal, he went back to his own tank the way he had come, looking quite innocent in the morning. Workers were amazed that a seemingly unintelligent animal was able to carry out such a trick.

LIZ PENNISI: A lot of the work is done in chimps and other apes because they're our closest relatives, and the idea is to put the chimps into a situation that they react to. And it turns out that competition for food is what motivates them to perform. So there's been a series of experiments, one of the more recent ones has to do with putting a chimp head to head with a human, and the chimp wants to reach for food and the human has the ability to pull the food away. And what the chimp readily figures out, is that if it kind of sneaks around a barrier that the human can't see, it can get the food. What that experiment is showing is that the chimp understands that the human is watching them and understands how to manipulate the situation to get what it wants.

COMMENTATOR: So I guess there's also been some interesting things done with birds as well, though, which aren't quite as close to us on the evolutionary relationship. We've had at least one study just this year that suggests that birds can remember, plan, or even perhaps, anticipate the future. Is that correct?

LP: Right. What happened is about ten years ago a couple of researchers realized that some of the skills that you see in chimps and social animals, including us, might also exist in social birds. And so they started a series of experiments, most of them take advantage of what they call caching behavior in which a scrub jay for example or a crow will take a tidbit of food, a piece of nut, whatever, and bury it. And all the experiments are based on the idea that, "OK, if some other bird is watching you bury the food, what do you do? And what they've discovered is that the bird is aware if somebody else is watching, the bird takes evasive action—it will go behind a barrier so that the onlooker can't see what it's doing. It will bury the food in one place and then come back and move it to another place.

COMMENTATOR: And I guess part of it sort of plays into this whole question of what cognition really is. I mean, isn't that sort of an extra layer of controversy or disagreement on this whole question?

LP: Oh right. I mean the definition of cognition and intelligence, even, if humans have to be the most intelligent beings, then we have to define intelligence in terms of what we can and cannot do. So what, one of the prevailing standards is something called 'theory of mind' and that is when you can assess what somebody else is thinking, can judge what somebody else might be doing, can take that information and use it at a later time. And at one point no animal was supposed to have any of that, and of course the experiments with chimps and even with the birds are showing that . . . well, they know about deception, they know when someone can see something they're doing, and they know how to manipulate that—what that person can see.

COMMENTATOR: Well Liz, it sounds like there's a lot going on on this front. Thanks for coming in today and chatting with us about some of it.

LP: Well, thank you.

page 88, Listening Skill

LIZ PENNISI: About ten years ago a couple of researchers realized that some of the skills that you see in chimps and social animals, including us, might also exist in social birds. And so they started a series of experiments. Most of them take advantage of what they call caching behavior, in which a scrub jay, for example, or a crow will take a tidbit of food, a piece of nut, whatever, and bury it. And all the experiments are based on the idea that, "OK, if some other bird is watching you bury the food, what do you do? And what they've discovered is that the bird is aware if somebody else is watching; the bird takes evasive action—it will go behind a barrier so that the onlooker can't see what it's doing. It will bury the food in one place and then come back and move it to another place.

UNIT 5: The Golden Years

Listening One, page 110, Preview

LESLIE MARTIN: The Longevity Project actually started in 1921, when Lewis Terman at Stanford recruited over fifteen hundred kids, boys and girls, to be part of the study. He planned to follow them into early adulthood to see if they grew up to be well adjusted, thriving people—he actually ended up studying them until he died.

page 110, Main Ideas

LESLIE MARTIN: The Longevity Project actually started in 1921, when Lewis Terman at Stanford recruited over fifteen hundred kids, boys and girls, to be part of the study. He planned to follow them into early adulthood to see if they grew up to be well adjusted, thriving people—he actually ended up studying them until he died.

HOWARD S. FRIEDMAN: And we picked up the study about twenty years ago and have been trying to see who lives long and who dies young, and why some people stay healthy and why some people become ill.

LM: We've published a lot of papers, and people always ask us questions about other studies: We'll start talking about one, and they'll say what about this? And what about that? And we decided that this was a really good time to put together all of the findings, in one spot, in one book, so that people who are interested generally about all the different things that lead to long life and health could find them in one place. There's a huge myth that is out there, which is that if you want to live a long life, you need a long checklist of do's and don'ts about all the right foods to eat, all the foods that you should never eat, all of the exercises you need to do, even if you hate them. And the Longevity Project is really a myth buster. What we discovered is that you don't need a long checklist in order to live a long life. It's really a lot simpler than that.

HF: There were many surprising and intriguing findings in the Longevity Project. One of those that amazed me the most was that hard work and even stressful hard work was not harmful. Actually, the people who work the hardest live the longest.

LM: What we found, and this is true in other, shorter term studies as well, is that cheerfulness and optimism really is a good thing, particularly if you're facing a short term crisis, you know, it sort of keeps you motivated if you expect that things will turn out OK. You may be more likely to hang in there with a treatment or some sort of a process that will get you back on your feet. But as a life approach, the children who are more cheerful and optimistic and kind of happy-go-lucky, they tended to take a lot more risks with their health. They had an attitude that was sort of . . . everything will turn out all right. And that tended to make them a bit more careless, which wasn't good in terms of their longevity. Probably the most surprising thing to me in the Longevity Project was the differences that we found for men versus women when they encountered divorce. Divorce certainly is stressful and a bad thing for anyone. But men were really able to improve their odds and ameliorate their risk by getting remarried after a divorce. That wasn't really so much the case for women. Women were just about as well off if they stayed single following a divorce.

HF: Of course, exercise in the form of physical activity is predictable for long life—it does help to keep you healthy. But not the kind of exercise that most people usually worry about, obsess about. It wasn't necessary to go to the gym, the same time every day, do a certain number of activities, keep track of how many steps you've taken each day. People who lived the longest, they didn't worry about things like that. They just lived a naturally active life. And that was sufficient. Many of the parents in this study were smart parents, and they had smart children in the study, and they thought, well, let's give them an advantage by putting them in school really early. But we found that starting first grade, a structured environment, too early, was really harmful and it led to problems in adolescence, for the children. In fact they died at a younger age. The Longevity Project doesn't burden you with endless lists of things to do to lead a long and healthy life. In fact, it shows that certain simple straightforward patterns can be developed, that anyone can develop, and that once you get on the right pattern, then you are much more likely to live a long and healthy life.

page 111, Make Inferences

Excerpt 1
SPEAKER: Divorce certainly is stressful and a bad thing for anyone. But men were really able to improve their odds and ameliorate their risk by getting remarried after a divorce.

Excerpt 2
SPEAKER: Of course, exercise in the form of physical activity is predictable for long life—it does help to keep you healthy. But not the kind of exercise that most people usually worry about, obsess about.

Excerpt 3
SPEAKER: In fact, it shows that certain simple straightforward patterns can be developed, that anyone can develop . . .

Listening Two, page 114, Comprehension

Tobey Dichter: I'm Tobey Dichter and I just turned 65. I am the founder of *Generations Online*.

[*Background*] Have you ever used the Internet? You have?

Commentator: Generations Online is a national non-profit that introduces the Internet and email to people over 65.

[*Background*] Click two times on the left. Just the left.

TD: We place it in places where they live and congregate. So senior centers, low-income housing . . . This happened when the Internet was starting to take on.

I think my mother kind of inspired this. I guess I was blessed with the older people in my life, like my mother, who died at age 85. They set the parameters for me. So I thought, it's really cool to be old and wise, and witty and then, as you met more and more older people, you realized that some just don't age as well. And that's what started me on the discovery. I was just curious. I would start to ask older people, well, you know, do you use the Internet? You must love it! Oh no, dear, I'm too old. Oh no, I'm too dumb. It broke my heart.

Woman: I'm Dorothy Gray, I'm 82 years old. It's not hard to catch on. Most things you do, cooking, or whatever, you follow directions. So it's the same thing with this. Follow directions, and you know how to use it.

TD: I had this wonderful job, big office: but this thing was tugging at me. And finally I left, after 30 years. And I never looked back.

[*Background*] Don't worry about the clicking.

[*Background*] Yo quiero ser independiente.

Woman: My daughter and my granddaughter are always the ones doing everything in the computer for me. I would like to be more independent and get my own information, so that way I don't have to bother them.

[*Background*] Tú sabes, hacer mis cosas . . .

It's hard enough to be old. It's much harder when everybody else is communicating in a certain fast way, and you're the only one left off. And I've had so many elders saying to me: They're leaving us behind. And there's too much to catch up to. There's way too much vocabulary—there are too many techniques.

Woman: I'm going to type in my name . . . yeah, this is the email over here right now. I learned the mouse, what is it, touching it and directing him . . . I can direct him to do what I want . . .

TD: We had one woman in the focus groups who said: "www means I'm never going to see it."

Woman: Well, it's good for you to know. It keeps your mind active, keeps you active . . . and the other thing is with the computer you can do a lot of networking.

I think working on this has changed me radically. It's given me a purpose that's driven not by the end product, but by the joys of each and every individual. I wouldn't want to be left off, so we can't leave them off.

page 115, Listening Skill

Excerpt 1

Speaker: I'm going to type in my name . . . yeah, this is the email over here right now.

Excerpt 2

Speaker: I learned the mouse, what is it . . . touching it and directing him . . . I can direct him (*laughs*) to do what I want.

page 124, Pronunciation

1. Why did you go there?
2. What did you see at the parade?
3. You can come, can't you?
4. They won't let you in without an ID card.
5. How do you get there?
6. Where do you live?
7. You can't come, can you?
8. Where do you go after class?
9. What do you think about that?

UNIT 6: Giving to Others

Listening One, page 134, Preview

Stacy Palmer: Actually, we don't know all of that much about what really motivates people to give. We know how often they give. And about half of Americans volunteer their time and 75 percent of people give money.

page 134, Main Ideas

Alex Goodwin: Probably most gestures of everyday kindness and generosity are never recorded. But when it comes to organized charities, fund-raisers make it their business to know who is giving and why. With us today is Stacy Palmer, editor of the fund-raiser's weekly bible, The Chronicle of Philanthropy.

Goodwin: Welcome, Ms. Palmer.

Stacy Palmer: Glad to be here.

AG: What studies have been done on volunteering and charitable giving?

SP: Actually, we don't know all of that much about what really motivates people to give. We know how often they give. And about half of Americans volunteer their time and 75 percent of people give money. There have been some polls that give some indication of what—what are some of the kinds of things that make people want to give. And usually, it's the passion for the cause. That's what they really care about. Whatever it is that they're involved with, they care about it a great deal. And that motivates them more than anything else—more than the tax benefits, more than the desire to repay somebody for something. They really care very, very much about whatever it is that they're getting involved in. And that's the biggest motivator.

AG: Do positive appeals work better than negative appeals?

SP: It's hard to tell. It depends on what the issue is. One of the things that politically minded causes often find is that when they have an enemy, they do very well. If they can say that this is the big threat to something, "You better do something now or else something bad will happen," people give in a big way.

AG: Well, what about the difference between volunteering time and volunteering money?

SP: A lot of people have differing attitudes on that, and both are very valuable. But I think people feel better after they volunteer. Writing the check feels good, but I think most people really f—when—when they go to volunteer, they see the direct effects of what they're doing. And that's much more rewarding to them.

AG: Now what's the magnitude of this in terms of percentage of the population? I mean, is there a figure at what-you know, at what percentage of the population give either their time and/or their money?

SP: About 50 percent of people say that they volunteer at least at some point, maybe, just, you know, a short-term volunteering project or something like that. It's a smaller percentage that actually volunteers once a week or—or something like that.

AG: Mm-hmm. Mm-hmm.

SP: But at least half of Americans say they volunteered at some time in the past year. Seventy-five percent of people said they made some kind of a cash donation, and that's often to some kind of a religious institution, which is what commands the biggest share of contributions, but also to multiple other causes. So most people in America do give something.

AG: What about social class? Is that as predictable as it should be?

SP: The very wealthy do give more often, and they give a little bit differently. They tend to like to go to these black tie benefits and do that sort of thing. And they also like to give with their name attached to it. People who are not in that wealthy class tend to give anonymously more often, and say that that's something that they prefer to do.

AG: Would you say that the less wealthy give a larger percentage of their income?

SP: The evidence is debatable on that, and that's something that economists really disagree on. And I think the biggest group of economists think that the poor do give proportionately more, but there's a strong argument to be made on the other side that the wealthy are giving proportionately more. So that's something that is continuing to be studied, and we hope at some point we'll get a more definitive answer with better data. Part of it is, how do you count what's giving? Is it giving when somebody helps their neighbor and gives, you know, a bunch of their winter clothing to somebody next door? Should you count that as part of charitable giving? It's not part of formal giving . . .

AG: No.

SP: . . . but it's certainly something that one would consider generous. The other problem is getting people to accurately say what it is that they've given in response to what they're being asked. Do you remember what you gave over the past year, honestly? Might you exaggerate it when somebody asks you, "Were you a giving person last year?"

AG: Sure.

SP: All of those things are what researchers are trying to factor out so that they get honest answers.

AG: Other than the—the thing we talked about a minute ago about ca—you know, caring about the cause, are there other reasons that people give? Are there other sort of universals that differentiate a giver from a non-giver?

SP: Usually, it's some kind of moral or religious feeling that also motivates a great deal of people to give. And it seems to come out of a feeling that it's important to, in some ways, give back to society.

AG: Mm-hmm.

SP: And that's often part of a family tradition or something that people have been taught all along the way, that that's something that's vital. And one of the things we're seeing a lot of is efforts to teach very young children how to give because it's clear that it is something that can be taught and something that the more people learn about as part of a tradition stays with them for all of their lives. So you even see kindergarten classes doing United Way fund-raising events. And I think we'll be seeing much more emphasis on teaching children because we can see that that really pays off. And you see in a lot of schools, too, they—this mandatory service requirement, where they actually have to do commer-community service to graduate. That's part of a way to show people, you know, "Here. I worked on a housing project or I helped clean up a river or I helped do something. Here's the difference that I made."

AG: Mm-hmm.

SP: And that seems to make a huge difference in helping people give all throughout their lives.

AG: Thank you very much, Ms. Palmer, for appearing on The Infinite Mind.

SP: Thank you.

page 135, Make Inferences

Excerpt 1

ALEX GOODWIN: Do positive appeals work better than negative appeals?

STACY PALMER: It's hard to tell. It depends on what the issue is. One of the things that politically minded causes often find is that when they have an enemy, they do very well. If they can say that this is the big threat to something, "You better do something now or else something bad will happen," people give in a big way.

Excerpt 2

AG: Well, what about the difference between volunteering time and volunteering money?

SP: A lot of people have differing attitudes on that, and both are very valuable. But I think people feel better after they volunteer. Writing the check feels good, but I think most people really f—when—when they go to volunteer, they see the direct effects of what they're doing. And that's much more rewarding to them.

Excerpt 3

AG: What about social class? Is that as predictable as it should be?

SP: The very wealthy do give more often, and they give a little bit differently. They tend to like to go to these black tie benefits and do that sort of thing. And they also like to give with their name attached to it. People who are not in that wealthy class tend to give anonymously more often, and say that that's something that they prefer to do.

Listening Two, page 138, Comprehension

KAI RYSSDAL: Something about winter and all those family gatherings must be inspiring us: Half of all charitable donations are made between Thanksgiving and New Year's. Or, maybe we just realize that the tax year is about to end. Some people, though, have the giving spirit year-round. Amy Radil introduces us to an anonymous Seattle resident who's become something of a guerilla philanthropist.

AMY RADIL: I had just done a story about a welfare mother who was having trouble feeding her children, when I got a phone message. The woman in the message, let's call her the Mystery Donor, said she would like to do something, anonymously, to help the woman in my story. She ended up paying off a $1,200 light bill to keep the woman's power from being shut off. Her career as a benefactor really began after she lost her husband.

DONOR: My husband died about three years ago and I had access to more money than I needed for expenses. So it was an opportunity to start giving money away.

AR: At age 58, the Mystery Donor lives in a pretty but not extravagant Seattle home. When her husband was alive they gave money but tended to focus on established charities. Now she acts on her own. Altogether she donates a quarter of her income each year, and she says that amount will increase over time. She says she often gives secretly because she's learned that money can change relationships. Her first secret donation was to a massage therapist she knew.

DONOR: She was a single mother and so this was really important work. And she broke her leg. And anybody who's been a single mother as I have knows what a catastrophe looks like on its way. And that looked awful to me. So what I did was to give her some money anonymously through having a cashier's check from the bank sent to her from another town.

AR: These small, personal gifts often go to helping single mothers. Their experience echoes her own years ago.

DONOR: I know what that feels like to feel desperate and need to care for a child. I was poor as a single mother for a period, looking for a job and had a one-year-old. I do recall one night where I had to decide whether to buy tuna fish or diapers. And it was down to that before I got my next paycheck. Of course we got the diapers.

AR: She describes the past three years as a learning curve in the art of philanthropy. She contributes hundreds of thousands of dollars each year to her cause of choice: sustainable farming. She belongs to a group, the Women Donors Network, that put her in touch with a University of Montana professor named Neva Hassanein. Hassanein had created a program to help local farmers supply the school's cafeteria food. The Mystery Donor wanted to help expand the program to other institutions. Hassanein says she then proposed having Americorps volunteers work with other colleges to replicate it.

NEVA HASSANEIN: And so we approached this donor with this idea and she loved it, was very excited. And it was in fact her prodding that got us to think outside the box.

AR: Hassanein says working with these freelance philanthropists has its advantages. They're more flexible and responsive than big foundations, she says, who can sometimes push their own agenda. The Mystery Donor says she may create a foundation one day, but right now she enjoys the freedom that comes from giving on her own.

DONOR: I really love flying under the radar and writing checks, you know, without having a structure. I certainly consult with a lot of people around what I do to make sure my judgment is as accurate as it can be, but right now this other way is good.

AR: Even when helping someone she knows, the Mystery Donor says she doesn't feel the need to ask whether they've received her gift. She says these gifts are more like being a secret Santa, where secrecy itself is part of the charm. In Seattle, I'm Amy Radil for Marketplace Money.

page 139, Listening Skill

Excerpt 1

REPORTER: These small personal gifts often go to helping single mothers. Their experience echoes her own years ago. "I know what that feels like to feel desperate and need to care for a child. I was poor as a single mother for a period, looking for a job and had a one-year-old."

Excerpt 2

REPORTER: The Mystery Donor says she may create a foundation one day, but right now she enjoys the freedom that comes from giving on her own. "I really love flying under the radar and writing checks, you know, without having a structure. I certainly consult with a lot of people around what I do to make sure my judgment is as accurate as it can be, but right now this other way is good."

page 154, Final Speaking Task, Step One

A Public Service Announcement

Close your eyes in Chicago and you can hear the sound of zebra braying in Africa. Look hard out your window in DC and you can see the snow-covered peaks of the Andes. Stand on a corner in LA and feel the hot wind of the Sahara brush across your face. The world is that small. We are that connected. Please visit earthshare.org and learn how the world's leading environmental groups are working together, making it so simple for you to make a difference, because we are many and we are one. Please visit us at earthshare.org to learn more. Earthshare. One environment: one simple way to care for it all.

UNIT 7: Do Your Homework!

Listening One, page 161, Preview

KAI RYSSDAL: I had a conversation a month or so ago with Steven Levitt about the Freakonomics of getting kids to get good grades. And how Levitt says we ought to just pay them. Fifty bucks for an A was what he got when he was a kid.

page 162, Main Ideas

KAI RYSSDAL: I had a conversation a month or so ago with Steven Levitt about the Freakonomics of getting kids to get good grades. And how Levitt says we oughta just pay 'em. Fifty bucks for an A was what he got when he was a kid. Me: not one thin dime. But that's a whole 'nother story. Anyway, Geri-Ellen Dow heard the segment and tweeted us a picture of two crisp $20 bills—one labeled "Great Expectations," the other labeled "The Odyssey"—and a note saying the money was there for the taking by her 14-year-old son if he read the books in question.

So of course we had to call her up to see what happened. Geri, good to talk to you.

GERI-ELLEN DOW: Thanks. It's nice talking with you, Kai.

KR: So you heard me talking to Steven Levitt about the Freakonomics of paying kids to study, and what did you do? Tell me about your experiment.

GD: Heh. I'm always looking for ways to motivate the kids because they don't seem to be really excited about school themselves.

KR: Shocking, shocking!

GD: Yeah, it is. So I thought that, well my son had two books to read over the summer—*Great Expectations* and *The Odyssey*.

KR: So how much were you going to pay them?

GD: So I figured $20 a book was reasonable.

KR: Oh man. See, I'm not going to read *The Odyssey* for $20.

GD: Yeah, you know, as it turns out, he felt probably that way as well. So what happened was, he finished *Great Expectations* maybe four days ago, five days ago, and then he started *The Odyssey* two days ago. And I just have to point out that school starts tomorrow.

KR: So you're going to get your $20 back.

GD: Well . . .

KR: No, are you going to give it to him? Come on.

GD: He's 250 pages into it. And the hesitation was he seems to be plowing through it, which I don't understand how you can do that.

KR: Yeah, no. You're going to pro-rate this then, is this what I'm hearing you tell me?

GD: We had a really heated discussion yesterday about whether I intended to pay him if he got it done before school or before the comprehensive test.

KR: Yeah, that's actually a very good point, which I should probably raise to Steven Levitt —you've got to define the terms of the agreement.

GD: Yes, and I was not clear on that. Although I think as it happened, and I had some different ideas about what I would have done if I was doing it over again.

KR: Like what?

GD: Well, I would have offered him more than $20.

KR: Yeah, you got that right.

GD: For a 500-page book that was written 2,000 years ago.

KR: Now, Levitt and Dubner, the guys behind Freakonomics, would say, 'Well, your sample size is a little small, and you need more information over time.'

GD: So you think I should maybe have more kids and do it longer, is that what you're suggesting?

KR: No. Well, that's a personal choice actually. But really, you need to do the experiment over a longer period of time so you can have more data, more information, right?

GD: And with more rigorous controls in terms of what the expectations are. Yes.

KR: Are you thinking you might do this again next summer? I guess you're going to wait and see how it goes, right?

GD: Yes, I'm going to wait. I don't know. I don't know.

KR: This is so fun, you are clearly conflicted about this.

GD: I am conflicted about it, yes.

KR: Huh. Well Geri, thanks a lot for your time.

GD: All right, thank you Kai.

page 164, Make Inferences

Excerpt 1

GERI-ELLEN DOW: So I figured 20 bucks a book was reasonable.

KAI RYSSDAL: Oh man. See, I'm not going to read *The Odyssey* for 20 bucks.

GD: Yeah, you know, as it turns out, he felt probably that way as well.

Excerpt 2

KR: Now, Levitt and Dubner, the guys behind Freakonomics, would say, 'Well your sample size is a little small, and you need more information over time.'

GD: So you think I should maybe have more kids and do it longer, is that what you're suggesting?

Excerpt 3

GD: We had a really heated discussion yesterday about whether I intended to pay him if he got it done before school or before the comprehensive test.

KR: Yeah, that's actually a very good point, which I should probably raise to Steven Levitt—you've got to define the terms of the agreement.

Listening Two, page 166, Comprehension

KIRAN CHETRY: Our next guest's article is raising a little bit of controversy: When it comes to raising successful kids, Chinese mothers have it right. Amy Chua is raising her children the way that she was raised, with a few hiccups along the way, but in a strict Chinese household, and she's written about her somewhat extreme parenting method in a new book. Here's an excerpt. "Here are some things that my daughters, Sophia and Louisa, were never allowed to do: attend a sleepover, have a play date, watch TV or play computer games, choose their own extracurricular activities, get any grade less than an A, and play any instrument other than the piano or violin." The book has people talking, certainly, it's generating a lot of controversy, and it's called "Battle Hymn of the Tiger Mother," and author Amy Chua joins us now. . . .

I had to laugh, Amy, because some of this resonated. My dad is from Nepal, and in the Asian culture, I mean, when you're a child, or a product of the Asian culture . . . and this is general . . . but you know, there is a greater emphasis on listening to your parents, and to studying. And also to just measuring up to their expectations of you—not what you want.

Let's talk first of all about some of those ideas, and of course, some people take issue with the fact that it said "Chinese," but you're coming, you're writing about what you know because that's what you know . . .

AMY CHUA: Of course, this is just my story, and I actually say early on in the book that I'm using this term loosely: I'm NOT speaking for all Chinese parents, and in fact it's more of an immigrant thing: You were just saying, you know, I know a lot of Guinean, Jamaican, Korean, Indian parents who have similar mindsets, and, similarly, I know many Chinese people who choose not to do this, partly because they didn't like it when it was applied to them.

KC: Well it's interesting, we are losing some of that as more of us grow up in America, and grow up in Western influences. My dad always had said to me that learning is a privilege, and going to school is a privilege. And he sort of carried that ethic with him. And he did impose that on me. I laughed in the book when you talked about if you get all A's and a B, an American parent would say, congratulations, you're doing great. And a "Chinese" parent, as you're putting it, would say, why the heck did you get a B? That's not acceptable!

AC: Did that happen to you?

KC: Of course!

AC: Right, I know, and I think this is one thing people don't understand: You have to put it in the family context. Every family's different. If you say that in some families, it could be really horrible, and harsh, and undermining. But I grew up with extremely strict but also extremely loving Chinese parents, immigrant parents. And for me, I mean, as a grownup looking back, their having high expectations for me coupled with love was really the greatest gift they could give me. I felt like I owed them everything. Which is why I tried to do it with my own two daughters. And with my first daughter, things went smoothly, but then, my second daughter came along, and that's when I kind of got my comeuppance. I mean, she and I are very similar, she's a fireball, you know—we both have hot tempers, we locked horns from day one, and again, at 13 she really rebelled, we began having terrible fights, a very dark period in my life, and I really began questioning everything I'd ever done, and that's actually why I wrote the book.

KC: So . . . in a nutshell, what can Western parents learn, though, about those high expectations? About the emphasis on studying that you talk about?

AC: I think that there are strengths and weaknesses to both the Asian and the Western models. They are almost mirror images of each other. Er . . . there are real strengths, though. I really think so. I think there is a question we are all confronting which is where does true self-esteem come from? I'm really a little surprised. It's almost like the idea of striving for excellence is a bad word, you know . . .

KC: Right . . . like maybe you're putting too much pressure on them?

AC: Yes . . . and that's true, by the way . . . I agree with that. If there's too much pressure, you get to a point where people are cracking, and they're miserable, you've got to pull back, that's the point of my book, in a way. I retreated. But short of that, if there's love, for many, many people, having high expectations, learning that you can do something that you thought you couldn't, that's a great feeling, and once you have that experience, in the future, you think: Wait a second. I once thought I couldn't do something and that through hard work and not giving up, I learned that I could do it. So you know, this is a good lesson. And also not making excuses. I find it interesting that these are called "Chinese values," you know, hard work, and don't give up, and don't make excuses, take responsibility, be self-reliant, I mean, the way I was taught. Because I think of those as really fundamental American values.

page 167, Listening Skill

Excerpt 1

AMY CHUA: . . . I actually say early on in the book that I'm using this term loosely: I'm NOT speaking for all Chinese parents, and in fact it's more of an immigrant thing: You were just saying, you know, I know a lot of Guinean, Jamaican, Korean, Indian parents who have similar mindsets . . .

Excerpt 2

AC: I find it interesting that these are called "Chinese values," you know, hard work, and don't give up, and don't make excuses, take responsibility, be self-reliant . . .

UNIT 8: Pros and Cons of Gaming

Listening One, page 186, Preview

INTERVIEWER: We spend more than 3 billion a year on gaming, more than we spend on film or music. And gaming has shed its nerdy image to become an essential part of youth culture. As a parent, I often wonder what effect it will have on my children. It's an immersive, interactive, cinematic experience, but is it too much for some people to handle?

page 186, Main Ideas, Part 1

RAFAEL ROSE: In the past five years, computer gaming has exploded in popularity.

TEEN A: "I love playing video games."

TEEN B: "I play games every day."

TEEN C: I've been waiting for this game for a really long time."

INTERVIEWER: We spend more than 3 billion a year on gaming, more than we spend on film or music. And gaming has shed its nerdy image to become an essential part of youth culture. As a parent, I often wonder what effect it will have on my children. It's an immersive, interactive, cinematic experience, but is it too much for some people to handle?

It's a fate 20-year-old Leo, not his real name, is trying to avoid.

LEO: you substitute the real world for this world. I mean two years I've been playing, 12 hours of the day, online, for two years if you want to look at it that way. It was fun while you're playing, but then when you think about the derogatory effect it's having on your life, then, um, then obviously, phh, you don't feel so good.

INTERVIEWER: His university work is suffering; he's lost contact with his friends and damaged his relationship with his family.

LEO: I would never inflict this game on anyone. This game is just a disease. It's just horrible. It's very hard to explain properly. You really, it's one of those things you really have to experience.

INTERVIEWER: He's now decided to go cold turkey and stop playing the game.

INTERVIEWER: When Allison Dando's son, Chris, started refusing to go to school, she had no idea why.

ALLISON: Initially we didn't connect it to the computer game playing at the start because it was just something that every boy did, and particularly a lot of the boys that we knew, and friends of ours. Yeah, we had the Internet, yeah, umm, both the children had computers in their bedroom, but there was nothing that particularly alarmed us.

CHRIS: It brought you into another world. Like, you'd be what you wanted to be.

INTERVIEWER: He was playing for up to 20 hours a day.

CHRIS: I remember there was one point where, uh, I think our Internet just went down, um, and I started sweating, and I actually started shaking, just because I couldn't play it.

ALLISON: Once I understood that this game was online, I'm saying, "Right, OK, well the answer to it is we'll cut off the Internet; that's it. And the response was just an outpouring of violence. He just went berserk.

CHRIS: I put on a boot and I kicked a hole in my sister's door. I just smashed anything I could see.

ALLISON: It was really scary.

CHRIS: It got to the point where, you know, my dad almost had to pin me down on the ground.

ALLISON: That was the point where we started to really understand from a parental point of view, "Gosh, this is dangerous! This is a dangerous tool in our house."

page 187, Main Ideas, Part 2

INTERVIEWER: I went to meet a world authority on the psychological impact of computer games.

PROFESSOR Mark Griffiths: The good news is that for the vast majority of people, video games is something that's very positive in their lives, but we have to take on board that there is a growing literature that suggests for a small but significant minority, things like gaming can be potentially problematic. My research has consistently shown people seem to display the signs and symptoms you get with the more traditional addictions.

INTERVIEWER: He says there isn't enough research to be certain how serious the problem is.

MG: People put money into alcohol and tobacco addiction, maybe even into gambling addiction, but in gaming addiction, it's kind of so new that people don't really see it as an important research area to look into.

INTERVIEWER: The little research that's been done suggests it's online games that cause the most concern.

INTERVIEWER: One award-winning games designer thinks it's time the industry accepts that some online games may encourage obsessive playing.

ADRIAN HON: I think people don't necessarily understand how powerful some game mechanics can be. It's one thing to think, "OK, I'm playing too much, but it's another thing to just stop playing because some games are designed in a manner that you just don't want to leave.

INTERVIEWER: He says powerful psychological techniques are used.

AH: The first one is by using this idea called the variable rate of **reinforcement**, which is basically like a jackpot, so it's a slot machine.

INTERVIEWER: The idea was developed after scientists discovered rats, taught to feed themselves by pressing a lever, would press it obsessively when the food appeared randomly.

AH: And people have found that this worked on humans as well. If you go and give people a lever to press or a button to press and then give them random rewards based on pressing that, you know, they'll do it all the time.

INTERVIEWER: In games, instead of food, you randomly get extra lives, or extra in-game **features** to keep you playing. The idea is to create a compulsion loop to keep us coming back for more. It's simple but powerful, and it's thought to explain why people get addicted to slot machines.

INTERVIEWER: I don't want to stop my son from gaming, but I'm going to keep an extra close eye on him to make sure he games safely.

page 189, Make Inferences

Excerpt 1

LEO: I would never inflict this game on anyone. This game is just a disease. It's just horrible. It's very hard to explain properly. You really, it's one of those things you really have to experience.

Excerpt 2

CHRIS: It got to the point where, you know, my dad almost had to pin me down on the ground.

ALLISON: That was the point where we started to really understand from a parental point of view, "Gosh, this is dangerous! This is a dangerous tool in our house."

Listening Two, page 192, Comprehension

JANE MCGONIGAL: There are a couple of concerns that come up often when we talk about video games. The first is addiction, and that's definitely a real problem. What I've discovered is that games do a better job, in many ways, of providing the things that we crave most, you know, whether it's a sense of satisfying hands-on work where we can really see the outcomes of our actions, or a chance to succeed and get better at something, to start out being really bad and then have this sense of mastery as we get better and better. Gamer addiction is not about, necessarily, the quality of the games being somehow fundamentally—they just grab us, and we can't escape—, it's really about what they offer us that the real world sometimes does a terrible job of offering us. And it is, hopefully, our goal to take those things that we get from games and find ways to have them in our real lives, too.

The other big concern that people have about games is violence, of course. There is no evidence that gaming makes you more violent. In fact, a study came out just last week showing that gamers who play violent games that require strategy with your teammates or cooperation with other players to beat the bad guys are actually much more cooperative in the game and in real life, that they're actually honing skills of cooperation, not skills of violence. This makes perfect sense because when you're playing a game with other players, you're not actually being violent, right? You have to actually work with the other players. You have to trust them to finish the game. You have to work with your teammates. You have to communicate. There's no actual violence involved, right? The actual effort involved is highly collaborative, highly trustworthy, highly social.

So, the message needs to be this is training for real life. You know, yes, games are escapist in that we do get to escape reality when we play them, but they're not just escapist. They're also returnist. We return to our real lives with real ways of thinking about what

we're capable of, real ways of solving problems more creatively. And this is the great news for the gamer generations, that we have spent our lives planting this seed, planting this capability, and now we can take those skills and abilities to real challenges, whether they're things like overcoming concussions the way that I used my gamer way of thinking to deal with that or tackling global challenges like climate change, and curing cancer, and overcoming political corruption. There are games to do all of these things now that you can play, you can bring your gamer abilities and help save the real world. So if you have a gamer in your life, or if you are a gamer, the good news is you are ready, they are ready to do extraordinary things in their real lives.

page 193, Listening Skill

Excerpt 1

The other big concern that people have about games is violence, of course. There is no evidence that gaming makes you more violent. In fact, a study came out just last week showing that gamers who play violent games that require strategy with your teammates or cooperation with other players to beat the bad guys are actually much more cooperative in the game and in real life.

Excerpt 2

You know, yes, games are escapist in that we do get to escape reality when we play them, but they're not just escapist. They're also returnist. We return to our real lives with real ways of thinking about what we're capable of, real ways of solving problems more creatively.

UNIT 1

"David Shenk responding to three questions about where genius comes from" © Big Think Products. All rights reserved. Reproduced by permission.

"Blue Jay: Julliard called this kid the greatest prodigy in 200 years." 5.3.2013 Copyright © 2013 CBS. All rights reserved. Reproduced by permission.

UNIT 2

"The Achilles Track Club Climbs Mount Kilimanjaro." Footage from My 9 News Courtesy of WWOR-TV, Inc. TM and (c) 1994. All rights reserved."

Carol Saylor—Wider Horizons is a project of WHYY, Inc. and Coming of Age.

UNIT 3

"Get Back in Bed," © Mudbath Productions. All rights reserved. Reproduced by permission.

"Expert Alert: Healthy sleep schedule key for students to hit the ground running." © 2010 Regents of the University of Minnesota. Used with permission.

UNIT 4

"The Infinite Mind: Animal Intelligence" excerpt from "The Infinite Mind" public radio series, programs on "Animal Intelligence" and "Altruism," produced by Lichtenstein Creative Media, © 2007, 2013 Lichtenstein Create Media, Incorporated.

"Cloaking Devices, Animal Cognition, Ancient Beads and More," from Science Podcast "Cloaking Devices, Animal Cognition, Ancient Beads and More" *Science* 23 June, 2006 [http://www.sciencemag.org/feature/mics/podcast/SciencePodcast_060623.mp3] Used with permission from AAAS.

UNIT 5

"Trailer transcript," from THE LONGEVITY PROJECT: SURPRISING DISCOVERIES FOR HEALTH AND LONG LIFE FROM THE LANDMARK EIGHT-DECADE STUDY by Howard S. Friedman and Leslie R. Martin, copyright © 2011 by Howard S. Friendman & Leslie R. Martin. Used by permission of Hudson Street Press, an imprint of Penguin Group (USA) Inc.

"Wider Horizons," author Tobey Dichter, is a project of WHYY, Inc. and Coming of Age.

UNIT 6

"Altruism" excerpt from "The Infinite Mind" public radio series, programs on "Animal Intelligence" and "Altruism," produced by Lichtenstein Creative Media, © 2007, 2013 Lichtenstein Create Media, Incorporated.

The Mystery Donor Amy Radil's "Sometimes charity is better a mystery" from American Public Media's Marketplace (c)(p) 2007. Used with permission. All rights reserved.

UNIT 7

"Bribing your kids to study, does it work?" From American Public Media's "Marketplace Tech" © (p) 2012. Used with permission. All rights reserved.

"Strict Chinese mom's key to kids' success/American Morning Chinese Mothers Superior?" Copyright © Wendy Sachs. All rights reserved. Reproduced by permission.

PHOTO CREDITS

THE PHONETIC ALPHABET

Consonant Symbols			
/b/	**b**e	/t/	**t**o
/d/	**d**o	/v/	**v**an
/f/	**f**ather	/w/	**w**ill
/g/	**g**et	/y/	**y**es
/h/	**h**e	/z/	**z**oo, bu**s**y
/k/	**k**eep, **c**an	/θ/	**th**anks
/l/	**l**et	/ð/	**th**en
/m/	**m**ay	/ʃ/	**sh**e
/n/	**n**o	/ʒ/	vi**s**ion, A**s**ia
/p/	**p**en	/tʃ/	**ch**ild
/r/	**r**ain	/dʒ/	**j**oin
/s/	**s**o, **c**ircle	/ŋ/	lo**ng**

Vowel Symbols			
/ɑ/	f**a**r, h**o**t	/iy/	**we**, m**ea**n, f**ee**t
/ɛ/	m**e**t, s**ai**d	/ey/	d**ay**, l**a**te, r**ai**n
/ɔ/	t**a**ll, b**ou**ght	/ow/	g**o**, l**ow**, c**oa**t
/ə/	s**o**n, **u**nder	/uw/	t**oo**, bl**ue**
/æ/	c**a**t	/ay/	t**i**me, b**uy**
/ɪ/	sh**i**p	/aw/	h**ou**se, n**ow**
/ʊ/	g**oo**d, c**ou**ld, p**u**t	/oy/	b**oy**, c**oi**n